Citizens
Uniting
TO RESTORE OUR
Democracy

Citizens
Uniting
TO RESTORE OUR
Democracy

Daniel Kemmis

University of Oklahoma Press : Norman

Publication of this book is made possible through the generosity of Edith Kinney Gaylord.

Portions of Chapter 8 are adapted from *Philanthropy and the Renewal of Democracy: Is It Time to Step Up Our Game?* Published by Philanthropy Northwest in collaboration with the Kettering Foundation (revised edition, 2016).

Library of Congress Cataloging-in-Publication Data

Names: Kemmis, Daniel, 1945– author.
Title: Citizens uniting to restore our democracy / Daniel Kemmis.
Description: Norman : University of Oklahoma Press, [2020] | Includes bibliographical references and index. | Summary: "Daniel Kemmis draws on history, democratic theory, and his own grassroots political experience to propose concrete steps by which citizens can restore democratic capacity and address the challenges of the twenty-first century"—Provided by publisher.
Identifiers: LCCN 2020010584 | ISBN 978-0-8061-6629-2 (paperback)
Subjects: LCSH: Democracy—United States. | Political participation— United States. | Civics. | United States—Politics and government—2017–
Classification: LCC JK1726 .K38 2020 | DDC 320.973—dc23
LC record available at https://lccn.loc.gov/2020010584

To Missoula and its devoted citizens
for sustaining my faith in democracy

Daniel Kemmis

Contents

Preface

This book's journey from conception to publication stretched across the better part of a decade. Most of that time was spent unpacking what had been contained from the outset in the two words of the book's working title: *Citizens Uniting*. The initial impetus for writing at all had been provided by the U.S. Supreme Court's January 2010 decision in *Citizens United v. Federal Election Commission*. Like so many others, I reacted to the early reports about the decision with dismay, guessing that it was going to inflict significant damage on an already badly ailing body politic. At a minimum, I felt motivated to contribute whatever little I could to healing this wound.

Because my own experience in politics and government seems always to call grassroots citizenship to mind whenever the subject of democracy arises, I found myself wondering what role that kind of grounded citizenship might play in any effective response to the *Citizens United* decision. But that got me only as far as the little private joke contained in the slogan of "citizens uniting." I still hadn't decided what to do with my initial outrage at the Supreme Court's ruling.

At first, I thought about simply writing a letter to the editor, so that at least my neighbors would know how I felt and what I thought should be done. I soon found, though, that I couldn't make much sense of what the Court had done without examining at least some of the decision's historical precedents. Educating myself on that background led to the further conclusion that I couldn't usefully describe the consequences of the decision without putting them in the context of a worsening complex of other wounds and diseases that were by then besetting the body politic.

If the decision itself opened up that broad a range of issues in need of exploration, the idea of citizens uniting in response to it was hardly less problematic. Even the word "citizen" had come under a cloud of sorts, and it would only darken as the decade progressed. I knew that, already in 2010, many of my neighbors and colleagues had grown uncomfortable with that word because it could all too readily be used to exclude people living in this country who cannot claim the formal status of American citizenship. Under those circumstances, many writers and activists had begun using the word "resident" when they would customarily have used "citizen." In fact, as the manuscript at last took on its final form nearly a decade later, the word assumed a new level of significance in public discourse when the Trump administration attempted to insert into the 2020 census form a question about whether or not respondents were U.S. citizens. The resulting controversy is relevant here only because it underscores that what the administration meant by the word was distinctly not the meaning of "citizen" that this book's title reflects nor the meaning that its argument examines. I stuck with the title despite these complications, in large part because I believe the deeper significance of the word "citizen" is too valuable to be lightly relinquished.

Citizenship is, of course, an ancient concept, rooted etymologically in the Roman republic and underlain by even older Greek origins. A citizen in this basic sense is one who cares for one's city or community and takes appropriate responsibility for the wellbeing of the *polis* or *civitas*. This core understanding of responsible citizenship is fundamental to the republican view of democracy on which this book rests. But that engaged form of citizenship has nothing to do with the documents in anyone's purse or wallet. Any given "undocumented" individual can be (and often is) a more fully engaged citizen in this basic sense than someone born into American citizenship but blithely oblivious to its democratic responsibilities. It is to all such engaged citizens, regardless of their legal status, that this book extends its invitation to unite in the work of healing democracy.

While this little historical foray may begin to explain what the word "citizens" is doing in the title of this book, it doesn't by any means account for my own determination to examine whether and how a united corps of citizens could contribute a meaningful response, either to the *Citizens United* decision itself or to the host of other wounds and diseases now afflicting our democracy. That argument unfolds as the book proceeds, but at this point I will simply say that I would never have undertaken, let alone finished, this book had not a lifetime of public service, including a fair amount of practical political experience, left me with a deep and abiding faith in the capacity of citizens to solve difficult problems together.

My confidence in democratic citizenship has been lastingly shaped by and rooted in my experience of serving the citizens of my hometown of Missoula, Montana, first as a legislator and then as their mayor during much of the 1990s. As I witnessed, day after day, my neighbors' remarkabe capacity to conceive and carry out a never-ending series of improvements to their community, I was reminded in the most tangible way that the word "citizen" is rooted in the active and effective care that people like my neighbors provide their cities or communities. If democracy means citizens governing themselves and, in the process, shaping the conditions of their own lives, then my experience both as an elected official and as a citizen of Missoula has been a decades-long education in the meaning and blessings of democracy, and especially of democratic citizenship. It was that experience, and the democratic faith it engendered, that kept me doggedly on the trail of the central question of this book: whether the same problem-solving capacity that had so inspired me as I watched it at work among my neighbors and fellow citizens could play any kind of meaningful role in addressing the problems that now infect our democratic institutions.

The question clearly invites a certain measure of skepticism. The problems facing our democracy are so big, so deeply entrenched, often so very much to the benefit of rich and powerful individuals, that we ordinary citizens would seem to have no real capacity for doing anything about them. I only compound this baseline doubtfulness by drawing many examples of the kind of citizenship I am invoking from my own small city in the northern Rockies, itself generally seen as a liberal enclave in the much more conservative state of Montana. I wouldn't blame anyone for asking how the view from this limited (and indeed privileged) perspective can contribute anything meaningful to the resolution of any of the major problems now besetting our republic.

Part of the answer is that, in fact, this kind of grounded citizenship is not going to provide a magic cure for our democratic woes. Neither will anything else. No one is going to provide *the* answer, and it would be strange if someone professing a deep faith in democracy were to claim—or even for a moment to imagine—that he knew the answer. If we are to succeed in getting our democratic body in better shape, we will do it democratically—which means at a minimum that any part of the solution I bring forward has to be subject to your additions or amendments.

Nowhere is this limitation more salient than in the respective roles to be played in this enterprise by various generations of citizens. The fact is that most of the work of healing our democracy is not going to be done by people of my age, regardless of how much we care or how invaluable we might consider our wisdom or experience. The various ailments afflicting our body politic have taken decades to reach their current state, and there will, unfortunately, be nothing quick about their cure. Reform and restoration will thus stretch across many years, and the state of reform at any given moment is going to be just that—a moment in what we must understand to be a long, slow, but also potentially creative and invigorating process, worthy of our patience and best efforts and the best efforts of our children.

I will be recruiting some of these younger citizens to assist in creating and curating the digital accompaniment to this book (including its website at citizens-uniting.org) as a means of keeping interested readers informed of new developments in the key arenas covered by the book. I know, though, that I will soon reach the limits of my own ability to keep pace with what must necessarily emerge in this arena. Old-fashioned by nature and by settled (if not curmudgeonly) choice, I have little capacity to imagine any of the forms or platforms that our children will employ either to reform or to practice democracy. I have faith that they will generally do it intelligently, compassionately, and well. I also believe they will do it better the more they know of the history and guiding principles of democracy.

Throughout a lifetime in government and politics, I have become steadily more convinced that the greater the challenges we face, the more crucial it becomes to pay attention to any lessons that history might offer about either the genesis of or possible solutions to those problems. This is an abiding conviction and one that I have naturally brought to bear on this book's examination of the biggest problem now facing our democracy: the preservation of democracy itself. But if I have naturally resorted to occasional historical sojourns in thinking about that problem, it should be evident enough to real historians that I remain an amateur in that field. The same is true of my forays into constitutional law and political theory. Neither an undergraduate focus on political theory nor a law degree provided me with anything like scholarly credentials in either of those fields. My passion for self-government has kept me reading and learning through the decades, though, so that, wherever possible in this volume, I attempt to provide guides to further reading by authors who do possess those credentials and the training to support them. Beyond that, the book's associated website will do its best to provide information about emerging scholarship in this arena.

The website will also make connections between current events, as they continue to unfold, and the book's major themes. The need for that kind of ongoing analysis was made painfully clear when the COVID-19 pandemic suddenly began consuming the world's attention early in 2020. By then, the book had reached the page proof stage, which meant that this paragraph would be its only significant reference to a world-transforming cataclysm. Yet the challenges which that tragic episode has laid before America and the world only sharpen the imperative to bring to a new level of problem-solving effectiveness all our means of human self-determination. This book is offered as one small contribution to that mighty and enduringly worthy endeavor.

Acknowledgments

My dedication of this book to the devoted citizens of Missoula barely begins to express my gratitude to them, or my regret at not being able to fill page after page with the names of those I know best and appreciate most. They, above all, have sustained my faith in the potential of democratic citizens here and everywhere to do what needs to be done, up to and including healing our badly damaged body politic.

I wrote most of this book at Break Espresso, one of Missoula's premiere coffee shops, depending on the always congenial attentiveness of the excellent baristas to get my dry cappuccino exactly right and depending too on another kind of stimulation that only a superb "third place" could provide. Because I've lived and worked in Missoula for nearly half a century now, I could often guess what was being discussed at any given table, even when my neighbors' voices reached me only as part of the overall buzz of conversation. While some of the encounters were purely social, I knew that many of them were concerned with various problems or opportunities confronting the community. I was constantly sustained by the realization that my neighbors could do (and were doing, every day) the hard and satisfying work of governing themselves.

Often a few city council members, Mayor John Engen, or former representative Pat Williams would add their voices to the hum. They, among many elected officials with whom I've worked over the years, have steadily deepened my conviction that politics is not only a high calling but that its best practitioners are indispensable to the healing of democracy. My successors in the mayor's office, Mike Kadas and then John Engen, by appointing me to several terms on the Missoula Redevelopment Agency (MRA) board, had provided me with an in-depth exposure to another crucial component of our democratic culture. Working for years with my board colleagues and the MRA staff on everything from affordable housing to skateboard parks and kayak waves brought home to me the real significance of citizenship as the care of one's city or larger community, as did the neighbors who served with me on the board that launched a lifelong learning institute and my colleagues on the board of the Missoula Farmers' Market. Even those forms of community building seem a little abstract when compared with what my next-door neighbors have taught me about democracy as our condominium association and its board reach agreement on when to pave the parking lot or how to pay for a new roof.

It was often board service, in fact, that provided me with a hands-on understanding of how millions of dedicated Americans have long been honing exactly those problem-solving skills that will be crucial to healing our democracy. I'm thinking particularly (and gratefully) of my colleagues on the boards of the Northwest Area Foundation and Philanthropy Northwest. I learned similar lessons from my service on the board of the Kettering Foundation (and then later as a Kettering associate), where I was privileged to engage for many years in the joint pursuit of that organization's mission of "making democracy work as it should." To those board colleagues, to the foundation's longtime president, David Mathews, and the entire staff, and, most especially, to John Dedrick for his unwavering support of my work, I owe far more gratitude than these few words can ever convey.

I found a similar willingness to stick with me when I went back to my first publisher, the University of Oklahoma Press, with the proposal for this book. Chuck Rankin was easing into retirement by then, but he persuaded his colleagues to take a chance on *Citizens Uniting*, passing the care of the book to his successor as editor in chief, Adam Kane. Adam and Steven B. Baker, the managing editor, shepherded the book to publication, ably assisted by Amy Hernandez and by Eva Silverfine's copyediting expertise and well-tuned ear for the English language.

Meanwhile back on the home front, Caroline Stephens devoted several weeks of focused effort to researching and preparing endnotes, assisted across the finish line by Sam Kemmis, home for a few weeks and impressed into something just short of indentured servitude.

Sam also helped me think through and launch the prototype for what Bob and Marc Jaffe, along with Ednor Therriault and Kate Whittle, have fashioned into the digital accompaniment to this book. Kate Paskievitch not only played a key role on that team but also carefully and conscientiously prepared the book's index.

Most of my family and many of my friends read chapters now and then or talked through with me the most challenging puzzles I was encountering. For that stimulation and support, I extend heartfelt, if utterly inadequate, thanks.

Every morning, Jean Larson and I spend an hour or so sitting in darkness or dim, dawning light, sipping coffee, checking in about family, friends, politics . . . life in general. Tentatively at first, and then with growing trust and finally with deep satisfaction, I started bringing to those conversations whatever was most stimulating or puzzling to me at that stage of the book's emergence. The person I there came to rely on as "Citizen Jean" never failed to bring to any given morning's challenge or conundrum some nuanced perspective that I in turn never failed to work into the text. Jean's insights don't get any footnotes, but they earned and she will always have my deepest gratitude.

Introduction

From Citizens United to Citizens Uniting

I had not been looking to write another book until I heard at the end of January 2010 about the U.S. Supreme Court's decision in *Citizens United v. Federal Election Commission*. As I set about examining the argument and the background of the ruling, the actual consequences of the decision and of its judicial offspring began to spread across the political landscape and to combine their toxic effects with other wounds and diseases already afflicting the body of the republic. One consequence was that, as the decade of this book's gestation progressed, the word "dysfunction" began to emerge as a kind of mantra among political observers, until it had become one of the most frequently invoked descriptors of our politics. It is important to remember that this sense of democratic malaise had thoroughly pervaded public consciousness and discourse long before the 2016 presidential election. Most of the major afflictions besetting the republic at that point still infect it today. These include the following:

- The ever-tightening grip of partisanship, which feeds the deepening inability of our political culture to identify or pursue the common good, routinely producing government gridlock, and making it nearly impossible to adopt effective or sustainable solutions to any of the major problems facing our society.

- Meanwhile, the influence of money and wealth over elections and governing institutions only continues to expand under the protection of a series of Supreme Court rulings.[1]
- The unrestrained roles of money and partisanship contribute to a feeling among most ordinary people that they aren't heard or empowered to influence the conditions of their lives in a democratically meaningful way.
- Election campaigns have grown much longer, much more negative, and far more costly than they would be if they were designed by the people they are meant to serve.
- Despite all that time and money, the system does not reliably assure that the most qualified (or even minimally qualified) candidates are nominated or elected. Instead, it too often puts in office people who seem more focused on securing their own reelection than on anything resembling the common good.
- The Electoral College and its nearly universal winner-take-all operating system now routinely narrow the presidential race to a handful of swing states, leaving citizens in other states effectively disenfranchised. Even worse, it far too often denies the presidency to the candidate who has won the majority of votes. This departure from the basic democratic principle of majority rule undermines still further the legitimacy of the presidential office.
- It is partisanship above all that prevents reform of the Electoral College system; at the same time, partisanship drives the redistricting process to create as many "safe" congressional seats as possible, leaving more millions of citizens feeling disenfranchised in those elections.
- The unrestrained role of partisanship reaches beyond elected office, so that it now openly dominates judicial appointments—especially to the U.S. Supreme Court. The worst effect of this unprecedented manipulation of the appointment process has been an erosion of the legitimacy of the Court itself in the public mind, regardless of the qualifications of any nominee.
- The widespread consternation occasioned by Donald Trump's 2016 Electoral College victory tended to obscure how thin the support of either major candidate had been prior to that election; indeed, it became clear by the end of

the campaign that most people were more inclined to vote *against* the candidate they most deeply loathed rather than *for* the one they thought could govern well.[2]

- What we see, then, is the chronic and progressive loss of legitimacy by all three branches of the national government.

- Meanwhile, the partisanship so determinative of the actions of elected officials is itself driven and sustained by deepening, ever more intractable ideological tribalism among voters themselves.

Again, almost all of these ills had already deeply infected our political system before the 2016 election cycle began. Nevertheless, Donald Trump's Electoral College victory that November roused such a widespread and intense reaction from so many voters, liberal and otherwise, that it very nearly obliterated any memory of this much broader and already well-advanced decline in the health of our democracy. In a sense this collective amnesia was perfectly understandable, given that we now had a person occupying the presidency who had lost the popular election by a large margin, a result that was surely not unrelated to the fact most Americans considered him thoroughly unqualified for the position. That state of affairs was only exacerbated in the following months, as an unprecedented and relentless stream of drama poured forth from the White House. The late-night tweets, the inexplicable policy gyrations, including spur-of-the-moment foreign policy pronouncements often deeply dismaying to America's longtime allies, the astonishing capacity of this political novice to act in ways no one would ever before have considered presidential—all of this theater commanded so much public attention that there seemed to be no time or energy left even to ask one fairly basic question: "How did we get ourselves into this fix to begin with?"

As this book went to press in the midst of the 2020 presidential campaign, Donald Trump had been impeached by a heavily partisan vote in the House of Representatives but saved from conviction by a similarly partisan tally in the Senate. By that time, the inflexibility of partisanship surprised no one, which rendered the outcome of the impeachment proceedings equally unsurprising.

Those most distressed by the Trump phenomenon therefore found their political attention focused almost exclusively on electing a new president. Regardless of the outcome of the 2020 election, however, we were still going to have to confront the backlog of problems that had so thoroughly beset our democracy before 2016. The real issue, from this point of view, was not so much Donald Trump but us. The real issue was what we had allowed to become of our democracy—and what we were going to do about it.

There were plenty of straightforward answers to the question of what had gone wrong in 2016, and many of them (like the undemocratic operation of the Electoral College) were perfectly valid. But just as I will argue that the 2010 decision in *Citizens United* cannot be reversed by glib slogans about corporate personhood or money as speech, so too what so many saw as the cataclysm of the 2016 presidential election would ultimately demand a response that looked further back than that election and further forward than the next one. What might it take, then, to shift our focus to that bigger picture? One step in that direction would be to recognize that the cumulative effect of all the wounds, diseases, and disabilities that have beset the body politic amount to nothing less than a crisis of legitimacy, not only for one particular administration, Congress, or Supreme Court but for our government as a whole. Yet that recognition can itself be overwhelming, leaving individual citizens feeling that there is nothing they can possibly do about any of this.

In that context, the ancient metaphor of Archimedes' lever may help us to imagine how we are going to meet the challenges confronting our democracy. We don't have to move the whole world, but the magnitude of the challenges now facing American democracy are gargantuan enough, and the resources at hand often feel insignificant enough, that we could well wish for a long and resilient Archimedean lever and a sturdy fulcrum resting on a secure enough foundation to enable us to move what sometimes seems an immovable burden. No one lever is going to suffice nor can any one book serve as a reliable manual for the job we have to do. Healing democracy can only be done democratically, which means that we can only do it in conversation with one another. In that spirit, I will suggest the possibility of a twenty-first century equivalent of the great democratic reform movement carried out by the Progressives a century ago. While I am by no means an uncritical fan of Progressive policies, what makes those reformers worth remembering now is not the particulars of their agenda but *"healing the ailments that plague our body politic*

their ability, in the face of deeply entrenched and well-financed opposition, to enact an astonishing and lasting suite of major democratic reforms. Those Progressive Era reforms included the enfranchisement of women (through the Nineteenth Amendment), the direct election of senators (codified in the Seventeenth Amendment), the creation in many states of powerful instruments of direct democracy, such as initiative and referendum, and, in some places, nonpartisan local elections.

None of that was easy by any means. There was concerted opposition from entrenched defenders of the status quo, just as there will be to every significant effort to restore democracy in our time. The good news is that several elements of such a movement have already begun to emerge. One aim of this book is to help readers identify any particular reforms that they might be motivated to support. More specifically, I will suggest that a sustained movement of democratic reform and restoration is going to require the creation of a "democracy lobby" at least as well organized, as well financed, and as effective in advancing the cause of democracy as the gun lobby has been in pursuing its objectives.

The feasibility of creating and sustaining such a powerful lobby rests on the assumption that millions of good citizens are both concerned enough about the current threats to their democracy and practiced enough in their own democratic competence to give such an instrument the heft and power necessary to advance the concerted and sustained work of healing the major ailments now afflicting our body politic. This is not to deny the magnitude of the challenge before us. While we will see that some democratic reform initiatives have made promising progress, others face immense hurdles. Effective reform of campaign finance law or of the presidential election system, for example, may not be possible without amending the U.S. Constitution. Again, such challenges can seem insurmountable, threatening to discourage us from undertaking any reform initiatives at all. But in the final analysis, challenge is what democracy is for. Either we're up to this one or we're not. I have no doubt that we are, in fact, equal to this challenge, provided we each bring what we are best situated to contribute to this effort to heal democracy.

In this book, which is intended as one contribution to that democracy-healing effort, I will sometimes draw on examples from my own experience in my native state of Montana, or my home community of Missoula. In no case is that meant to suggest that there is anything special about Missoula or Montana, let alone about my own experiences. The illustrations are valuable only insofar as they motivate readers to substitute stories from their own communities and their own lives. It is only from that very personal material that we have any hope of drawing the strength and wisdom we are going to need for the long struggle of revitalizing our democracy. This book is centered on the conviction that the multiple wounds and diseases now afflicting our body politic can best be healed by mobilizing and leveraging with renewed intensity this fundamental form of democratic citizenship. How that might happen will take a book to unfold.

In chapter 1 I will take a quick look at the history, rationale, and possibilities for reforming the Electoral College as a kind of warm-up exercise for examining the other big challenges now confronting us. That example underscores, among other things, what a stumbling block unconstrained partisanship can be, not only to solving society's major substantive problems but also to addressing the challenges confronting democracy itself.

Parties aren't going to disappear, though, and under the right conditions, they can actually help democracy work for us. In chapter 2 I argue, however, that partisanship in our day has become all too much like quicksand, pulling everything, including democratic reforms, into its mire. Do we, the people, really have what it takes to rescue our governing institutions from that deadly entanglement?

The most compelling reason for believing we do have that capacity is simply that, even while our major political institutions have fallen into deepening dysfunction, we as a people have maintained an impressive capacity to solve problems and realize opportunities closer to home. Because we so often take this grassroots republican vigor for granted, in chapter 3 I inquire how this solid democratic ground might afford us a base from which to rescue our floundering institutions.

In the same spirit, in chapter 4 I remind readers that we have done something very much like this, imperfectly but impressively, a century or so ago, even amending the Constitution several times in the process. In the presence of our too-often-overlooked democratic capacity, that history should fortify our hope that we can again meet historic-scale challenges to our democracy.

Perhaps the supreme test of that hope is what the Supreme Court has now done to one of our ancestors' most solid and widespread reforms: protecting elections against the corrupting influence of concentrated wealth, including that accumulated by corporations. In chapter 5 I begin to inspect those campaign finance decisions, taking a hard look through democratic eyes, searching for the rulings' deepest democratic flaws and injuries but also using that search to remind us of why we care so deeply about (and have so much faith in) our time-honored republican principles and practices, not least free speech itself.

Citizens United invited corporations into the electoral arena from which our ancestors had barred them—decimating in the process a social compact with corporations that, as I remind us in chapter 6, had been (and still is) crucial to any modern society remaining the master rather than the servant of the economic creatures it has generated. This isn't the first time our highest court has undermined the people's control over key elements of their society, but no genuine democracy can allow as few as five persons to prevent the rest of us from determining for ourselves the basic conditions of our existence.

To get back on top of this situation (and indeed to invite the Court to help us do so if it chooses), in chapter 7 I examine the even bigger problem buried in the entire series of campaign finance rulings, reaching back more than forty years. The deepest judicial injuries to democracy have arisen from an interpretation of the First Amendment that has departed radically from the democratic principles of the nation's founders. Unfortunately, society at large has been deeply complicit in this departure from our republican foundations.

Recalling why free speech is so essential to any meaningful form of self-government reminds us that many citizens have actually been getting better at that kind of democratic problem-solving speech at exactly the same time that our highest court has been undermining democracy and the other two branches have become less capable of solving the biggest problems facing our society. Moreover, as I suggest in chapter 8, while some forms of accumulated wealth have been turning our democracy into an outright plutocracy, the wealth concentrated in philanthropic institutions is being increasingly steered toward strengthening democracy in an inspiring variety of ways.

Meanwhile, as I recount in chapter 9, citizens have recently been uniting around a range of democratic reforms that are now poised to coalesce into the twenty-first-century equivalent of the Progressive movement, especially if they are accompanied by the creation of a powerful democracy lobby. In that spirit, the *Citizens Uniting* website (at citizens-uniting.org) provides opportunities for any of us to discover and make our own contributions to the strands of the emerging reform movement, as we join forces in the hard but worthy work of getting our democratic body back in shape.

As we do that, we may simultaneously position our nation to play a newly constructive role in the family of nations. As I briefly recount in the epilogue, the version of American exceptionalism that has insisted that we are the nation that must show the rest of the world how to be democratic has not only lost its luster but has become a positive hindrance to our contributing meaningfully to the resolution of global problems. America's return to a humbler and more historically accurate understanding of our democratic strengths will enable us to contribute much more constructively to the crucial work of global self-determination.

1 Electoral College Reform
A Warm-Up Case Study

The mode of appointment of the Chief Magistrate of the United States is almost the only part of the [proposed Constitution], of any consequence, which has escaped without severe censure . . . from its opponents.

* * *

It was desirable that the sense of the people should operate in the choice of the person to whom so important a trust was to be confided. This end will be answered by committing the right of making it, not to any preestablished body [such as Congress], but to men chosen by the people for the special purpose . . .

* * *

It was equally desirable, that the immediate election should be made by men most capable of analyzing the qualities adapted to the station, and acting under circumstances favorable to deliberation, and to a judicious combination of all the reasons and inducements which were proper to govern their choice. A small number of persons, selected by their fellow-citizens from the general mass, will be most likely to possess the information and discernment requisite to such complicated investigations.

* * *

This process of election affords a moral certainty that the office of President will seldom fall to the lot of any man who is not in an eminent degree endowed with the requisite qualifications. . . . It will not be too strong to say that there will be a constant probability of seeing the station filled by characters preeminent for ability and virtue.

—*Alexander Hamilton*, Federalist *No. 68*

When the votes had all been counted for the 2016 presidential election, Hillary Clinton led Donald Trump by nearly three million votes (65,844,969 to 62,979,984).[1] In percentage terms, Clinton had garnered the support of 48.3 percent of the total votes to 46.2 percent for Trump. But because Trump had won 304 votes in the Electoral College to Clinton's 227, the clear second choice of the American people would be inaugurated as their president.[2] Four previous second-place finishers in the popular vote had also become president, most recently in 2000, with George W. Bush's Electoral College victory over Al Gore.[3] As with all the previous elections of second-place finishers, Gore's half-million vote edge over Bush in 2000 had been much narrower than Clinton's substantial margin over Trump. In 2000, it had been the Supreme Court's willingness to be drawn into Florida's vote-counting controversy, and the resulting 5–4 decision in Bush's favor (the five justices in the majority all having been appointed by Republican presidents), that had been the main focus of public attention.[4] The Court's activist role, with its partisan aura, somewhat overshadowed the equally crucial role of the Electoral College system in enabling the runner-up to win the election.

In 2016, with the popular margin much wider than in 2000, the Electoral College came under considerably sharper criticism, with some citizens even trying to persuade official electors to ignore the votes in their states and instead vote for the national popular vote winner. That did not happen, but it did underscore that in a period of fragile popular faith in so many governing institutions, any instance of the people's second choice being elevated to the presidency was bound to worsen an already widespread sense of disenfranchisement and governing illegitimacy. When the discrepancy between the popular vote and the Electoral College tally grows as large as it did in 2016, that discontent is naturally and correspondingly deepened. Clearly, by 2016, the Electoral College could no longer be said to have "escaped without censure" as Alexander Hamilton found that it had in 1787. In fact, the mechanism had been one of the most controversial features of the Constitution for a very long time. As reported by the reform organization FairVote, "Over the history of our country, there have been at least 700 proposed amendments to modify or abolish the Electoral College—more than any other subject of Constitutional reform."[5]

It was not surprising, then, that the 2016 Electoral College victory of such a clear loser in the popular vote stirred up one more wave of discontent with the entire Electoral College system. Still, it was almost immediately evident that the strength of this discontent would not by itself be enough to bring about change in the system. Within days of the election, retiring Senator Barbara Boxer (D-CA) introduced a resolution calling for abolition of the Electoral College, but no one thought it had any chance of even getting a hearing in the Republican-controlled Senate (as in fact it did not.)[6]

Given this apparently intractable situation, any reader might reasonably ask why Electoral College reform should be the first topic we tackle here. It certainly doesn't appear to be low-hanging fruit on the tree of reform, ripe for the plucking—nor is it even necessarily the most crucial reform we might undertake in the cause of democracy. Still, the antimajoritarian operation of the Electoral College constitutes a highly visible presenting symptom of that far more pervasive unhealthiness that now afflicts our body politic. The Electoral College is also appropriate as a preliminary case study because there are features of this particular malady that can prepare us to address other democratic wounds and diseases with sharper discernment.

For example, anyone who is serious about changing the presidential election system has to be in it for the long haul, and in this sense the effort to make the election of the president more genuinely democratic is similar to many of the other arenas of democratic reform that we will examine. In each case, I will argue that sustaining the requisite level of commitment against inevitable disappointments and setbacks will depend substantially on taking a longer and deeper view than our increasingly superficial political culture generally affords us. Here, I aim to use Electoral College reform to get us started thinking about how we might, in this and in every other case of democratic failure, seek that broader and deeper view. In particular, I will suggest how a more nuanced understanding of both history and basic democratic theory can, in the long run, enhance the likelihood of our actually making a difference with something as democratically injurious and yet as difficult to change as the Electoral College.

Part of the purpose here, as with later chapters' examination of other ailments in the body of democracy, is to use the study of those wounds and diseases to remind ourselves of some basic democratic principles and enduring democratic strengths that we have tended to overlook or to take for granted. Often those strengths turn out to be embedded in the origins (if seldom in the current operation) of the now-dysfunctional institution or practice. To anticipate one leading example: while preserving the governing power of states had been part of the original rationale behind the Electoral College, it really doesn't perform that state-empowering function any longer. Yet a reinvigorated federalism is going to prove indispensable to democratic renewal generally and is very likely to play a key role in Electoral College reform itself. In those rather unexpected terms, then, recalling the republican origins of a dysfunctional mechanism can strengthen the conceptual underpinnings of democratic reform.

It turns out that getting to the bottom of what is so democratically damaging about something like the Electoral College (or the Supreme Court's campaign finance rulings) is going to be one of the best ways of strengthening our understanding—and therefore our effective deployment—of enduringly healthy democratic practices. In those double-edged or dialectical terms, it will be helpful to examine the most democratically damaging features of the Electoral College, both as it was established by the Constitution and as it has been institutionalized in the actual practice of presidential elections.

The core problems with the Electoral College can be roughly catalogued as follows:

- It institutionalizes a raw numerical inequity that consistently gives some American citizens greater influence than others in the choice of our president.
- It can (and has already twice in this young century) put the second choice of the people in the nation's highest office, thus undermining not just in theory but in hard fact the basic democratic principle of majority rule.

- It has created a situation in which a small handful of "swing states" exercise almost total dominance over presidential elections, leaving the citizens of the vast majority of our states essentially disenfranchised.

Against this variegated background of democratic shortcomings in the Electoral College system, three main paths to reform have emerged, each of which would, if successful, address one or more of the undemocratic features of the Electoral College system:

- A constitutional amendment abolishing or fundamentally altering the Electoral College
- An interstate compact that would have the effect of abolition, without requiring a constitutional amendment
- State-by-state reforms to replace the winner-take-all mechanism currently employed in all but two states, in this way reducing or eliminating the swing state dominance of presidential elections

Before turning to those paths to reform, or to the problems they seek to address, we will be well served by reminding ourselves of how the Electoral College came to be in the first place, beginning with the grounds originally put forth to justify this peculiar institution. Those grounds fell into two main categories: (1) ensuring that the best available person was chosen as president; and (2) preserving the influence of the individual states in the federal system. I argue that neither of these objectives can any longer serve as a valid justification for the Electoral College, and that this, in conjunction with the previously delineated catalogue of the institution's undemocratic features, justifies at least one more in the long series of efforts to abolish or alter that system. But because those efforts have had so little success in the past, it is worthwhile to start with the main arguments in favor of the system. What we see is that behind each of these justifications for the Electoral College lie some very important and powerful principles of self-government that cannot simply be brushed aside. The institution they defend no longer fulfills those principles, and it needs to be modified or replaced. That is far more likely to happen, though, if the change is accompanied by the preservation, if not the strengthening, of the principles that have underlain (and repeatedly used to justify) its existence. This same dialectic of seeking out and nurturing the democratic principles underlying no longer democratic practices and institutions will be repeated with several of the other democratic ailments and efforts to heal them that we will examine in later chapters. With that in mind, let's take a closer look at the main justifications that have been advanced for creating or retaining the Electoral College.

The passages quoted at the outset of this chapter from Hamilton's *Federalist* No. 68 present quite a complex set of justifications for the Electoral College, combining elements of majoritarianism with a more aristocratic strain. Never a democrat or anything like it, Hamilton nevertheless acknowledged that "it was desirable that the sense of the people should operate" in the selection of the president.[7] But Hamilton was quick to note that this popular role needed to be carefully circumscribed. As he explained, while the people would be directly (and in that sense democratically) engaged in choosing the members of the Electoral College, the people would not themselves be choosing the president. Instead (and in Hamilton's view appropriately), they would be choosing the men that they most trusted to choose, in turn, the best person to serve as president.[8] Hamilton clearly imagined these wise electors deliberating among themselves before choosing that best person for the office of president. In these terms, the Electoral College was simply part of the broader fabric of the Constitution, which sought to strike a sustainable balance between democracy (rule by the many) and aristocracy (in the root sense of rule by the best or most able).

It was probably never realistic to think that the Electoral College could serve as the kind of deliberative body that Hamilton described in *Federalist* No. 68, especially given that the Constitution itself directed that the electors chosen by the people were to gather in their respective states, not in a central location where they might all, after careful deliberation, decide who was best suited to be the president.[9] Still, it was possible to imagine the electors, in those state-by-state gatherings, discussing among themselves who was the best person to lead the nation—a picture that contemplates a process quite different from one in which the people themselves, by majority vote, selected the president. This more deliberative, more aristocratic, less majoritarian approach was clearly how Hamilton saw the Electoral College operating.

But if that vision was ever realistic, it no longer bears the slightest resemblance to reality.

One feature of the 2016 election made that contest's overthrow of majority rule especially troublesome, and troublesome in a sense that goes to the very heart of representative democracy, while turning Hamilton's "choice of the best" defense of the Electoral College precisely on its head. In chapter 8 I will examine more closely the theory of democratic representation; for now, it is enough to note that one of its foundational premises is that the people at large are capable of choosing officials who are, in turn, capable of governing. This minimal justification for representative government is so basic that we almost never bother to articulate it or even to think about it. It is relevant in this context, though, because it provides a potent reminder of why majority rule is usually the best form of democratic decision making and therefore why the antimajoritarian features of the Electoral College are so problematic.

It is a basic fact of political life that in any given situation, on any given issue or question, there are bound to be many different opinions, including some seriously misplaced or counterfactual opinions. But, as James Surowiecki argued so persuasively in *The Wisdom of Crowds*, more often than not the collective judgement of a large number of people comes closer to sound and accurate conclusions than any one individual (or indeed any minority) is likely to come.[10] It is because of the general soundness of its conclusions that collective wisdom can safely tolerate (while isolating or otherwise rendering relatively harmless) the outlying opinions.

Crucially, in 2016, a very substantial majority of Americans were quite firmly convinced that Donald Trump was not qualified for the office he was seeking.[11] In terms of the fundamental republican premise that the people at large are capable of selecting the most competent among them for public office, something is seriously wrong with the system by which that office is filled if the person judged by most voters to be unqualified is nevertheless allowed to assume the office. In the 2016 presidential election, the key node of that defective system—the mechanism that allowed for the election of a person thought by most voters to be unqualified—was precisely the Electoral College. If Hamilton's conclusion that the operation of that institution would guarantee "that there will be a constant probability of seeing the station filled by

characters preeminent for ability and virtue" had ever been justified, the election of 2016 seemed to have obliterated that justification for good.[12]

The second of the original justifications for the Electoral College has nearly as little contemporary evidence to support it, but
because it has more practical force in terms of keeping the institution in place, it will require closer examination. We have first
to remind ourselves in more detail of the historical origins of the
Electoral College.

The Constitution that was proposed by the convention delegates in 1787 provided that each state was entitled to the same
number of electors as there were members of its congressional delegation.[13] If the delegates in Philadelphia had adopted the Virginia
Plan, which they first considered, both houses of Congress would
have been apportioned by population, and the Electoral College
would thus also have reflected that one-person-one-vote principle.
But once the Great Compromise emerged, securing to the small-
est state the same number of senators as the largest, this departure
from majoritarianism carried over into the Electoral College, and
thus into the choice of the chief executive.

Since every state elects two senators, regardless of its population, small states are and always have been automatically over-
represented, not only in the Senate itself, but by implication in
the Electoral College as well. Thus Wyoming, with three electoral votes representing slightly over half a million residents, has
roughly four times as much clout per capita in the Electoral College as Texas, where thirty-two electors represent nearly twenty-
five million people. In the fundamentally important terms of
equal voting power, this feature of the Electoral College is clearly
undemocratic, and much of the energy behind Electoral College
reform has always been aimed at this inequity. That energy gets
a boost whenever a second-place popular vote finisher secures a
majority in the Electoral College, since it is precisely this unequal
apportionment of Electoral College votes among the states that
enables this to happen.

Under these circumstances, it becomes especially important to
recall why this inegalitarian feature got built into presidential elections in the first place. In fact, there was a very strong (and indeed
strongly democratic) reason for it. That reason becomes clear when
we remember that many of the leaders of the American Revolution

who were most passionate about the necessity of the people being in control of their governments (revolutionaries who believed that it was precisely for such control that they had risked their lives) were for that very reason extremely skeptical about the proposed Constitution's transfer of so much governing authority from the states to the national government. Those skeptics included such undoubted patriots as Patrick Henry and Sam Adams. These and other passionate advocates of democracy believed that the people could effectively govern themselves in small, accessible polities like the states; they had sincere doubts that they could remain in control of a powerful governing entity that reached across thirteen states. They were convinced that, to the extent the proposed Constitution transferred sovereignty from state governments to the nation, it was going to undermine the practice of self-government as it had come to be experienced—and treasured—in America.

In this, they drew support from one of the most persuasive and respected of Enlightenment thinkers, the Baron de Montesquieu, who had argued in his *Spirit of the Laws* that any authentic republic must be confined to what we might now call a human-scale territory. "It is natural for a republic to have only a small territory; otherwise it cannot long subsist," Montesquieu had written—and many of America's most passionate republicans were certain that he was right.[14] Their individual colonies, which had become their states, and to which most of them now referred as their "countries," operated at the scale that Montesquieu had approved—a scale at which they themselves felt that they had been able to establish genuine republics. Many of them were deeply fearful that a nation of the size contemplated by the proposed Constitution must necessarily fall prey to the evils against which Montesquieu had warned.

The defenders of state sovereignty had therefore been especially diligent about protecting those features of the proposed Constitution that maintained a meaningful role for the states within the new structure. One of those was the U.S. Senate, where it could be argued that the states were represented *as states*, since they were all equally represented in that body, and also since it was the state legislatures that would choose senators. The proposed Electoral College, by assigning to each state a number of electors corresponding to the size of their congressional delegation, blended the Senate's representation of states with the House's representation of individuals in the selection of the president. The role of the states as states in the presidential selection process appeared again with a vengeance in the way the Constitution addressed the possibility that sometimes no presidential candidate might receive a majority of the electoral votes. Article II provided that the choice of the president then fell to the House of Representatives, but rather than giving each member of the House a vote in that choice, the document provided (and still provides) that each *state* would have one vote.[15]

These and other safeguards of state power in the proposed Constitution were still not enough to overcome the distrust of many Americans about this powerful new national government. It was this uneasiness that would eventually produce the Bill of Rights, the promise of which these democratic federalists extracted as the price for permitting their states to ratify the Constitution. All of the limitations on government action set forth in the first eight amendments were aimed at the new national government and intended to prevent the worst abuses that Montesquieu had thought must proceed from a big, centralized state. That catalogue of limitations on the new government was reinforced by some boilerplate in the Ninth Amendment ("The enumeration in the Constitution, of certain rights, shall not be construed to deny or disparage others retained by the people")[16] and then capped off in the Tenth with an explicit declaration of state power: "The powers not delegated to the United States by the Constitution, nor prohibited by it to the States, are reserved to the States respectively, or to the people."[17]

I have made this brief foray into constitutional history simply as a reminder that the structure of the Electoral College emerged from a complex set of circumstances and beliefs, not least among them being the widespread conviction within the revolutionary generation that self-government depended substantially on the continued empowerment of individual states within the national structure. The relationship of democracy to federalism has, of course, had a very complex history. From John C. Calhoun to George Wallace and beyond, federalism in its narrowest, states-rights guise has repeatedly been invoked in the cause of racial oppression, a fact that has left many Americans convinced that federalism is itself inherently oppressive. That conclusion may not be substantially softened by the reminder that James Madison and Thomas Jefferson had been among the first to invoke a strong version of federalism with their authorship of the Virginia and Kentucky resolutions in 1798, not in defense of slavery but in opposition to the oppressive Alien and Sedition Acts.

More to the point of the democratic challenges of our own time, we will see repeatedly in later chapters of this book that the work of healing our body politic in the coming years is very often going to have to be carried out at the state (or indeed, the local) level. Whether it is a matter of regaining democratic control over campaign finance or of implementing electoral reforms that can begin to loosen the stranglehold of the two-party system, it will be crucial that individual states have the freedom and authority to experiment with procedures that the nation as a whole may not yet be prepared to embrace. That use of state sovereignty to test new forms of self-government represents federalism in its most fundamentally democratic dimension. By contrast, the vestige of federalism that continues to cling to the structure of the Electoral College contains none of this kind of self-governing creativity; instead, it seriously undermines the core belief that the people are in charge of their own government.

I confess that I have not always viewed the Electoral College in this light. In fact, if a proposal to abolish that institution had come before the Montana legislature when I was serving there in the 1970s and 1980s, I may well have voted against it, and precisely on grounds of democratic federalism. At that time, Montana was defending its adoption of the nation's highest coal severance tax against an interstate commerce challenge that eventually made its way to the U.S. Supreme Court. Meanwhile, many of us were advocating restrictions on the development of nuclear power in our state that would likely have faced a similar challenge if we had succeeded in passing that legislation. With the defense of Montana's sovereignty over its own environment very much on my mind, and feeling the vulnerability of that sovereignty to national preemption, I remember arguing with non-Montanans in defense of our disproportionate representation in the U.S. Senate and thereby in the Electoral College. I would still argue in favor of a muscular federalism, but I no longer believe that the inequities built into the Electoral College contribute anything meaningful to genuine federalism.

Still, a lively appreciation for the value of federalism should keep us open to exploring the possibility that states (and especially

small states) might be more willing to relinquish the disproportionate power they enjoy in the Electoral College if they were
persuaded that the price they would pay for that element of a
democratic reform package is more than compensated by a genuine commitment to federalism in other components of the package. That commitment would have to be substantive to have this
effect, but it might not hurt if democratic reformers could sometimes acknowledge that the Tenth Amendment is actually a valid
component of the Bill of Rights and that its guarantee of state sovereignty may yet prove to be the bulwark of democracy its authors
designed it to be.

In fact, that resurgence of the republican essence of federalism
could occur in a truly consequential way in the course of pursuing
certain of those democratic reforms that are most likely to emerge
initially at the state or local level. Some of those reforms (especially in the campaign finance arena) are almost guaranteed to face
court challenges. When they do, the opportunity is likely to arise
to defend the reform, at least in part, on Tenth Amendment "powers reserved to the states" grounds. Since that is territory that has
been occupied almost exclusively by conservatives in recent times,
its invocation in the cause of democratic reform might come as a
surprise in some quarters—including among conservative judges.
The point here is not to make a detailed argument about the
Tenth Amendment but to invite conversation about how a genuine commitment to federalism might become an active part of a
reform agenda and how it might, in the process, begin to loosen
the determination among many Americans to defend outmoded
vestiges of federalism—like the Electoral College—that have become inimical to the cause of democracy.

Enticing as that prospect may be to some reformers, this discussion of federalism (and conservatism) brings into focus another
dimension of the Electoral College picture that seems likely to
keep effective reform at bay for the foreseeable future. That dimension is partisanship—a factor whose growing dominance of our
self-governing institutions and practices has, as I will detail in the
next chapter, become both one of the major diseases afflicting our
body politic and a leading barrier to curing other diseases. If the
Electoral College systematically undermines the exercise of democracy in presidential elections, the fact that the institution now
so reliably advances the interests of one party (the Republicans)

means that, at least for the time being, partisanship is likely to be a major barrier to Electoral College reform.

In the next chapter I will explore the role of parties and partisanship in resisting a whole range of democratic reforms. For now, though, we should note that, historically, the role of parties in the specific arena of Electoral College reform has actually cut both ways. Let's start with the first change to the Electoral College, which became the Twelfth Amendment to the Constitution. Article II, Section 1 of the Constitution originally provided that "[e]ach State shall appoint, in such Manner as the Legislature thereof may direct, a Number of Electors, equal to the whole Number of Senators and Representatives to which the State may be entitled in the Congress. . . . The Electors shall meet in their respective States, and vote by Ballot for two Persons, of whom one at least shall not be an Inhabitant of the same State with themselves."[18] Because that original language was drafted before political parties appeared on the American scene, it did not provide for what we now take for granted as a key feature of the process, namely a team from the same party being elected as president and vice president. Instead, the Constitution originally gave each elector two votes and mandated that the candidate with the greatest number of electoral votes would become president, while the runner-up would serve as vice president.[19]

Already with the 1796 election, this mechanism had produced the anomalous result of Thomas Jefferson serving as vice president under John Adams, while openly opposing many of Adams's policies.[20] By the 1800 election, two major political parties had been fully formed, but the constitutionally mandated Electoral College remained blind to their commanding presence. In particular, that original system provided no easy way for either of the new political parties to elect a team as president and vice president. In this regard, the Federalists proved savvier in 1800 than Jefferson's Democratic Republicans. The Federalist electors, while casting all their first-choice votes for Adams, arranged to have one of their electors cast his second vote for someone other than their vice-presidential candidate, Charles Cotesworth Pinckney. Jefferson and his running mate, Aaron Burr, overlooked this crucial maneuver. As a result, when the election was concluded, Jefferson and Burr had each received 73 electoral votes. Adams had garnered 65 votes and Pinckney a strategically diminished 64.[21]

By the terms of the Constitution, this threw the runoff election between Jefferson and Burr into the House of Representatives, where each state was entitled to one vote. Partisanship now temporarily took a back seat to personal ambition, as Burr spent several weeks exploring the possibility of persuading Federalist members of the House to support him rather than Jefferson. In the end, Alexander Hamilton, finding his distrust of the wily Burr outweighing his dislike of Jefferson's politics, persuaded James A. Bayard, the sole congressman from Delaware and a Federalist, to break the stalemate by abstaining on the next ballot, thus putting Jefferson in the White House.[22]

This fiasco, which came very close to turning into a full-blown constitutional crisis or even a civil war, soon produced the Twelfth Amendment to the Constitution, which implicitly recognized the fact of political parties by providing that "[t]he electors shall meet in their respective states and vote by ballot for President and Vice-President . . . ; they shall name in their ballots the person voted for as President, and in distinct ballots the person voted for as Vice-President."[23] By allowing in this way for teams to run for the two positions, the Twelfth Amendment recognized implicitly the role that political parties had come to play in America.

If nothing else, this rather bizarre chapter in our constitutional history might serve as a reminder that when a political institution like the Electoral College fails to serve the needs of a self-governing people, it can and should be changed. That happened again in 1961, with the adoption of the Twenty-Third Amendment, which finally gave citizens of the District of Columbia a voice in presidential elections by granting to the District a number of electoral votes not to exceed those allotted to the least populous state.[24]

While there have been hundreds of efforts since the adoption of the Twelfth Amendment to correct the fundamental inequities built into the structure of the Electoral College, the only attempt that showed any real chance of succeeding arose a half century ago, in the wake of the 1968 presidential election. During that tumultuous year (which brought the assassinations of Robert F. Kennedy and Martin Luther King Jr. and bloody suppression of demonstrations outside the Democratic National Convention in Chicago), a very serious third-party candidacy by Alabama Governor George Wallace complicated the center-court face-off between the Republican nominee, Richard Nixon, and the Democrat, Hubert Humphrey.

In the end, Nixon defeated Humphrey both in the popular vote (31,785,480 to 31,275,166) and much more decisively in the Electoral College (301 to 191).[25] Wallace, with just under ten million popular votes, commanded forty-six Electoral College votes, all from his native South.[26] Had either Wallace or Humphrey (or both between them) captured thirty-two more electoral votes, Nixon would have fallen short of a majority in the Electoral College, which would have thrown the presidential election into the House of Representatives. That possibility, which had been very real up until election day, alarmed both major political parties enough to unite them in putting serious Electoral College reform proposals before Congress in 1969.[27] Both Nixon and Humphrey went on record in favor of reform, and in September 1969, a proposal to abolish the Electoral College passed the House by the overwhelming margin of 338 to 70.[28] The Senate version of the resolution faced a filibuster, however, and the measure died the next year when a combination of southern and small-state senators rallied enough votes to defeat two separate attempts to end the filibuster.[29]

That attempt to abolish the Electoral College has appeared for the time being to be the high-water mark of outright repeal efforts. The 1976 contest between Gerald Ford and Jimmy Carter produced another attempt at repeal, this one introduced into the Senate by Indiana Democrat Birch Bayh, but that proposal was eventually defeated in the Senate by a vote of 51 to 48 and was never considered by the House.[30] While there have been several subsequent proposals to abolish the Electoral College (including Senator Boxer's token gesture following the 2016 presidential election), that route to reform has appeared to be blocked for the time being.

Meanwhile, though, a different approach to the same objective has gained some notable momentum. Launched in February of 2006, the National Popular Vote Interstate Compact (NPVIC) is an ingenious and well-organized effort to nationalize presidential elections without amending the Constitution. It seeks to do so by utilizing the constitutionally authorized mechanism of an interstate compact. Such compacts are familiar in many arenas of public policy, from water allocation (where states along the Colorado River, for example, have agreed about how much water each state can draw from the river) to insurance product regulation. The NPVIC would bind each participating state to award all of its electoral votes to the presidential candidate who receives the most popular votes nationwide in that election.[31] By its express terms, the compact would not take effect until it had been adopted by enough states to provide a majority of the electoral votes needed to elect a president (that is, 270 of the total 538 electoral votes). Since the compacting states would constitute a majority in the Electoral College, their agreement to cast all of their votes for the national popular vote winner would automatically elect that person as president.

The compact effort had passed both houses of the California legislature by August of 2006 (at which point it was vetoed by Governor Arnold Schwarzenegger.) That veto was the first of two by Schwarzenegger, and other governors have also blocked adoption in their states.[32] Still, the effort continued, slowly adding states year by year (including California, where Governor Jerry Brown signed the legislation in 2011).[33] By the summer of 2019, the proposed compact had been approved by fifteen states plus the District of Columbia, with a combined total of 196 electoral votes. It was, at that point, well over halfway toward its own triggering goal, and it had passed at least one house in eight other states, with seventy-five additional electoral votes.[34]

Whether this particular reform effort will finally succeed or not is still very much an open question. Its first years had produced heartening success, but they had also revealed what a challenging road this would be. Rescission efforts were launched in some of the states where both the legislature and governor had previously approved the compact, and the initiative's savviest supporters knew that resistance would only stiffen as the goal drew nearer. Furthermore, even if the compact were to garner support in enough states to pull its own internal trigger, Article I, Section 10 of the U.S. Constitution seems to imply that it could not actually go into effect without congressional approval.[35] Since Congress has never approved any of the proposals for abolishing the Electoral College that it has seen over the centuries, it is not clear why it would approve this very indirect method of doing the same thing. Supporters of the compact argue that congressional approval is not constitutionally mandated, and it is conceivable that the Supreme Court (which would almost certainly be called on to settle the matter) might agree. Short of that, it is also possible that Congress would approve the compact if there were a powerful and persistent enough push behind it.

The NPVIC may or may not achieve its objective of making presidential elections more democratic. Whether it succeeds by its own terms or not, however, the project has the potential to contribute in less tangible ways to the larger, longer-term work of democratic reform. The sheer amount of organizing activity that is required to get both houses of any state legislature to approve the compact, and to persuade the governor to sign it, can be viewed not only as it affects the fate of the compact itself but also in terms of the democratic muscles that are being strengthened in the process. Those muscles will be indispensable in the equally long and hard battle to reclaim democratic control over campaign finance law or to contain partisanship within the bounds of effective self-government. In the meantime, there is one largely untested path to Electoral College reform that could be pursued on a state-by-state basis, potentially bringing into play, on behalf of reform, the very forces of federalism that we noted previously as part of the earliest justification for this institution.

As it turns out, one major problem resulting from the operation of the Electoral College—the undemocratic privileging of swing states in presidential elections—is fully within the control of each state and is therefore amenable to a robust exercise of just the kind of democratic federalism that people like Sam Adams and Patrick Henry supported. So, let us put the swing state problem on the table, tracing its roots directly to their grounding in the Electoral College and then examining how individual states could use their retained sovereignty to address this problem.

While the disproportionate representation of small-population states is the feature of the Electoral College that receives the most attention, and while that disproportion is certainly problematic in one-person-one-vote terms, it is no longer the only source of harm to democracy arising from our method of electing the president and should therefore not be the only focus of reform. In a nutshell, however disproportionate the Electoral College representation of Wyoming may be to that of California, no voter in either of those "safe" states enjoys anything close to the influence of voters in Ohio, Florida, or any other "swing state" when it comes to presidential elections. That disproportionate influence is directly

attributable to the Electoral College, but this undemocratic feature of the process could be eliminated by the action of individual
states without changing a word of the Constitution.

First, let's get clear about the problem, starting with some
numbers. In the 2012 presidential election, Barack Obama's massive "ground game" included the staffing of just under eight hundred campaign offices around the country. Exactly twenty-five of
those offices were located in the twenty-five states that the campaign staff knew from the outset they were either certain to carry
or certain to lose in November. By contrast to that one-office-per-
state allotment, over four hundred of Obama's offices (an average
of eighty offices per state) were concentrated in the five key swing
states of Colorado, Florida, Iowa, Ohio, and Wisconsin. In fact, 87
percent of the Obama offices were concentrated in just twelve
states.[36] Not by coincidence, those were the same twelve "in play"
states (and they were the only states) in which either Obama or
Mitt Romney or one of their running mates actually set foot during the crucial weeks between Labor Day and Election Day.[37] The
remaining thirty-eight states were taken for granted by both campaigns because they were viewed either as sure wins or certain
losses. The Romney campaign, meanwhile, did not even open field
offices in two-thirds of the states, concentrating all 284 of its offices in the sixteen states where Romney's campaign saw a chance
(but not a certainty) of either winning or losing.[38]

The picture is essentially the same if we look at advertising
expenditures. In that arena, the pattern of focusing on swing states
and ignoring all others was well documented for the 2012 election cycle, but it was by no means confined to that election. In
the final six months of the 2012 campaign, over 99 percent of all
advertising dollars were spent in (and on) just ten states.[39] But as
early as 2004, CNN reported that 52 percent of all the advertising
expenditures by either the Bush or Kerry campaigns were concentrated in three swing states, while the three largest (but "safe")
states of California, New York, and Texas were all but ignored.[40] In
2008, 95 percent of the combined advertising of both campaigns
was concentrated in fourteen swing states—the same states that
received 99 percent of the visits by either a presidential or vice-
presidential candidate.[41]

None of this is intended as a criticism of the decisions of any
of these campaigns or their professional staffs. They are making

exactly the decisions that our system of presidential elections dictate that they should make. The point here is that the Electoral College system has created a hugely undemocratic bias that reaches far beyond the disproportionate weighting of small and large states. Whether you live in California or Wyoming, you are essentially disenfranchised in the presidential election, not because of the size of your state's population but because you live in a "safe" state. As an individual, your vote is of next to no significance, and if you don't know that, the candidates do—and they act accordingly by ignoring you.

This radical disenfranchisement of "safe state" voters is directly attributable to the Electoral College system, and it would be eliminated if that system were ever to be removed from the Constitution. This is what Republican senator (and later presidential candidate) Bob Dole pointed out in a 1979 Senate speech in favor of abolishing the Electoral College. "Were we to switch to a system of direct election, I think we would see a resulting change in the nature of campaigning," Dole predicted.[42] He even argued that this would give voters in many small states more power than they now possess. "While urban areas will still be important campaigning centers, there will be a new emphasis given to smaller states," Dole continued. "Candidates will soon realize that all votes are important, and votes from small states carry the same import as votes from large states. That to me is one of the major attractions of direct election. Each vote carries equal importance."[43] Finally, Dole zeroed in on what in our day has become the central disenfranchising dynamic of the Electoral College system: the exclusive emphasis on swing states. "Direct election would give candidates incentive to campaign in states that are perceived to be single party states," Dole concluded. "For no longer will minority votes be lost. Their accumulated total will be important, and in some instances perhaps even decisive."[44]

As Dole was arguing, this swing-state problem would be eliminated if the Electoral College were to be abolished. But this increasingly damaging consequence of the Electoral College system could also be substantially addressed on a state-by-state basis, without the need to amend the Constitution. How can that be, if the Electoral College is part of the Constitution? The root of swing-state dominance in presidential politics does not lie in the wording of the Constitution, however, but in the nearly universal practice of allotting all of a state's electoral votes to whichever candidate secures a plurality of that state's popular vote. This winner-take-all system has been adopted by every state except Maine and Nebraska. Those two outliers have chosen to allocate their electoral votes according to the number of popular votes received by the presidential candidates in each of the state's congressional districts.

Without examining this approach in detail here, a moment's thought will reveal that if more states followed this practice, the pattern of campaign spending, candidate visits, and voter disenfranchisement outlined above would be substantially altered. It would be even more radically transformed if states began apportioning their electoral votes according to the proportion of the popular vote each candidate won in that state—a change that would be perfectly consistent with the current language of the Constitution. If all of California's electoral votes were not guaranteed to go to the Democratic presidential candidate but were divided proportionately according to the popular vote, every Republican Californian's vote would suddenly matter—and the candidates would prove it by showing up. And if Wyoming's three electoral votes were allocated proportionately, a Wyoming Democrat might know that two of those votes will surely go to the Republican candidate, but if Democrats can muster a third of the popular vote, they will have a say in the Electoral College.

It is entirely within the power of each state to determine the method by which its electoral votes are allocated. So why do forty-eight states and the District of Columbia choose and stubbornly maintain a system that radically disenfranchises so many voters? The handful of swing states might resist any change to a system that attracts so much candidate attention to their states—and certainly their media outlets could be expected to resist any innovations that would deprive them of a remarkable bonanza (now expanded exponentially by the Supreme Court's campaign finance lawmaking). In the vast majority of states, however—those in the taken-for-granted, nonswing category—we have to look for some other explanation for the perseverance of this undemocratic winner-take-all system.

There is, in fact, a very powerful explanation: partisanship. Short of a total abolition of the Electoral College (or its effective abolition by something like the proposed interstate compact), the

Democratic Party would resist to its last breath any reform that would threaten its guaranteed grip on all of California's electoral votes. The Republican Party has long had the same motivation to protect its hold on all the electoral votes from Texas. No matter how deep and broad the frustration of ordinary citizens may be with a presidential selection process that almost none of them would design this way if they had a choice, the iron rule of partisanship seems likely, at least for the foreseeable future, to keep us mired in that spot. It's time to take a broader and more in-depth look at the multiple ways that partisanship has come to make self-government more challenging than ever—including making it harder to enact healing reforms.

2   Partisan Quicksand

Among the numerous advantages promised by a well constructed Union, none deserves to be more accurately developed than its tendency to break and control the violence of faction. The friend of popular governments never finds himself so much alarmed for their character and fate, as when he contemplates their propensity to this dangerous vice. . . .

By a faction, I understand a number of citizens, whether amounting to a majority or a minority of the whole, who are united and actuated by some common impulse of passion, or of interest, adverse to the rights of other citizens, or to the permanent and aggregate interests of the community. . . .

The latent causes of faction are thus sown in the nature of man; and we see them everywhere brought into different degrees of activity, according to the different circumstances of civil society. . . .

It is in vain to say that enlightened statesmen will be able to adjust these clashing interests, and render them all subservient to the public good. Enlightened statesmen will not always be at the helm.

—*James Madison*, Federalist *No. 10*

The bulk of this book was written during one of the most severe and extended periods of congressional dysfunction in American history. Extreme and unrelenting partisanship was the chief culprit. As I began working on this chapter in October 2013, for example, the national government was more than a week into a massive shutdown, caused entirely by partisan maneuvering. With another debt limit deadline approaching, a now utterly familiar game of brinkmanship was in full swing, and again it was all about maneuvering for partisan advantage. That specific crisis was eventually resolved, but the heart of the "resolution" was merely a postponement of any real decisions to some future date (a date that had itself been chosen primarily on the basis of electoral considerations). That particular series of "kicking the can down the road" episodes had at that point already been going on for more than two years. To call any of this "governing" would be to stretch that word nearly beyond recognition. But if this all-too-familiar travesty of democracy is primarily the result of unbridled partisanship, those who care most deeply about self-government have little choice but to take a closer look at the roots and dynamics of partisanship.

Let's start by reminding ourselves of the historical dimensions of America's love-hate relationship with political parties. No one better exemplifies both sides of that dichotomy than James Madison. Although Madison, in the passages quoted above from *The Federalist Papers*, was writing about "faction" rather than political parties as we know them, the major factions that concerned Madison in that essay were already well on their way to coalescing into parties. Madison was, in 1787, still clinging to the hope that America could forestall the formation of actual political parties, which he, like most of the founders, saw as one of the major diseases of the English body politic. Yet within a decade of composing *Federalist* No. 10, Madison himself was deeply engaged with his friend and mentor, Thomas Jefferson, in creating the first fully organized American political party.

Madison and Jefferson's motivation in abandoning their opposition to parties provides an excellent introduction to the subject of what still today makes partisanship such a powerful political force. Jefferson found himself marginalized within the administration of George Washington, where he served as secretary of state, unable either to enact policies he favored or to forestall those proposals of Treasury Secretary Alexander Hamilton that he strongly opposed. He had sought the presidency when Washington stepped aside in 1796 but narrowly lost that election to John Adams.[1]

Under the rules written into the original version of the Constitution, this meant that Jefferson would spend the next four years serving as Adams's vice president. Opposed almost as strongly to Adams's policies as he had been to Hamilton's, the vice president gradually assumed the role of leader of the opposition to the Adams administration. From that ambiguous position, Jefferson, aided at every step by Madison, launched a much more serious and concerted pursuit of the presidency (and control of Congress) than the Virginians had mounted in 1796. Their newly fashioned political party was key to that effort. After the bizarre standoff with his own running mate, Aaron Burr, which we examined in chapter 1, Jefferson emerged the victor and assumed the presidency in March 1801.[2]

While Jefferson and Madison, like most of the other founding fathers, had hoped that America might manage to govern itself without political parties, there was from the outset at least one bright side to the emergence of parties in terms of democratic practice. Jefferson and Madison's decision to create a political party to advance an alternative set of policies to Hamilton's capitalist and pro-British agenda would enable them to provide a clear choice for voters in 1800 and in a series of subsequent elections. To the extent that the emergence of organized political parties enabled Americans to choose intelligently and meaningfully among contrasting sets of policies, parties were (and are) an important element of the machinery of democracy.

The role that parties play in providing choices among clusters of policy options is only meaningful, though, if the parties are then able to deliver in terms of actually shaping and enacting policy. The desire to control the levers of power (or the institutions of government) was for Jefferson and Madison and still is today the major motivation for creating and maintaining political parties. This is so basic that it may seem not worth saying, but if we don't keep this simple fact in focus, we run the risk of fooling ourselves into expecting parties to behave in some way that is contrary to their nature. Their nature is to seek and maintain power. If they did not do that, parties would have little if any democratic significance.

It is also important to recognize that the care and advancement of democratic institutions can itself constitute at least a portion of the cluster of policies that any given party promotes. Jefferson and Madison certainly saw their "Democratic Republican" party in those terms, and the party they created still proudly bears the Democratic title. (In all fairness, it has to be noted that there have been times when the Republican Party has been a better friend of democracy than the party that still carries democracy's name.) That history aside, we come here to a hard fact: even though parties can play a key role in democracy, either by providing voters with clear policy choices on economic or social issues, or even by advancing initiatives that strengthen democratic governance, that is not what primarily shapes or drives stable political parties. It is the motivation to seek and maintain power that fundamentally defines and shapes parties. It is this motivation, above all, that gives them a life of their own and an overwhelming incentive to guard and advance the interests of that self-perpetuating organism that a political party actually constitutes.

The repeated appearance of parties in the course of history is testimony to their organic nature. Not surprisingly, they have been less prevalent in dictatorships or other forms of autocracy, but even there court factions have often exhibited behaviors that would be replicated by full-blown parties. Wherever anything resembling republican forms of government has taken root, parties have become a prominent (if often unwelcome) element of the political ecosystem. Both Jefferson and Madison would have been familiar with the history of the Optimates and Populares of the Roman Republic, as with the Guelfs and Ghibellines of thirteenth-century Florence. Much more proximately, the Whigs and Tories had been alternating in power in London as very sophisticated political parties for over a century by the time of the American Revolution.

In fact, the leaders of the American insurrection had seen enough of the British party system to know that the interests of either party did not reliably coincide with the broader interests of the society or body politic. In this sense, parties clearly fall within the category of Madison's "factions," "united and actuated by some common impulse of passion, or of interest, adverse to the rights of other citizens, or to the permanent and aggregate interests of the community."[3] Yet the historical inevitability and indeed the republican value of parties soon caught Madison in their sweep, and by the end of the century he had played a major role in launching the United States on its partisan path. Now, well over two centuries

later, the conflict between the common good and the interest of
political parties is clearer than ever, as the two national parties
maneuver endlessly for electoral advantage, while the very major
problems confronting the country too often go unattended, owing
largely to the iron grip of partisanship.

This Madisonian story presents what may fairly be called a
paradox of democracy. Without parties to present citizens with
legible choices among policy clusters, and without the ability to
follow through on those policy choices by controlling governing
institutions, representative democracy would be all but unwork-
able. And yet the ability of the polity to solve its problems is now
all too often hindered or altogether stymied because parties *by
their nature* take on a life of their own, and relentlessly pursue
their own interests.

Both in terms of their historical persistence and their ever-
present capacity to undermine democratic practices, parties are
very much like that other humanly indispensable and democratically problematic phenomenon that we will examine in later
chapters: money. And just as money, by its very nature, will seek
what its owners perceive as value wherever it can find it (until
society says, "This is not for sale!"), so too political parties, by their
nature, will use all means reasonably available to achieve their
end of securing, maintaining, or expanding their power. To expect
either money or parties to behave differently *on their own* is at best
naive. In a thriving democracy, though, neither money nor parties
are left entirely on their own, and in particular, such a democracy
must and will guard its own most fundamental processes against
the corrosion of too much money or of excessive partisanship.

A first indispensable step toward containing partisanship
is to recognize and understand as fully as we can the variety of
means by which parties seek or maintain power. One illuminat-
ing example is provided by a phenomenon with which Americans
have become intimately familiar and thoroughly disgusted in recent years: legislative brinkmanship. Writing this paragraph on
the fourteenth day of the October 2013 shutdown of the national
government, I heard ringing in my ears the nearly universal refrain
of my friends and neighbors over the preceding two weeks: "Why?
What's wrong with them?" Without seeking to excuse this deplor-
able pattern of congressional dysfunction, I have to confess that
I understand at least a little about why legislative leaders behave

in ways that seem utterly irrational to most citizens. I understand it because, on a far more modest scale, I've been there. Some of what I learned there may help to illustrate this all-but-inescapable partisan dynamic.

I served in the Montana legislature years ago and eventually came into leadership positions in the House of Representatives, starting when my party's caucus elected me minority leader in 1980. I understood that in placing me in this office, my colleagues expected me to focus whatever legislative skill I might possess on making my party look good and the other party look bad in order to enhance the possibility of our gaining the majority in the next election. With help from our Democratic governor and a well-organized state party, we succeeded at that, and with the Democrats now commanding a majority in the House, I was elected Speaker. Because the Republicans still controlled the Senate, we experienced a classic case of divided government. And with it came a classic case of legislative brinkmanship.

Montana's constitution limits legislative sessions to ninety days. The hard edge of that adjournment deadline provided the context for a thoroughly partisan game of legislative "chicken." Early in the session, I had introduced a bill that would have enacted a key component of my party's economic development platform. With our majority, we Democrats had no trouble getting the bill through the House, but the Republican Senate amended it substantially (in ways calculated to appeal to and broaden the Republican base). The House, on a party-line vote rejected the Senate amendments, which meant that a conference committee would have to be appointed to iron out the differences between the House and Senate versions of the bill. As Speaker, it fell to me to name the House members of the conference committee. I almost never appointed myself to conference committees, but because I was the bill's chief sponsor, and because of its importance to the party, I did include myself in this slate of conferees. We sent our list to the Republican president of the Senate and waited for him to name the Senate conferees. And waited. And waited.

By the eighty-fifth legislative day, we understood that the bill might well expire for lack of a conference committee. We were not, however, totally unprepared for this eventuality. A key Republican bill, sponsored by the Senate president, Stan Stephens, was now heavily amended by the House and returned to the Senate.

President Stephens named his conference committee members for that bill, with his own name at the top of the list. I now waited a day or two before naming the House conferees, as the clock ticked down toward the mandatory adjournment. I no longer remember which of us eventually called the other, but at a carefully choreographed time, we each named the other half of the two conference committees, and as those groups argued themselves into the ninetieth day, we finally found a mutually acceptable compromise on each bill, releasing them simultaneously for final votes on the floor of each chamber. With the adoption of both conference committee reports, the only order of business remaining in either chamber was a motion to adjourn sine die. My gavel fell in the House within minutes of President Stephens declaring the Senate adjourned.

I haven't told this story because I take any pride in it; in fact, I know that most of my readers and even most of my friends will think I could have found some way to avoid behavior that might justly be called childish. As I tell the story, I feel a little embarrassed about it myself. I find some companionship if not consolation in Abraham Lincoln's having admitted that he regretted an episode in which he led several of his fellow Whig legislators in jumping out a second story window of the Illinois capitol to deprive the Democratic majority of a quorum on a vote of particular importance to Lincoln's party.[4] The point here is not to romanticize such behavior but simply to acknowledge that a certain amount of this kind of gamesmanship seems to come with the territory of representative government. At a minimum, it is surely part of what accounts for the popularity in legislative circles of the quote so often attributed to Otto von Bismarck that one should avoid watching either laws or sausages being made. Beyond that not altogether helpful reminder, there are a couple of observations that may clarify the role of brinkmanship and other such classic legislative maneuvers in a working democracy.

We might note, for example, that in most cases these seemingly childish games actually arise, at least in part, from the crucially important democratic struggle between competing policies or principles. Lincoln and his Whig colleagues did not jump out of that window purely for the fun of it but because they were intent on blocking a piece of legislation being pushed through by the Democratic majority. Stan Stephens and I didn't hold one another's bills hostage because we were too immature to think of anything better to do with our time but because we and our political parties were promoting alternative policies that were both consequential and controversial. And, as this chapter was emerging into its first draft form, the Republicans and Democrats in Congress were not lurching from one deadline to another out of stupidity but because they held (and intended to have the American people choose between) two quite different views of how to deal with fiscal crises and other major problems facing our nation.

This is not to say, however, that we should simply bite our tongues and accept these patterns of brinkmanship. In fact, the partisanship that drives them has continued to intensify to the point that it threatens the democratic governance it is supposed to serve. In the legislatures of Illinois in the 1830s or Montana in the 1980s, the democratic, policy-sorting value of this kind of partisan gamesmanship may have come close to balancing the damage it undoubtedly inflicted on the people's faith in their representative institutions. But this is now all too seldom the case. Partisanship has now become so pervasive and so corrosive that it threatens the very fabric of democracy. And this disease cannot be cured simply by "throwing all the rascals out." The problem is much deeper and much more systemic than that.

The metaphor running through the remainder of this chapter is that of quicksand. Imagine democracy as a road we've been walking along for some time. Not infrequently it gets a little muddy, and we get frustrated with the mud and try various ways of getting around it or cleaning it off our shoes. But we seem now to have wandered into something more dangerous than mud. We seem to be sinking, and the harder we struggle, the deeper we sink. This is partisan quicksand, and, like actual quicksand, what makes it so dangerous is its deadly combination of different elements, all coagulating in one place and time. Actual quicksand consists of sand, water, clay, and salt. No one or two of those elements makes quicksand, but when all of them come together, it can create a very dangerous amalgam. As it happens, the partisan quicksand in which so many of our democratic institutions are now mired is also made up of various elements, and it is their interaction that makes them so hazardous.

The forms of legislative gamesmanship that we have been examining constitute one of the more or less enduring ingredients of partisan quicksand. Mixed in with this in our time are more systemic or structural ingredients, including the role of the Electoral College in presidential elections, established practices of legislative and congressional redistricting, the Senate filibuster practice, judicial appointments, and judicially imposed campaign finance rules. Each of these elements is itself a crucial point of attention for citizens hoping to restore truly democratic practices to our governing institutions. At the same time, these individual components have combined to create the partisan quicksand that now so often prevents our government from solving any of our problems. Worse, the quicksand draws into its grip the very efforts at reform that we might hope would heal our democracy. To get a clearer picture of how this devilish dynamic works, we will briefly examine several of these structural factors, focusing on how they contribute to the quagmire of partisanship. Our eventual aim will be to discover and describe solid democratic ground on which we might stand while we pursue the long, hard work of pulling our institutions out of the quicksand. But first, painful as it may be, we need to become more familiar with the nature of this quicksand as it works to entrap so many efforts at sensible reform. In the preceding chapter, we examined in a preliminary way how partisanship works to stymie Electoral College reform. Now let's add in some of the other quicksand ingredients, beginning with the way we draw congressional and legislative district boundaries.

REDISTRICTING

As we noted earlier in this chapter, the driving force behind political parties is and has to be the acquisition, maintenance, or expansion of governing power. One of the chief means of perpetuating partisan power, gradually honed to a fine art in recent times, is congressional and legislative redistricting. Whenever and wherever they can, parties influence the drawing of district lines in a way that optimizes the party's chances of winning and holding a majority of the seats representing those districts. One side effect of this dynamic is the creation of an inordinate number of "safe" seats, where the election of one party's candidate is all but guaranteed.[5] This works both ways: the dominant party in any given state not only guarantees itself as many safe seats as it can generate, but since one party is seldom so dominant that it can make every district safe for itself, the majority party will often draw boundaries that concentrate the other party's dependable voters in the fewest possible number of sacrificial districts that then become as safe for the opposition as any of the majority's districts are for them. These two complementary processes have come to be known as "cracking" and "packing."

This deeply embedded dynamic contributes materially to the dysfunction of legislative bodies in this way: the safer a district is for either party, the more certain it becomes that the decisive choice will be made in the primary election, where that party's candidate will be chosen. That candidate is then all but guaranteed to win the general election: that's what it means to run for a "safe" seat. With a smaller electorate almost always in play in a primary than in a general election, the most aggressive and committed bloc of voters within the majority party all too often determines the result in that preliminary but decisive contest. The overall effect, now thoroughly documented and widely bemoaned, is the election of ideological purists from both ends of the spectrum, out of all proportion to the actual numbers of such ideologues among the citizenry.

What is perhaps less obvious at first blush is that ideological purity is nearly the opposite of a commitment to problem solving. The all-but-guaranteed result of this partisan redistricting dynamic is pervasive legislative dysfunction, both at the national level and in many state legislatures. The cause-and-effect relationship between reapportionment and gridlock is too complex to be examined in detail here, but an instance of my own, incidental involvement in the reapportionment process might serve as an illustration of how the quicksand-like logic of reapportionment, like the operation of the Electoral College, traps well-meaning officeholders and citizens in its partisan grip.

As with every other state, Montana's redistricting process kicks in once the results of the national decennial census are available. A certain amount of partisanship is built into the Montana process because the state's constitution gives majority and minority party leaders in the legislature the responsibility of naming four of the five members of the reapportionment commission. Those four members are then given the opportunity to name the fifth member, who is to serve as chair of the commission. If they cannot agree on that choice, the Montana Supreme Court names the chair.[6]

The two rounds of redistricting occasioned by the 1990 and 2000 census counts had created an escalating cycle of partisanship here in Montana, which then carried its memories and its momentum into the 2010 round. Democrats had claimed that the map drawn after the 1990 census deliberately favored Republican legislative candidates and that this accounted for Republicans controlling both houses of the legislature in all five of the biennial sessions elected under that plan. The next commission, appointed after the 2000 census, had a 3–2 Democratic majority, which adopted a plan that Republicans claimed was specifically designed to elect Democrats.

That tit-for-tat background was very much in play as a new commission swung into full gear in 2012. The four members appointed by the legislative leadership had been unable to agree among themselves on a fifth member to chair the commission. As the state constitution provided, they each made recommendations to the Montana Supreme Court.[7] That body, however, knew from past experience that if it chose any of the nominees from that list, the result would almost certainly be another 3–2 partisan split on the commission. The justices therefore exercised their constitutional prerogative to name someone not on any of the submitted lists. They chose a former Supreme Court justice who had retired a few years earlier to launch a mediation practice.

With its chairman in place, the commission set to work. The Republican members requested the commission's staff to prepare three maps for comparison purposes: one driven primarily by the criterion of equal population for each district, one seeking to minimize the division of political jurisdictions like counties and cities, and one attempting to reflect the rural and urban "communities of interest" in the state. The staff also prepared a map based roughly on the approach used by the previous commission. Finally, the two Democratic members of the commission prepared their own map, dubbing it the "communities plan."[8]

The commission launched a series of hearings around the state to take public comment on these five draft plans. As it happened, the first hearing was held in Missoula, and since I was convinced that reapportionment is one of the key entry points to democratic reform, I felt an obligation to weigh in.[9] I knew that the Missoula Democratic Party had been urging people to support the plan drafted by the commission's two Democrats. As a lifelong Democrat who had been honored by my party with leadership positions in the legislature, and backed by that party in two mayoral elections, I would not lightly oppose a proposal that most Democrats had been persuaded was not only correct on the merits but also likely to contribute to the prospects of future Democratic majorities.

In the end, though, I decided that the Democratic plan was designed to give more weight to partisan considerations than to meaningful, inhabited places. I presented both written and oral testimony to the commission in which I pointed out that, when I served in the legislature in the 1970s and early 1980s, my legislative colleagues and I had customarily referred to our districts not by number but by place-names. No one then knew or cared that I represented District 94, but it meant something to them when I said that I represented the University district or when my colleagues spoke about representing the Rattlesnake Valley or South Hills.

I went on to point out that in the three rounds of redistricting that had occurred since then, meaningful places had become a steadily less important factor in the drawing of legislative maps. Legislators now rarely gave place-names to their districts, referring to them instead by the meaningless numbers that have been assigned to them. That was because the districts weren't primarily places any longer. They were instead what all too many legislative and congressional districts have become across the country: a set of census tracts pieced together by careful calculation of partisan advantage. In Montana, I argued, both parties had contributed to that process over the last several rounds of redistricting.

I suggested that the commission had an opportunity to make place a genuine counterweight to party, in the service of good governance, by paying as much attention as possible to where people call home—what they think of as their community or their neighborhood. That, of course, would mean paying little or no attention to the partisan makeup of any particular district—the one consideration that had outweighed all others in the previous two rounds of redistricting. I went on to evaluate in these terms the five maps that the commission had before it. The map presented by the Democratic commissioners was not at the bottom of my list, but it was nowhere near the top. I could feel the icy stares of my Democratic friends drilling into my back as I presented my testimony. This was partisan treason, pure and simple.

What I want to emphasize here is not so much the argument I was advancing about making districts correspond to real places but rather how uncomfortable I felt in taking a position at odds with the one endorsed by almost all my fellow Democrats. And the point of that is not to congratulate myself for swimming against the stream but rather to underscore how deeply rooted the dynamics of partisanship actually are. If I, neither holding nor seeking a partisan office, felt so keenly the expectation to line up behind the Democratic redistricting plan, how much more strongly would that pressure be felt by anyone in a position to advance the partisan cause? It is precisely that pressure that drives the creation of safe legislative and congressional districts across the country, with the resulting election of inordinate numbers of ideological purists to the U.S. House and to an increasing number of state legislatures. That pressure and those results are a direct reflection of the ancient, inherent, self-perpetuating dynamics of partisanship. And they contribute very substantially to the partisan quicksand from which even the best-intentioned of elected officials cannot extricate themselves without the assistance of democratic citizens standing on firmer ground. I will examine in a later chapter how that kind of citizen rescue is beginning to show promise of reforming the reapportionment process (and we will see there how the Supreme Court has been drawn into, and then refused to be drawn further into, this arena[10]). But first we need to identify a few more ingredients of the quicksand of partisanship.

CAMPAIGN FINANCE

This subject will be treated at some length in later chapters, but we have to examine it briefly here because it is both an important component of the partisan trap and a good illustration of why the quicksand metaphor is so helpful in understanding the affliction of excessive partisanship.

In the last week of January 2012, various reform groups marked the second anniversary of the Supreme Court's *Citizens*

United decision and several members of Congress introduced new resolutions aimed at amending the Constitution to overturn that ruling.[11] But the big news on this front came within two weeks of the anniversary, and it was a chilling reminder of the effect that *Citizens United* was now having on American politics.

Early in February, President Obama's re-election organization announced that he was reversing his earlier position and would now encourage his supporters to contribute to a "super PAC" of the kind that *Citizens United* and its judicial offspring had unleashed on the political landscape two years earlier. Here was one more indication for skeptics (not excluding myself) that the "change we can believe in" mantra of the 2008 Obama campaign was far more easily promised than delivered in the real world of Washington, D.C. Obama's campaign manager, Jim Messina, outlined those realities in an email to campaign supporters. Declaring that "we will not play by two sets of rules," Messina explained:

> The President opposed the *Citizens United* decision. He understood that with the dramatic growth in opportunities to raise and spend unlimited special-interest money, we would see new strategies to hide it from public view. He continues to support a law to force full disclosure of all funding intended to influence our elections, a reform that was blocked in 2010 by a unanimous Republican filibuster in the U.S. Senate. And the President favors action—by constitutional amendment, if necessary—to place reasonable limits on all such spending. But this cycle, our campaign has to face the reality of the law as it currently stands.[12]

Messina was stating the simple, hard facts, and his point was that it would have been the equivalent of tying one hand behind his back for Obama to have taken any other course. The point here is not to quarrel with the decision of Obama or his advisors but rather to use this development to illustrate how, in the arena of campaign finance, even the best intentioned of politicians are trapped in something very like quicksand. That conclusion is reinforced by the recollection that this was actually Barack Obama's second retreat from a progressive position on campaign finance. Having all but promised to limit the amount of money he would raise privately for his 2008 presidential bid, in order to use the system of public financing, Obama reversed course in June of that year, declaring that his campaign would be supported entirely by private contributions. "It's not an easy decision, and especially because I support a robust system of public financing of elections," Obama said at that time. "But the public financing of presidential elections as it exists today is broken, and we face opponents who've become masters at gaming this broken system."[13]

Again, my point is not to second-guess the decision that Obama made in 2008 but to underscore this recurring theme: when operating within a money-corrupted system, both parties are convinced that they have to play by that system's written and unwritten rules or risk defeat in a quixotic adherence to principle. This is what we mean by quicksand. Let's examine one more ingredient of this deadly mixture, now from the intertwined perspective of the U.S. Senate and the Supreme Court.

THE SENATE AND THE SUPREME COURT

Because the U.S. Constitution provides for the election of two senators from each state, the boundaries of their "districts" never change, which means that redistricting has no influence on either the membership or the behavior of the Senate. Even without any help from that quarter, however, the Senate has devised and perfected its own unique contributions to congressional dysfunction. Those contributions have come primarily in the form of the Senate filibuster and the associated cloture rule. It sometimes seems as if, when no other feature of our national government can stop us from solving major problems, we can always count on the filibuster as a last barrier to effective problem solving.

As with redistricting, this wound to the body of democracy had been kept open by the powerful dynamics of partisanship. Strangely enough, it was also partisanship that began to reform the filibuster rules in the years between 2013 and 2017, as the two parties engaged in a round of tit-for-tat use of the so-called nuclear option. Always lurking in the Senate rulebook as a potential way for the majority party to change the filibuster rules by a byzantine series of simple majority votes, the threat of the nuclear option had been marched out for years by frustrated Senate majorities from both parties. That game of threat and counterthreat moved into new territory when the nuclear option was first actually deployed in 2013. Stymied by repeated Republican use of the filibuster rules to block many of President Obama's nominations to various positions, and especially to district and circuit court judgeships, the Democrats under majority leader Harry Reid at last stopped threatening and on November 20, 2013, actually deployed the nuclear option to remove any presidential appointments except those to the Supreme Court from any threat of a filibuster.[14] Minority leader Mitch McConnell and other Republican senators loudly protested that the rights of the minority were being trampled, along with sacred Senate traditions, but they could not stop what the majority party had finally decided to do.

That was where things stood as I finished the first draft of this chapter. That draft contained a prediction that, whenever the Republicans again found themselves in control of both the Senate and the White House, they would be all but certain (and might indeed feel bound by the threats of reprisal they had made in 2013) to avenge what they saw as a naked use of majority power to oppress the minority. Such a prediction required no extraordinary powers of foresight; indeed, it was widely assumed among Senate watchers. The only real questions were (1) when the Republicans would get that opportunity, and (2) whether they would use it to remove the threat of Democrats filibustering a Supreme Court nomination or to remove the threat of the minority party preventing passage of substantive legislation—the two arenas that remained subject to a filibuster.

Regardless of how those two questions would eventually be answered, it seemed entirely possible in 2013 that the dynamic the Democrats had set in motion might well carry itself to the point of dismantling the filibuster altogether. If so, that in itself could be counted as a significant democratic reform. But that it would have come about in a way that seriously deepened partisan divisions should give all "small d" democrats pause, especially since it turned out that the next phase in the story went hand in hand with the deepening politicization of the Supreme Court.

That chapter began with Justice Antonin Scalia's entirely unexpected death in February 2016, followed by the audacious stonewalling by Senate Republicans of President Obama's Supreme Court nomination.[15] That gambit had paid off when Republicans held their Senate majority in the 2016 election while

Donald Trump scored his Electoral College victory and proceeded to nominate Neil Gorsuch to fill the vacancy.[16] Before Gorsuch could be seated, though, the Senate would have to go through one more drama, which brings us back to the filibuster rule. With Republicans now in control of both the Senate and the White House, all the pieces had fallen into place for demolishing the next layer of the filibuster rule.

Even then, however, that result was not a given. Democrats could have simply chosen not to bring the filibuster mechanism into play in the Gorsuch confirmation process. They knew to a certainty that Gorsuch was going to be confirmed one way or the other—either by a straight up-and-down vote, which Republicans were guaranteed to win, or by Republican deployment of the nuclear option to prevent a Democrat filibuster. By signaling their intention to filibuster the nomination, Democrats more or less intentionally brought on the removal of filibuster protection, not only for this Supreme Court nomination but for all subsequent ones. Accordingly, on Thursday, April 6, 2017, Mitch McConnell led his Republican caucus through the same series of minutely choreographed procedural votes that Harry Reid had used in 2013, and the deed was done.[17] The next day, by a vote of 54 to 45, the Senate confirmed the nomination, and the following Monday, Gorsuch took the oath of office in the Rose Garden, with Donald Trump at his elbow.[18]

This entire saga of the Senate filibuster rule had been a tale of deepening partisanship, and partisanship might eventually drive it further yet. It is already clear that any time one party controls both the White House and the Senate all federal judicial appointments, including those to the Supreme Court, can from now on be as partisan as that party chooses. The filibuster threat may well be removed from substantive legislation next. That may not be an altogether bad thing—but no matter how we assess the pros and cons of something like the filibuster, this story is clearly one of intensifying partisanship—including an ever-deeper partisan divide within the judicial branch. That metastasizing of partisanship is one of the most serious illnesses in our body politic. The tit-for-tat story of filibuster erosion shows how partisanship feeds on itself, just as earlier I showed how partisanship is one of the major hindrances to the healing of other wounds.

The events that put Neil Gorsuch (and then Brett Kavana-ugh) on the Supreme Court had, among other side effects, very probably ended any real chance of a judicial reversal of *Citizens United* for the foreseeable future. But if those events had thus put the task of reclaiming democratic control over the election process back on the shoulders of the people, those same events also helped to underscore how much else now rested on our shoulders. One indication of the resulting challenge to democratic citizenship arose from the way that the entire episode had deepened still further America's partisan divide. Indeed, from the moment that Justice Scalia's heart failed until Justices Gorsuch and Kavanaugh took their seats, raw partisanship had been a prominent factor at every turn. This is quicksand indeed. But there is more.

Perhaps most sobering of all is the realization that it is not just politicians or their professional consultants who are driving partisanship to exert ever-greater dominion over our governing institutions. Citizens themselves, often motivated by an unquestionably sincere desire to make things better, are steadily making this part of the picture worse. That conclusion was documented quite persuasively in June 2014 when the Pew Research Center released the results of a major study of ideological divisions within the American electorate. The report drew on several years of sampling public opinion and on a massive new survey of ten thousand citizens that provided a high-resolution snapshot of current attitudes, poised against the background of long-term trends. The picture that emerged came as no surprise to any close observer of American public life, but it did provide conclusive evidence of a number of fairly depressing features of our ailing democracy. "Republicans and Democrats are more divided along ideological lines—and partisan antipathy is deeper and more extensive—than at any point in the last two decades," the report concluded, adding ominously that "these divisions are greatest among those who are the most engaged and active in the political process."[19]

The Pew report demolished any inclination we might have to lay the entire blame for the increasing polarization of American politics on politicians. Citizens are deeply complicit in this polarization, and the more politically engaged they are, the more they seem to contribute to this phenomenon. Any hope that the healing of democracy might emerge directly from the mobilization of democratically engaged citizens seems to be seriously impaired by these findings. At a minimum, a citizen-centered strategy of democratic reform and revitalization has to proceed with an unblinking recognition of this state of affairs.

What do these findings mean within the context of this book's major themes of an ailing body politic and the role of citizens in healing it? A radical decline in the problem-solving capacity of democratic institutions might naturally provoke citizens to try to secure their most cherished policy objectives by the deployment of raw political muscle to elect enough officeholders to turn those policies into law. There is nothing wrong with that kind of activity; indeed, it is an essential ingredient of any healthy practice of representative democracy, as I noted earlier in describing the initial appearance of organized political parties on the American scene.

One reason that political parties seem indispensable to any serious effort at self-government is simply that the enterprise of living together on some portion of the earth's surface is guaranteed to raise questions about how best to do that. Such questions have plagued humans throughout our species' history. What is our tribe or clan going to eat? Should we grow food or hunt it? Where will we live? Who is going to decide? These and myriad other questions—almost never posed this starkly but always crucial to the enterprise of being human—inevitably began to sort themselves into patterns of various kinds, one of which was almost always whether it would be better to stick with the accustomed ways of doing things or try somebody's new idea. Thus, in a rough, general way, it became nearly inevitable that there would emerge a conservative and a more progressive or experimental approach to the endless stream of questions that being human will always present.

I am not pretending to say anything even mildly profound here, let alone anything definitive about the origin of political parties. The point is only that the challenge of being human necessarily produces different approaches to that enterprise. In those rare instances where humans have decided to let the whole (or some substantial part) of the group make the decisions, these self-governing people are bound to be drawn to different approaches and different groupings of approaches. This is all made more complicated—and the stakes are raised substantially—when the differences involve seriously conflicting interests, such as those of ethnicity or race, class, age, or gender. Sometimes those differences become so commanding and intractable that they result in revolution or civil war. Short of that, those who hope to maintain a self-governing, republican (as opposed to authoritarian) mode of making the hard decisions inherent in being human have to find some way of coming to terms with the inevitable, passionate and consequential disagreements among the citizens of any republic about how best to resolve those issues. The willingness of substantial numbers of people to acknowledge (and figure out how to live with) the inevitability of such disagreements is an indispensable feature of a self-governing polity.

It is in these terms that we must view (and address) the deepening intensity of polarization that the Pew study documented as characterizing active citizens in our own time. At a minimum, that deepening tribalism is itself a key ingredient of the partisan quicksand that stymies so much serious democratic reform. The more convinced we become that the "other side" is not only wrong about particular substantive issues but is so set in its ways that it cannot be worked with, the more inclined we are to focus our political energy exclusively on keeping "their kind" out of office and putting (or keeping) "our kind" in. This dynamic then merges with the more institutionalized forms of entrenched polarization, like the creation of "safe seats" through redistricting. Whatever it takes to keep the dangerous wrongheadedness of "those people" in check is what we should do. And of course, the more of it "we" do, the more "they" do. In this way, the quicksand of partisanship sucks in not only politicians but the most politically engaged citizens as well.

Again, there is nothing inherently wrong with democratic citizens pursuing either their interests or their ideals by supporting one or another political party, just as there is nothing inherently inappropriate about those parties playing a role in governing or, for that matter, with money playing a role in elections. Yet these factors have all contributed to the deepening dysfunction of our representative institutions. In every case, the problem arises from the unchecked or immoderate scope of the factor in question. Money and partisanship are both inescapable components of politics, but that doesn't mean that either should be allowed to operate without limits. Voting for people who share our ideological positions is perfectly consistent with representative democracy, but only if it is balanced by a concern for electing people with the skills required to transcend ideology in order to identify and secure the common good. Until millions of solid, democratically experienced citizens begin explicitly choosing candidates by this standard, the passionate ideological tribalism now so prevalent among voters will continue to exacerbate the deadly suction of partisan quicksand that has all but immobilized our governing institutions.

That seems to have been precisely the case with one of the most dramatic, surprising, and, for millions of Americans, alarming manifestations of partisan quicksand in our time: the elevation of Donald Trump to the presidency. When Trump announced his candidacy on June 16, 2015, most political observers were simply amused at the idea of this notoriously self-centered and impulsive real estate developer and reality TV host seeking the presidency. For months (indeed, well into the 2016 primary season) it was simply assumed that common sense would eventually prevail and that one of the experienced Republican governors, senators, or House members would secure the nomination. As Trump finished ahead of all of them (while still never winning a majority of votes) in one primary after another, however, his opponents at least had to take him seriously enough to launch what came to be called the "Never Trump" movement. By then, though, it was too late, and as the Trump bandwagon continued to roll to the convention and beyond, the irresistible pull of partisanship began to assert itself. Some Republican leaders still refused to support Trump, but most fell in line, so that after he took office, even his most bizarre or internationally destabilizing spasms of impulsiveness aroused only fainthearted protests from elected Republicans.

What could possibly account for this wholesale abandonment by respected Republican leaders of the most minimal standards of presidential competence? There can only be one answer, and it has everything to do with how the most ideologically committed citizens contribute to the dynamics of partisanship. From the summer of 2016 on, any Republican officeholder or candidate who voiced serious or sustained criticism of Trump risked arousing the wrath of the hard-core ideological base of the Republican Party. That base was only a portion of any Republican officeholder's electoral majority, but without it, most of those elected officials concluded that they themselves could not continue to win elections, nor could the party maintain its control of the presidency or of either house of Congress. It was this same dynamic that made it all but certain that very few Senate Republicans would vote to convict Donald Trump of the impeachment charges the House Democrats had raised against him.

Those charges were themselves in no small part a response to very similar dynamics on the Democratic side of the aisle. The leadership of that party had been reluctant even to open an impeachment inquiry, fearful of a backlash if they impeached Trump but failed to convict him. In the end, pressure from the more liberal base of the party moved the leadership to launch impeachment proceedings, even though the prevailing wisdom held that the Republican Senate would not provide the votes necessary for conviction. In that event, the fate of the Trump presidency would go back to the voters, where the deepening tribalism on both sides, so compellingly documented by the Pew study, would play to its conclusion. That conclusion would still be subject to the peculiar mathematics of the Electoral College, of course, but even if this time around the winning candidate turned out to be the choice of the majority of voting citizens, the deepening ideological polarization within the body politic would continue to afflict our governing institutions well beyond 2020, as it had well before 2016.

This chapter has centered on the argument that many of the worst dysfunctions in our governing institutions resemble quicksand, in which even the best-intentioned elected officials often find themselves trapped. Now we see that some of the most potent citizen reactions to governing dysfunction have simply deepened and thickened the quicksand. This book, though, arises from the conviction (1) that citizens actually occupy firmer republican or democratic ground than they often recognize, (2) that citizens, occupying that far more solid self-governing ground, might have the primary responsibility for pulling their elected officials out of the mire, and (3) that in any event it is through citizens uniting on that ground that our democratic institutions are most likely to be restored.

Perhaps the picture we are looking at (and indeed living in) is one in which the politically most active citizens, while they may have one foot on solid democratic ground, are themselves mired in quicksand up to their knees with their ideologically leading leg.

All the more reason, then, to gain as much clarity as we possibly can about the nature of the firm ground on which that other foot is planted. That ground definitely exists, and there is good reason to turn to it as a reliable base from which we can begin drawing our governing institutions from their dysfunction. But that is going to depend on growing numbers of our most active citizens, from across the ideological spectrum, putting steadily more weight on that solid democratic footing. The next chapter provides a preliminary testing of that ground.

3 The Solid Ground
of Everyday Citizenship

Everyone knows how genuinely troubled the United States is
at the level of national politics and governance. It is natural to
assume that these disorders must reflect a deeper rot across
the country.

Serious as the era's problems are, more people, in more
places, told us they felt hopeful about their ability to move
circumstances the right way than you would ever guess from
national news coverage of most political discourse.

Would it make any difference if more people understood
that the local progress they see was not an isolated anomaly
but part of a trend?

Even as the country is becoming worse in obvious ways—
angrier, more divided, less able to do the basic business of
governing itself—it is becoming distinctly better on a range
of other indicators that are harder to perceive.

—James Fallows, May 2018

On January 8, 2011, while U.S. representative Gabrielle Giffords
conducted a "Congress on Your Corner" meeting with constituents in a supermarket parking lot in Tucson, Arizona, Jared Lee
Loughner drew out a handgun and shot her and eighteen other
people before he was subdued and arrested.[1] Giffords survived her
nearly fatal head wound, but six people died, including federal district court chief judge John Roll and a nine-year-old girl, Christina

Taylor Green.[2] On January 12, President Obama flew to Arizona to speak at the memorial service for the slain victims.

A TALE OF TWO MEMORIALS

In the immediate aftermath of the shooting, some commentators had blamed rhetoric from the political right wing for contributing to the emotions that seemed to have led to the shooting; in particular, they pointed to the political action committee website of former Alaska governor and Republican vice presidential candidate Sarah Palin, which had "targeted" the districts of Giffords and others with pictures of crosshairs on an electoral map. In his Tucson speech, though, President Obama called on Americans to use the occasion to deepen our commitment to civility. "Rather than pointing fingers or assigning blame," he suggested, "let's use this occasion to expand our moral imaginations, to listen to each other more carefully, to sharpen our instincts for empathy, to remind ourselves of all the ways that our hopes and dreams are bound together."[3]

I remember thinking that it was an excellent speech, with just the right message for the somber occasion. Most Americans no doubt hoped that the Tucson tragedy might help to produce the civil spirit that the president invoked. Indeed, that spirit seemed to manifest itself a few days later, when many members of Congress responded to Senator Mark Udall's suggestion that the traditional partisan seating chart be scrambled for the State of the Union address.[4] Could a senseless act of violence that had nearly killed one of their colleagues induce representatives and senators not only to sit together across partisan lines but to work together to resolve the serious problems the country was facing? Anyone committed to the cause of American democracy would naturally hope for that result.

At the same time, most of us probably recognized how slim the chances were that one tragic occasion, one thoughtful speech, or one night of congressional collegiality could have that kind of lasting effect against the tide of partisanship, brinkmanship, cynicism, and anger that all too deeply pervades our political culture. By August of that same year, as congressional gridlock brought the nation to the brink of default on the national debt, we pretty much had our answer.

And yet . . .

Just a few days after President Obama spoke in Tucson, I had occasion to attend another memorial service—this one in Missoula, to mark the unexpected passing of someone I'd known and worked with for many years. During my tenure as mayor of Missoula, I had appointed Hal Fraser to the Missoula Redevelopment Agency (MRA) board, and then for many years after leaving city hall, I served with Hal as a member of that board, which he was then chairing. In that capacity, I and my fellow board members had found deep satisfaction in working together on projects stretching from trails to skateboard parks, from helping to make Missoula home to one of the most vibrant downtowns in the Northern Rockies to building a world-class kayak wave in the very heart of the city. Not one of those projects had been our board's work alone, of course, and certainly none of them had been Hal's alone, but as an MRA board member, as a banker, or simply as a dedicated citizen, Hal Fraser had worked for decades with hundreds of other citizens on these and scores of other projects that had steadily made Missoula a better and better place to work, play, and raise families.

So, when my fellow board members and I joined the Fraser family to honor and remember him that Saturday in January, we found ourselves surrounded by roughly one thousand other people, all bound in one way or another to Hal. But as I looked around that room, I became aware not only of these folks' connections to Hal Fraser but of the countless strings of connection, crisscrossing the room and binding us all to each other. These were the connections that we had forged in working together on those dozens of community-enhancing projects, many of which were fondly, sometimes humorously, recalled that day.

Hal had been a moving force in all of them. But he would have been the first to remind us that he didn't make any of them happen. He knew better than any of us that they could only happen in one way: by people from many different backgrounds and points of view looking beyond their differences and uniting around a common cause, which was always the cause of a better community. They could only happen, in President Obama's words a few days earlier in Tucson, by getting people to "expand our moral imaginations, to listen to each other more carefully, to sharpen our instincts for empathy, to remind ourselves of all the ways that our hopes and dreams are bound together."[5]

Those words were fully appropriate to that occasion of national grief. However wise, though, and however heartfelt, we could hardly expect a few words spoken in the wake of one day of tragic violence to heal a political culture worn down by decades of multiple assaults on the practice of democracy. But that should not blind us to what my neighbors and I bore witness to in Missoula that same week. It is worth pausing to reflect for a moment on how and why the transitory collegiality of the 2011 State of the Union address stands in such sharp contrast to the lasting effect of a lifetime like Hal Fraser's, a lifetime quietly committed to practicing the very principles of civility that President Obama had invoked in Tucson.

At a time when more and more Americans are questioning whether our national democracy is capable of doing what needs to be done in the face of ever more daunting challenges, it is well to remind ourselves that every day, thousands of citizens are doing just what Hal Fraser did for a lifetime. If American democracy manages to restore itself, it will be in large part because of those good citizens who are, without fanfare, "listening to each other more carefully, sharpening their instincts for empathy, reminding themselves of all the ways that their hopes and dreams are bound together."[6] This communal base of a healthy democratic culture is tremendously important, and I am convinced that the healing of larger democratic institutions can succeed only by drawing more deliberately and intelligently than ever before on the perpetually demonstrated capacity of people to work with their neighbors to identify and realize the common good.

There is a danger, though, of sentimentalizing this phenomenon and therefore failing to reap its full harvest. Community spirit is a great good thing, but purely on its own the kind of motivation that Theda Skocpol calls "local do-goodism" can go only so far to withstand or transcend the forces of greed and prejudice that seem to motivate most people most of the time.[7] Even at the local level, then, we need to take a little broader and perhaps more hard-headed look at the sustaining and sustainable sources of democratic vitality. I am convinced that what we find there is much more substantial and far more capable of contributing to the healing of our larger institutions than any amount of "do-goodism" could ever be. But to gain any real confidence in this solid ground of active citizenship, we have to examine much more closely how it actually works. In particular, we need to revisit that strand of American political pragmatism called "enlightened self-interest."

ENLIGHTENED SELF-INTEREST
AS A DEMOCRATIC ENGINE

The idea of enlightened self-interest has a deep and significant place in the history of American democracy. It was first and most famously identified by Alexis de Tocqueville in volume two of his classic work, *Democracy in America*. Since Tocqueville's original formulation carries nuances that will prove useful to us, we will begin with his original way of phrasing it (which was in French, of course). Tocqueville wrote of Americans' embrace of *la doctrine de l'intérêt bien entendu*, which is usually translated as "the doctrine of interest properly understood."[8] What this implies is that one's self-interest can be either well or poorly understood and that the choice has consequences that reach beyond the individual making it. At least in the instances that Tocqueville highlights, a proper understanding of one's self-interest required that broader interests also be taken into account, including, most often, those of one's neighbors.

Armed with that concept, Tocqueville set out to understand "how the inhabitants of the United States almost always know how to combine their own well-being with that of their fellow citizens."[9] He concluded that "American moralists do not claim that one must sacrifice oneself because it is great [i.e., noble] to do it; but they say boldly that such sacrifices are as necessary to the one who imposes them on himself as to the one who profits from them."[10] Or again: "Americans . . . show how the enlightened love of themselves constantly brings them to aid each other and disposes them willingly to sacrifice a part of their time and their wealth to the good of the state."[11]

However accurate this observation might once have been, most of us would probably say that it doesn't sound much like the America (or the Americans) that we now know. At a time when "no new taxes" has practically become our national motto, when our political system seems incapable of addressing potentially disastrous budget deficits either by increasing revenue or tightening up "entitlements," it is difficult to discern "how the inhabitants of the United States" are now inclined "to combine their own well-being with that of their fellow citizens."[12] Yet those among us who have undertaken to fill elected or appointed offices are often acutely aware that without some widespread willingness among the citizenry to constrain immediate, individual self-interest for the common good, governing becomes all but impossible. The question then becomes where that willingness can come from, how it can be cultivated, and whether it can be scaled up sufficiently to heal the pervasive dysfunction of our larger governing institutions.

The willingness to transcend narrow self-interest for the sake of a greater good might come from some pure altruistic desire among the people themselves to do right by their neighbors. In fact, we almost always see that kind of motivation widely at work in the immediate aftermath of a natural disaster like an earthquake, hurricane, or flood. A considerably smaller but not insignificant number of people habitually bring such altruistic motives to any act of citizenship, including voting for the candidates most likely to pursue policies consistent with these motives. But this kind of selfless altruism does not seem to be widespread or durable enough to sustain democratic governance by itself. Those who are primarily and steadfastly motivated by it are rarely a majority of voters, while the more widely shared episodes of altruism sparked by cataclysms always seem to fade out again when public attention gets diverted to something else.

This gloomy picture might lead us to despair of the possibility of a democracy ever being able to address big problems like climate change, racism, poverty, or crushing public indebtedness—problems that seem irresolvable without a widespread willingness to transcend narrow perceptions of self-interest. It is in this challenging context that I propose to take a hard look at Tocqueville's argument that the pursuit of enlightened self-interest was in his day and still is a crucial feature of Americans' capacity for self-government.

One more caveat is in order at this point. Even at its best, an enlivened perception or practice of enlightened self-interest will not provide a silver bullet that can resolve all our democratic challenges. At most, it might prove to be one element among many that could contribute to our capacity to solve together the problems we now face. But those problems are big enough and urgent enough that we cannot afford to overlook any substantial resource that might enhance our ability to address them. It is with those modest but hopeful expectations that we might most fruitfully examine the role of enlightened self-interest in public life today. What will soon become apparent is that, pessimistic as we might be about the general shape of our public life, we could all name many instances of how the identification and pursuit of enlightened self-interest on the part of citizens has resulted in projects or policies that have enhanced our communities or the lives of their residents. If that is so, then we have to ask whether this still-vibrant strain of democratic citizenship has anything substantial to contribute to the healing of our larger political body.

A TYPICAL EXAMPLE

To begin to get a grasp on how enlightened self-interest works, and how it might become more pervasive, I will draw again on my own experience in my hometown of Missoula, Montana. Beyond my knowing it best, there is nothing about Missoula that makes it a better source for such examples than any other community. There may, however, be something about local communities as a class that makes them more amenable than larger polities to the mobilization of enlightened self-interest. That is a major theme in Benjamin Barber's hopeful work on the role of cities in revitalizing democracy, *If Mayors Ruled the World*.[13] We will keep our eye on that possibility as we consider this home-grown case study.

Missoula is a small city (now roughly seventy thousand people) nestled in a mountain valley in western Montana.[14] The confluence of three rivers made this an inevitable spot for settlement, and the city naturally centered itself along the Clark Fork River, between the two rail lines and the highway that carried people and goods through the valley. Enlivened by multiple opportunities for outdoor recreation and leavened by the presence of the University of Montana, Missoula had, by the 1970s, become a modestly cosmopolitan oasis in the midst of the sparsely settled reaches of the Northern Rockies. The downtown was clearly the heart of the community, comprising a vibrant mix of retail and office activities.

But that all changed, and changed dramatically, in the late 1970s. One of the rail lines, the Milwaukee Road, went bankrupt, closed its depot, and tore up its tracks. At about the same time, a new regional shopping mall was built on the south end of town, two or three miles from the center of town. Overnight, Missoula's vibrant downtown was almost totally eviscerated, as one store after another closed its doors and boarded up its windows. After a period of something resembling catatonic shock, the few remaining merchants and other business owners eventually agreed to do what they could to stop the hemorrhaging and, if possible, to find a way to breathe new life into Missoula's downtown. One or two of them had heard of a mechanism called "tax increment financing" (TIF) that was being used in other states to revitalize declining urban neighborhoods.[15] Since Montana law did not yet allow the use of TIF, the city's leaders went to the legislature to see if they could secure authorization for that redevelopment tool.

I was serving in the Montana legislature at that time, representing a Missoula district, so I was expected to support this initiative brought forward by my hometown. While I didn't think of it in those terms at the time, I now understand that a form of enlightened self-interest lay at the heart of the political support that had been mobilized behind the legislation among various elements of the Missoula community. City and county governments, as well as the elementary and secondary school districts, had to be willing to forego for several years their respective shares of any increases in tax revenues that might result from downtown revitalization so that the new revenue (the increment) could be plowed back into the downtown in the form of further redevelopment investments. In this sense, the hundreds of communities across the country that have used TIF to revitalize downtowns or other ailing neighborhoods have all relied implicitly on the operation of enlightened self-interest to make the process work. In fact, when we turn to the question of whether there are particular governance mechanisms that encourage the mobilization of enlightened self-interest, we should put TIF on that list. First, though, a little more of the Missoula downtown story will flesh out the concept of enlightened self-interest more fully.

Having secured the authority to create an urban renewal tax-increment district, and having created the Missoula Redevelopment Agency (MRA) and supplied it with a citizen board to govern the district, Missoula was faced with the dilemma that confronts so many such efforts: TIF depends entirely on the creation of more taxable value within any new district, but by definition the district is in decline. This is almost literally, then, a matter of pulling yourself up by your own bootstraps. How, exactly, do you do that?

In Missoula's case, fortuitous events created a small amount of increment soon after the district was formed, but with only a few thousand dollars to invest, the new governing board was still hard-pressed to decide on the most effective way to deploy those slender resources. The default answer would have been to use these scarce public resources to leverage some private investment (like helping one of those boarded-up stores meet fire codes so it could reopen and start paying taxes again), which would, in turn, generate more increment to be used to leverage more private investment, and so on. Not surprisingly, there were several downtown merchants (or prospective merchants) who urged the newly appointed MRA board to take that approach and, specifically, to help *their* businesses survive. But some of the board members had a slightly different idea.

While Missoula had grown up along the Clark Fork River, and while the downtown in particular had centered on the river, Missoula had, throughout its history, paid very little attention to the river other than as a barrier that it had to build bridges across. Like many other river communities, Missoula had dumped garbage in and alongside the river and had made no effort to provide riverfront trails or parks. The heightened environmental awareness of the late twentieth century, though, combined with the abandonment of the Milwaukee railroad line next to the river, had led some Missoulians to begin dreaming of a chain of riverfront parks, connected by trails, including one along the old rail bed. Now, some of the MRA board members suggested that reclaiming the riverfront might be the most effective way of reversing the decline of the downtown. What if that small accumulation of increment were to be invested in the development of a new riverfront park in the very heart of the downtown? "But parks don't pay taxes," the skeptics reminded the board. "You'll never turn redevelopment into a self-perpetuating engine that way."

In the end, the board adopted a mixed approach, making some investments to leverage particular private developments but putting a major share of its scarce resources into public amenities, like those parks and trails. The strategy worked, and Missoula's downtown is now generally recognized as one of the most robust and inviting in the Northern Rockies. The string of trails and parks and the still-expanding number of other public amenities they have catalyzed have been key to the revitalization of a downtown that had very nearly died. The board's approach has proven itself to be good public policy. But it could never have been launched or sustained without a very clear and extensive identification and pursuit of enlightened self-interest on the part of those downtown merchants and other business leaders who were willing to forego immediate public assistance to benefit their own enterprises directly in favor of the much more indirect benefits provided by those public amenities.

This story is not presented because there is anything remarkable about it but precisely because there isn't. This kind of thing happens day after day, year after year, in communities across America, and every good citizen of any American community could tell any number of similar stories. (These are precisely the stories that Deborah and James Fallows have told in their 2018 book, *Our Towns: A 100,000-Mile Journey into the Heart of America*.[16]) The point here is simply to suggest that if we dig deeply enough into those stories we might come to a clearer understanding of whether (and if so, how) enlightened self-interest continues to play the democratic role that Tocqueville identified and how that role might be expanded within the structure and culture of American democracy.

With that objective in mind, let's go back to the Missoula story to see if we can gain a clearer understanding of how the identification and pursuit of enlightened self-interest might nurture democracy itself. How, for example, does this story compare with the democratically discouraging scenarios that we see unfolding so often at the level of the national or even many state governments? One striking difference is the nearly total absence of ideological considerations in this local story. What predominates instead is a straightforward problem-solving mindset. The community is confronted with a clear and pressing problem: the collapse of the downtown in the case of Missoula and many other cities. In our case, a few people knew about a mechanism (TIF) that might help address that cataclysm. The decision to pursue that approach was purely pragmatic; it would be difficult to detect any trace of ideology in it. Much the same was true of the later decision to invest some of the scarce public resources in reclaiming the riverfront.

While various people might have greater or lesser attachment to "green" amenities like trails and parks, the driving consideration around which a consensus could form was the pragmatic question of what would most effectively contribute to the sustainable revitalization of the downtown.

It is precisely this pragmatic baseline that Tocqueville identified as the democratic essence of enlightened self-interest. Americans, he believed, were so good at the democratic pursuit of the common good not because of any particular ideology, and not even because of altruism, but because their hardheaded, pragmatic assessment of their own long-term self-interest so often led them to the conclusion that they were more likely to thrive and prosper if their neighbors and their community were also thriving and prospering. In those terms, Tocqueville would not have been the least bit surprised to see Missoula's merchants willing to forego some immediate benefits to their businesses in return for making the downtown in general a more appealing place. They were certainly pursuing their own interest, but it was their interest *bien entendu*, as our visitor from France would have said.

It seems apparent that the connection Tocqueville drew between enlightened self-interest and democracy is still fully in play in instances like the Missoula story (and in those stories across the country that the Fallows' book recounts).[17] In such cases, the identification and pursuit of enlightened self-interest becomes all but indistinguishable from the practice of democratic citizenship. And the more thoroughly a community cultivates this kind of civic culture, the more difficult it becomes to distinguish enlightened self-interest from community spiritedness. The initial intersection isn't far to seek. For many of the people that we have described as pursuing their enlightened self-interest, the most prominent guidepost to that goal was the recognition that a thriving and attractive community would provide the most promising setting in which their own enterprises could thrive and prosper.

In some cases, that calculation may have been quite explicit, but in most others, it lay further in the background. For some, a certain amount of community spiritedness will have been mixed with the pursuit of enlightened self-interest from the outset. Regardless of the proportion of these ingredients early on, the trajectory over time is likely to be in the direction of gradually more public spiritedness enriching the mix, as participants become more comfortable with each other and as they share in the celebration (and mutual congratulation) of their public enterprises. So, in Missoula, every new riverfront park dedication, every opening of a new trail segment stirred in more people a sense of pride in what they had accomplished together.

For many of the downtown merchants, the fact that an attractive riverfront was bringing more people back downtown certainly did not escape their attention, and it was likely to make them more supportive of the next engaging riverfront project. But most of them came to appreciate and enjoy those projects for their own sake, so that, at a certain point, it became nearly impossible to distinguish between public spiritedness and an awareness of where any one entrepreneur's enlightened self-interest resided. In fact (and I think this is essentially what Tocqueville was saying), the most potent and reliable contribution to public spiritedness is often a lively, engaged, and widespread pursuit of enlightened self-interest. And, as John Dewey argued in another classic work on the pragmatic strain of American democracy, the resulting sense of shared purpose is also (and not incidentally) the surest route to a sustainable practice of democracy. In *The Public and Its Problems*, Dewey wrote:

> Wherever there is conjoint activity [like restoring a dying downtown] whose consequences are appreciated as good by all singular persons who take part in it, and where the realization of the good is such as to effect an energetic desire and effort to sustain it in being just because it is a good shared by all, there is in so far a community. *The clear consciousness of a communal life, in all its implications, constitutes the idea of democracy.* (Emphasis added)[18]

Let's take just a minute to digest this passage, and in particular the last sentence. It seems safe to say that if most Americans were asked to express "the idea of democracy," they wouldn't go directly to "the clear consciousness of a communal life."[19] The common perception is that democracy is about elections. From that perspective, the kind of active citizenship we've been describing here is either invisible or irrelevant to democracy. The guiding purpose of this chapter, though, is to suggest that the major problems that beset representative democracy cannot and will not be addressed in any meaningful or lasting way without drawing very deliberately on the civic strength residing in the very different kind of democracy we find operating every day in every one of our communities. It is this "clear consciousness of a communal life" that Dewey identifies as constituting "the idea of democracy."[20] But that suggestion invites us to examine more closely the relationship between electoral democracy and the kind of hands-on, problem-solving citizenship we have been observing at the community level.

One of the great virtues of *The Public and Its Problems* is Dewey's analysis of how elected officials fit into his citizen-centered picture of democracy. For there to be a democratic public at all, Dewey argues, there has to be the capacity among substantial numbers of citizens to identify (and then to agree to pursue) common objectives. But because a fair share of the actual work of pursuing those objectives often has to rest with government, he says, "we come upon the primary problem of the public: to achieve such recognition of itself as will give it weight in the selection of official representatives and in the definition of their responsibilities and rights."[21]

Dewey's way of saying this may sound a little obscure, but his thought is so deeply relevant to our own contemporary situation that it is worth spending some time untangling it. If we were to apply Dewey's analysis to the current crisis of democracy, we might say that in our day the "primary problem of the public" is for the American citizenry "to achieve such recognition of itself"—and in particular of its own enduring democratic vitality—"as will give it weight" not only "in the selection of official representatives" but in reasserting democratic control over "the definition of their responsibilities and rights."[22] That, in essence, is the work of democratic reform that now lies before us. Until American citizens find a way to unite in saying, for example, "our elections need to be *our* elections; they need to be structured and financed in a way that serves *our* needs as democratic citizens," democracy will not be restored to anything like a satisfactory state in this country. That restorative work will inevitably take the form of specific initiatives concerning, for example, campaign finance and the structure of elections, and will therefore depend substantially on the engagement of elected officials. But the heart of the matter is that the democratic public must, in Dewey's phrase, "achieve such recognition of itself" that it can effectively redefine its relation to those officials.[23]

In these terms, the practice of local democracy provides absolutely indispensable lessons about the appropriate relationship between citizens and those they elect to represent them. In particular, the way self-government works at the local level far more often manifests itself as a matter of shared responsibility between citizens and officials than it does at other levels of government. To a certain extent, this difference is an inescapable consequence of scale, but even so, there are crucial features of the local relationship that must now be adapted to larger scales as we undertake the work of restoring health to the body politic. So let us take a minute to examine local democracy in this light, turning again for illustration to the story of Missoula's downtown revitalization.

Having eventually been appointed to the redevelopment agency board by my successor in the mayor's office, I became convinced during my decade or so of service there that downtown redevelopment had largely succeeded because it had been pursued as an ongoing and steadily strengthening partnership between public officials and various private entities. The relevance of this to a healthy democracy will become more evident if we take time to explore the relationship between the often-used phrase "public–private partnership" and the less common but increasingly important concept of "governance." The partnership phrase is fairly self-explanatory, but the word governance is not. Most of us understand that governance means something different than (although somehow overlapping) "government." Without attempting a comprehensive definition of "governance," I want to suggest that the ongoing, evolving public–private partnership of Missoula's downtown revitalization effort has been a classic case of what we mean by democratic governance—and therefore of what we mean by democracy itself.

From the multitude of examples that might now be invoked, consider just one from the early days of the effort to bring the downtown back from the brink. In keeping with the decision to invest some of its scarce resources in developing public amenities along the river corridor, the MRA board focused initially on the riverfront acreage nearest the heart of the downtown. Until then, the highest and best use that had been discovered for this location had been the striped asphalt of a parking lot. The MRA now began exploring the possibility of converting some of the parking to park-land. Drawing on a previous planning effort, the agency included an outdoor amphitheater and events ring in the park's design.

As the plans slowly took on the more tangible form of an attractively landscaped (but largely unpeopled) green space, business leaders began discussing how to use the new park to draw more people to the downtown (and sometimes to their businesses). Acting through their private, nonprofit Missoula Downtown Association (MDA), these entrepreneurs told the MRA board that, if the agency would provide a brick surface and some public restrooms in the area adjacent to the amphitheater, the MDA would pay for and erect a festive circus-style tent there. The MDA then proceeded to organize a weekly event called "Out to Lunch in Caras Park" to occur every Wednesday noon throughout the summer. They lined up local bands to perform in the amphitheater, and they invited downtown restaurants and other vendors to set up stands under the tent to sell food to the people they hoped would show up. Only a handful of people did appear that first summer, and only a few more the next year, but the MDA stuck with it, devoting some of its precious dues to getting the word out, and gradually Out to Lunch at Caras Park began to snowball. Now over thirty years old, it has become a staple feature of the weekly summer routine of hundreds of Missoula families, not a few of whom visit downtown shops or other businesses before or after lunch.

So here we have a civic success story of a kind that will surely be familiar to anyone reading this chapter. (The story will teach its democratic lessons more effectively if you take a minute to call to mind a similar example from your own experience.) One fairly clear lesson from this and similar stories in other communities is that the identification and pursuit of enlightened self-interest lies very near the center of this picture. While we could easily focus on Out to Lunch as an intrinsically good thing, well worth pursuing for its own sake, the truth is that it would not have happened without the self-interested motivation of downtown businesses. As Tocqueville would have predicted, these entrepreneurs came to see that their true interests (their interests "properly understood") could best be pursued by creating something of benefit not only to themselves but to the larger community.

Enl-self just stated again

The pursuit of that enlightened self-interest led to a vibrant public–private partnership of a kind that most civically active

Americans know well. In democratic terms, the revitalization of Missoula's downtown, to which the Caras Park project was meant to contribute, was a straightforward case of what John Dewey described as the organic emergence of a democratic public.[24] Something needed to be done (the downtown needed to be revitalized), but because no single individual or company could accomplish this in isolation, it became a shared, or public, problem. Government resources (especially tax increment funds) were mobilized as one component of the solution, but while the MRA and the Missoula Parks and Recreation Department could design, build, and maintain a park, this was decidedly *not* a case of "if you build it, they will come." To get people to the park (and to the larger downtown) in sufficient numbers, engaging activities had to be imagined, designed, launched, and maintained. City government played a much smaller role than citizens in that work. This helps to illustrate why the word governance has become so useful in describing a long-term undertaking like the reinvigoration of Missoula's downtown. From Caras Park through countless succeeding "public–private partnerships" to the more recent development and implementation of a downtown master plan, the work has always entailed government but has almost never been done by government alone. Without ever (to my knowledge) using the word, Missoula's city officials and civic leaders have engaged in democratic "governance" to achieve the goal of downtown revitalization they had set for themselves three decades ago.

The role of democratic citizenship is clearly crucial in this context. Everyone involved—the MDA and its members, the city government and its elected officials and employees, that particular branch of city government charged with redevelopment (the MRA) and its paid staff and volunteer board—all of us are involved in a common task of taking care of our city. In that sense, we are all city-stewards ("citi-zens"), and we all take that role pretty seriously. Some of us have some very particular responsibilities and roles within that picture: some are elected to their positions; some are hired and paid for theirs; some are appointed but unpaid; many are volunteers compensated by nothing but civic pride or enlightened self-interest and carrying no other title than that crucial one of "citizen." But we are all engaged together in taking care of our city, and it is absolutely clear that our city would not be the community we love so well without the contributions of all these individuals and organizations. The reason this matters so much, though, is that something very much like this story from my hometown is true of thousands of communities and millions of citizens across the country.

Let's take a minute to remind ourselves of where we are in our analysis. This chapter is one of several that will explore the enduring or emerging sources of democratic strength on which we might plausibly draw in the long labor of healing the major wounds to our body politic that are now of such widespread concern. If democratic citizenship is a key source of that strength, and if that kind of citizenship has remained most vibrant at the community level, it seems that the more we know about the factors that nourish and sustain that kind of citizenship, the better positioned we will be to bring that source of strength to bear on the work of healing larger democratic institutions. What emerge so clearly at the community level are two major insights into democratic health. One has to do with the blending of enlightened self-interest with community spiritedness that arises from the sustained practice of problem-solving citizenship. The second is revealed in the sharing of responsibility for the common good among elected and appointed officials on one hand and citizens on the other. I want to close this chapter with a little further reflection on that second, rather subtle but I believe crucial, feature of a healthy democracy.

We saw in chapter 2 how the dynamics of partisanship can trap even the best intentioned of elected officials (especially at larger scales of government) in practices that seriously undermine democracy. Building on the quicksand metaphor, I suggested that politicians can't escape this quagmire without help from someone standing on more secure democratic ground. In particular, while elected officials will have a crucial role to play in enacting and maintaining the reforms required to bring our democratic institutions back to a state of health, the political forces at work are so powerful that there is no way that elected officials can accomplish almost any of those reforms on their own.

The argument here is that a major part of what it will take to mount and sustain an effective democratic reform movement will be a marked shift in the way millions of citizens experience and enact their relationship to elected officials. If they currently see themselves primarily as voters, constituents, or occasional petitioners, they will have to begin seeing themselves instead as colleagues in the task of making things work—including making democracy itself work. At a minimum, there will have to emerge a mind-set more like the one so many people now bring to their relationship with local officials. "Yes," these more self-aware citizens might say to a governor or member of congress, "by virtue of your election and your office, you have some very particular responsibilities, but you are still part of this larger team that we all play for as we move the ball down the field together. The office we have chosen you to fill for a while is a crucial component of our team's struc-ture, but so is the office I and my neighbors hold—the office of citizen. Things would go downhill in a hurry if we weren't doing our jobs. Most of what makes our lives or that of our friends or families most satisfying is actually the result of what citizens have done, or what we have done in partnership with our local officials. Some of what works well is certainly the result of what you and your colleagues have done in the more exalted roles to which we have elected you. We genuinely appreciate that. But please don't forget that the office you hold is actually our office, and the work you do is work we share."

There is nothing new about voters reminding elected officials in one way or another that "you work for us." The tenor of that message, as it is usually delivered though, is almost always one of anger, or at least of discontent. The impact of the message in that form rests on the fact that "we can replace you if we choose." That is an important reminder in any representative democracy and one that must always lie ready to hand. But what if those officials started hearing not only "remember that you work *for* us," but also, "remember that you work *with* us"? That is a message that I be-lieve must become second nature to millions of good citizens if an effective movement of democratic reform is to take root and flourish. It is the kind of message that should come naturally from the lips of engaged and active citizens, accustomed to relating to their local officials in just that way.

As I will suggest in a later chapter, the work of democratic re-newal that is now called for will almost certainly require millions of citizens creating something like a democracy lobby powerful enough to begin reshaping our institutions of self-government. To anticipate that chapter briefly: I will turn in that context to the National Rifle Association as an example of how something like a democracy lobby might become effective enough to meet and overcome the profound challenges facing our republic. We will pay particular attention there to two key strengths of the gun lobby: first, the millions of people who own firearms whose physical power they can directly experience and control, and second, the availability of a constitutional provision that vastly enhances their sense of empowerment. I am convinced that there are even more millions of people who hold in their hands and exercise regularly the skills and practices of everyday citizenship, and furthermore that there exist constitutional foundations of democratic citizenship that will prove far more solid and empowering than anything provided by the Second Amendment. Unfortunately, those foundations have been buried under decades of undemocratic judicial pronouncements, particularly in the arena of campaign finance. We will thus seek, in chapter 6, a sharper understanding of how deeply undemocratic those campaign finance rulings have been and, at the same time, seek to uncover the solid republican ground on which we can hope to see millions of citizens uniting in the great democratic challenge of restoring the vitality of our self-governing institutions. First, though, we need to recover an embodied sense of just how democratically potent that kind of citizenship continues to be. I'll offer two more brief stories to illustrate that point.

This book has mainly been written at two or three of my favorite coffee and breakfast spots around Missoula. These are some of Missoula's classic "third places"—those gathering spots, neither homes nor workplaces, where a tremendous amount of the shaping of any community takes place. This chapter in particular has unfolded primarily at Break Espresso, during a stretch of summer days when a classic case of democratic governance has played out at a neighboring table. The main actors in this tableau are two of Missoula's senior civic leaders, Dan Lambros and Tom Boone. Lambros was one of the founders of what would become the city's premiere real estate company, while Boone carried forward and significantly expanded the law firm his father had launched in 1946. I have known both men for many years and have had several opportunities to appreciate the contributions that they and their families have made to Missoula's cultural and civic life. Tom was a regular at Break Espresso, stopping by frequently to pick up a cup of coffee to take to the office. I had never seen Dan there before, though, and never saw Tom stay long enough to sit down, so when I saw them at a table together one morning, I knew something must be up. When I confessed my surprise to them, Dan filled me in on their enterprise.

He told me that the Boone and Lambros families had returned from a trip to Europe with a shared inspiration about one more way to improve their hometown. While traveling in Portugal, they had been struck by the beauty of a number of illuminated bridges. "These lighted bridges were not only works of art in themselves," they later explained in an op-ed piece, "but they also . . . added a stunning architectural feature to the overall city landscape. We came back thinking we should light a Missoula bridge, too."[25] The travelers inspired a few of their friends with their enthusiasm, and together they took the idea to the park board (which endorsed it) and then to the city council. At that point they began to encounter a number of concerns about long-term maintenance costs and possible effects on wildlife or on the cultural and historic value of the river. The day I first encountered Dan and Tom together at the coffee shop, they were preparing for the first of what I would witness as a series of face-to-face meetings with individual city council members to hear these officials' concerns, to try to reshape their bridge lighting proposal in response, and, if possible, to persuade the council members of the public value of this evolving initiative.

It took many months of intense deliberation and negotiation, and a fair amount of private fund-raising, but eventually two bridges in the heart of Missoula were tastefully illuminated to widespread acclaim for their contribution to both safety and aesthetics. As a resident of the adjacent neighborhood, I've now had countless opportunities to appreciate this enhancement to community life. But I also appreciated the opportunity to watch this little example of democracy in action as it unfolded there at Break Espresso. If citizenship is fundamentally a matter of caring for one's city—and by extension of caring for our communities at all scales, up to the global—then what I had witnessed was just one more example of the kind of citizenship that had made my time as mayor so deeply satisfying.

When I left the mayor's office, I had been asked the usual round of questions about my experience there, including the standard questions about my proudest achievements and the most important lessons I had learned. I had learned plenty, of course, but I found that I was having a hard time naming my proudest

achievements, simply because everything I actually did take pride
in had so clearly not been "my" achievement at all. I recalled, for
example, how we had expanded our trail system many miles further along the riverfront and out into the forests surrounding the
city—and then I remembered all the different kinds of work, all
the endless problem solving by countless citizens and officials that
had enabled those trails to come into being. I was especially proud
of one new riverfront park that we had created where for decades
we had dumped fill dirt and construction debris—and I was reminded of the patient, savvy work of the citizens who drafted,
promoted, and passed the open space bond that had enabled us
to buy the land and of the creative work of another set of citizens as they sought to design the park in a way that worked not
only for the surrounding neighborhood but also for the birds and
beavers that depended on that particular kind of riparian habitat.
I was acutely aware of how little of all that I myself had done or
indeed could have done, given my own very narrow range of skills
or expertise.

When I finally got around to answering the question about the
most significant lesson I had learned from my years in the mayor's
office, I found myself saying I had learned that Missoula was several thousand times smarter than I was or ever would be. And that
was the simple truth. The point, of course, is not about my ig-
norance but about the community's collective intelligence. That
ability to figure out what needs doing and to fashion a workable
way of getting it done was something I might have noticed from
other vantage points, but from the one that I had been privileged
to occupy in city hall, it had become inescapably clear. What that
lesson boiled down to was a profound appreciation for democratic
citizenship in the root sense of people learning how to take care of
their city and help it to realize its potential.

It was only against the background of that remarkable, persistent exercise of effective citizenship that I could make any
kind of honest assessment of my own role in any of the communal achievements that I so proudly recalled. Clearly there is a role
for political leadership in these situations. Among other things, a
good politician can often play a catalytic role in helping citizens
with diverse interests recognize—and stay together long enough
to realize—their shared interest. Having found myself playing
that role frequently as mayor, and having so often been gratified

by what I saw my neighbors go on to accomplish, I had been indelibly reminded of how democracy thrives when elected officials share with engaged citizens the responsibility of governing. The hopeful news is that exactly this kind of shared governance occurs thousands of times every day. I am convinced that the practice of citizenship that brought Dan and Tom back to that table morning after morning for their meetings with city council members is something so broadly shared across this country, so powerful and persistent and so fundamentally democratic that it will eventually lead to citizens uniting in the work of restoring our larger governing institutions to a corresponding state of health.

The magnitude of that challenge can hardly be exaggerated, and skeptical readers could be forgiven for asking whether a handful of citizens figuring out how to put lights on bridges over a western river is really going to help us in any meaningful way to meet such overwhelming challenges to our democracy as the antimajoritarian operation of the Electoral College or wealth-privileging Supreme Court rulings on campaign finance. When we stop to think that neither of those democratic afflictions may be curable short of amending the Constitution, it is easy to fall into despair. As one step on the path to regaining our democratic self-confidence I want to invite us to journey back roughly a century to a time when our ancestors brought their own home-grown, self-governing capacities to bear on another set of challenges to democracy no less daunting than ours, leaving us a legacy of inspiration to carry us through the hard, healing work that now lies before us.

4   Drawing Hope from History

Recalling the Progressive Movement

The cure for the ills of Democracy is more Democracy.

—Jane Addams, 1902

Our remote little farmhouse on the high, dry, windy plains of eastern Montana offered very few fine adornments beyond the bare necessities of the hardscrabble life my parents had managed to scrape out and hold together in that forbidding place. One exception, though, caught and commanded my attention as early as any memory I've retained. Within a rich, dark walnut oval frame, a photo of a handsome, middle-aged man with a neatly trimmed beard was more subtly framed by a cloud-like background silhouette of a figure vaguely suggestive of George Washington. This stately gentleman was "Uncle Walter," only a little later coming more clearly into focus for me as my father's uncle, and thus my great-uncle. He was still living when I was a boy; in fact, as an ordained Methodist deacon, he had baptized me when I was five or six. But his pastoral calling had always taken second place in my mind to what had earned him that elegant walnut frame and the aura of that Washingtonian nimbus—namely his long-time service in the Montana legislature. Elected as quite a young man to the House early in the century, he was still serving in the Senate in the early 1950s. As awed by his august career as the portrait's presentation intended me to be, I more or less put him alongside Yogi Berra in my boyhood pantheon of heroes to be revered, if not emulated. I'm still a Yankee fan to this day, thanks mostly to the exploits of their remarkable catcher back then, and while I never became much of a baseball player, I did manage to translate my admiration for Uncle Walter, first into a childhood fascination with politics and eventually into a legislative career of my own.

Most of us could tell such stories about how some admired adult inspired us to walk a path in life that we might otherwise have bypassed. The way that Uncle Walter did that for me is of no significance outside my own life, but his story, seen as part of the larger story of his generation of involved citizens and statesmen, presents just the kind of inspiration that I believe we now need as we search for what we can do, individually and together, to heal the deep wounds and diseases from which our democracy is suffering. Specifically, I want to invite us on a very brief journey back to the Progressive Era of a century ago, to recall the remarkable array of history-changing reforms that emerged from those decades and at the same time to fix firmly in our minds the fact that the people who brought about all of those democracy-strengthening reforms are now worth remembering, not because they were better than— or in any other essential way different from—us, but because their democratic faith can still inspire us to do what needs to be done in the service of democracy in our own troubled time. In fact, it is exactly the way they brought the living of their daily lives into their democracy-healing politics that might now inspire us to do the same. To begin to see how that inspiration could work, I'll return to Uncle Walter for another moment or two.

My hero-inspired fascination with politics led me while still a boy to begin researching Walter's career. I soon discovered that during his tenure in the Montana House of Representatives, Walter had departed from his parents' Republican loyalty long enough to run as a Progressive candidate during Theodore Roosevelt's "Bull Moose" attempt to regain the presidency in 1912.[1] Walter's parents may well have shared his enthusiasm for Roosevelt, if only because they had claimed their pioneer homestead in the lower Yellowstone valley in 1884, the same year that Roosevelt had established his "Elkhorn Ranch" about sixty miles across the North Dakota badlands from the Kemmis farm. Roosevelt would soon return to New York, but the Kemmis family would stay put, building a school on their homestead for young Walter and his siblings and for the growing number of neighbor children who were showing up as a stream of new homesteaders settled in the valley. By the time Walter ran for the legislature under the same label as Roosevelt, their two lives had followed very different paths, but the confluence of their politics in 1912 is part of a tale that might still inspire anyone concerned about the well-being of our democracy. Their journeys, along with millions of other stories of both political leaders and ordinary citizens, coalesced into what we now call the Progressive movement.[2]

That movement produced one of the greatest waves of democratic revitalization in American history, including hundreds of amendments to state constitutions and the largest cluster of national constitutional amendments since the adoption of the Bill of Rights. Political leaders, from the world-famous like Theodore Roosevelt to the obscure like Uncle Walter, played an indispensable role in that phenomenon. But their role was underlain and indeed overshadowed by the active engagement of millions of ordinary citizens. And behind that popular floodtide lay the element that still gives the Progressive movement the capacity to inspire us today: the unflagging commitment of those multitudes of citizens to do whatever was required to rescue their democracy from the multiple threats that assailed it. As Jane Addams, one of the preeminent figures in the Progressive movement put it, "The cure for the ills of Democracy is more Democracy."[3] It was, in the end, a gigantic and sustained surge of democracy that gave the Progressive movement the capacity to play its historic role—and perhaps the capacity to inspire us to a similarly effective effort on behalf of our democracy.

I should note here that I am by no means an uncritical fan of the Progressives. Many of their policies, and even some of their principles, seem to me to have been misplaced, and as a consequence, some of their successful reforms have created problems that continue to afflict us today. The Progressive emphasis on the role of professionalism, for example, can be seen as undermining democratic governance insofar as it overlooked or devalued local knowledge or folk wisdom. We in the West have sometimes chafed under that substitution of professional for lay knowledge in the management of the public lands, for example, so that even some of us who genuinely appreciate the work of Progressives like Roosevelt and Gifford Pinchot in protecting public lands have been less enthralled by this disempowering feature of the governing system they created for those lands. That privileging of professional over local knowledge has been at play also in the vastly different arena of municipal governance, where the city manager form of government promoted by the National Municipal League (which Roosevelt helped to create) has, in those cities that have adopted it, replaced the popular election of chief executives by the appointment of professional managers.[4] While reasonable people have continued to disagree about the pros and cons of the council-manager form of government, many of us who have been elected and held accountable in the strong mayor system have questioned on democratic grounds the Progressives' determination to professionalize the executive branch of municipal government.

Despite such arguably undemocratic side effects of the Progressive agenda, however, the movement did far more to advance than to weaken the cause of democracy. The democratic significance of Progressivism shines forth, for example, in the exceptional breadth of the movement's scope, touching as it did on so many major dimensions of American life. That breadth is instanced in the two vastly diverse examples I just cited, both promoted by Roosevelt. Indeed, the protean energy of that one reformer, capable of leaving his fingerprints on our contemporary experience of arenas as diverse as public lands and city government, stands as a kind of personal incarnation of the reach of Progressivism into so many significant dimensions of American life.

That breadth is clearly reflected in Maureen A. Flanagan having organized her 2007 book *America Reformed* "around four major ideas of progressivism: social justice, political, economic, and foreign policy."[5] Our interest here is not in the particulars of that catalogue so much as in its reach into so many crucial dimensions of human life. What that range underscores is that the movement was fundamentally about people making a concerted and sustained effort to determine the major conditions of their own lives. And because that ability to influence the circumstances shaping our lives is the very essence of democracy, the Progressive movement was, above all, a democratic movement. As Flanagan puts it, "At stake in all proposed reforms was the definition of American democracy."[6] What we find motivating all of the major reforms and reformers, then, was the growing awareness that, in various settings, people were not able to determine the conditions of their own lives as fully as they thought they should. Millions of ordinary citizens added their energies to this remarkable democratic movement when they set out to do something about the various ways that they saw their institutions falling short of—or actively hindering—genuine democratic self-determination.

Even the most cursory glance at the Progressive Era will remind us of the phenomenal range of its activities. There is the social dimension, most memorably institutionalized in the settlement house movement launched by Jane Addams.[7] The social focus of the movement was also reflected in the two vastly different arenas represented by John Dewey's educational reforms on the one hand and the temperance movement on the other.[8] Social reforms shaded over into the economic field with agitation around child labor and other factory conditions. In both the social and the economic arenas, reformers did not shy away from becoming politically engaged by pushing for progressive legislation—and when necessary for constitutional amendments like the Sixteenth Amendment reversing the Supreme Court's abrogation of a Progressive-inspired income tax law.[9] Sometimes the reformers pushed beyond where the nation was ultimately ready to follow, as with the ill-fated Eighteenth Amendment imposing prohibition on the country.[10]

But one dimension of this reforming activity is of special significance in our own time, namely that the reformers were so willing to change the very structures of democratic self-governance whenever existing institutions or practices stood in the way of their shaping the conditions of their lives in the social or economic arenas. At least four instances of that level of reform will enlighten our search for inspiration for our own time: civil service reform, direct election of senators, women's suffrage, and such mechanisms of direct democracy as initiative and referendum. Across this range, the reformers did not shrink from taking on the very heavy lift of constitutional revision if that proved to be the only way to democratize their governing institutions. Sometimes those amendments took place at the state level, but in the case of senatorial elections and women's suffrage they produced, respectively, the Seventeenth and Nineteenth Amendments to the U.S. Constitution.[11]

One of the first places we see this willingness to carry reform into the structures of self-government itself was in the city—not least the city to which Theodore Roosevelt returned after his ranching adventure in Dakota Territory. Once back in his native metropolis of New York, the young Roosevelt became steadily more involved in reform politics, joining other reformers in taking on the Tammany Hall "machine" that had so long run the city, as its counterparts did in most other American cities. As Flanagan put it in *America Reformed*, "Businessmen bribed municipal officials for business favors and the politicians delivered these favors for a price. In some cities it seemed as if every official was 'on the take.'"[12]

Crucial to the power of the machines was the "spoils system," which rewarded those most reliably loyal to the bosses with public jobs of all kinds. Civil service reform, seeking to base public employment on merit rather than party loyalty, was among the leading objectives of the emerging reform movement. One of Roosevelt's biographers gives us a flavor of how the cause of civil service reform swept multitudes of citizens into its stream, and thus into the larger river that became the Progressive movement. For this author, too, democracy lay at the heart of the matter:

> The fact remains that thousands, even millions, lined up behind the banner, and they were as evangelical (and as strenuously resisted) as any crusaders in history. To them Civil Service Reform was "a dream at first, and then a passionate cause which the ethical would not let sleep." . . . It sought to restore to government three fundamental principles of American democracy: first, that opportunity be made equal to all citizens; second, that the meritorious only be appointed; third, that no public servants should suffer for their political beliefs. . . . Few converts believed in the above principles more sincerely than Theodore Roosevelt.[13]

In fact, TR was so active in that cause that President Benjamin Harrison appointed him to the newly created Civil Service Commission in 1889.[14] He quickly (and characteristically) became the most active member of that body, serving there until 1895.

Meanwhile, back in the West, the practice of self-government entered a promising but at the same time challenging phase as the last of the old frontier became settled enough for several territories to seek admission to the union as new states. In 1889, the same year that Roosevelt began his tenure at the Civil Service Commission, Montana, North and South Dakota, and Washington would all be granted statehood, a transition that was accompanied in each state by the eminently democratic process of writing new constitutions. If the years between 1889 and 1920 produced some of the most creative activity on behalf of democracy in American history, that movement of democratic renewal was especially vibrant in the states west of the Mississippi. I focus most of the remainder of this chapter on the role of this region in the Progressive reforms, not because I believe that other regions played less important roles but because I know more about the lives these ancestors of mine and their neighbors lived, and therefore I can more readily demonstrate how they translated the living of those lives into democratic reform.

One good entry point into that regional concentration of reforming energy is by way of the writing and revising of constitutions. While fashioning the institutions and procedures by which they and their children would govern themselves might be seen as a quintessentially democratic activity on the part of western settlers, they were in fact undertaking that task under the shadow of some of the same threats to genuine self-government that had come to afflict the rest of the country. In this region, big-city political machines were far less of a hindrance to democracy than another of the scourges of the Gilded Age: the inordinate political power of concentrated wealth. That power threatened to dominate the creation of several of the brand-new political jurisdictions that were being formed in the process of moving from territorial status to statehood. Montana's constitution, for example, was drafted at a convention presided over by one William A. Clark.[15] A true son of the Gilded Age, Clark had made a fortune from the copper ore underlying Butte, Montana, and eventually spent part of that fortune buying votes from Montana legislators to make himself a U.S. senator.[16] As it turns out, Clark's efforts to buy a seat in the U.S. Senate played a significant role in building support for what would become the Seventeenth Amendment to the Constitution.[17] That incident can therefore serve to illustrate several of the dysfunctional features of late-nineteenth century American politics that eventually mobilized millions of Americans (including thousands of Montanans) to lend their energy to a great movement of democratic reform.

Under the terms of the original Constitution, U.S. senators had for over a century been chosen by their state legislatures. As the nineteenth century progressed, this method of selection had left the Senate particularly subject to many of the corruptions of democracy that the reformers were beginning to address by century's end. As the Center for Legislative Archives summarizes the background to the Seventeenth Amendment, "Several state legislatures deadlocked over the election of senators, which led to Senate vacancies lasting months and even years. In other cases, political machines gained control over state legislatures, and the Senators elected with their support were dismissed as puppets. In addition, the Senate was seen as a 'millionaire's club' serving powerful private interests."[18]

The average senator had always been wealthier than the typical American, but in the decades following the Civil War, the number of very wealthy men holding Senate seats rose steadily. Not surprisingly, so did the tendency of the Senate to support policies that advanced the interests of those plutocrats. William A. Clark became a poster child for that complaint.[19] As Timothy Egan put it in a *New York Times* column in 2010:

> After gaining control of much of the world's copper supply, the 19th-century robber baron William A. Clark set out to buy a seat in the United States Senate. Openly, he went about bribing Montana legislators, $10,000 a vote, the cash paid in monogrammed envelopes.
>
> Mark Twain called Clark "as rotten a human being as can be found anywhere under the flag," but the senator did not show any shame. "I never bought a man who wasn't for sale," he said.
>
> It was corruption such as this that led to the 17th Amendment, which allows direct election of senators by the people, not state legislators. And it was stone-hearted, Gilded Age titans like Clark who prompted this populist movement in the West.[20]

Our interest here is not in the Seventeenth Amendment itself, or in the intensely venal nature of people like William A. Clark. What we want to remember is that, when their institutions became so dysfunctional that someone like Clark could be sent to the Senate, the people of Montana and of the nation at large finally did something about it. More to the point, they did something about it in the face of what could easily have felt like overwhelming odds. Then as now, amending the Constitution required two-thirds votes in each house of Congress to submit an amendment to the states and then approval by three-fourths of those states.[21] Reformers had managed to get proposals for direct election of senators through the House on one or two occasions, but the chance of that happening in the Senate, where every member had benefited from the old system, seemed nonexistent. The story of what happened next is summarized by an account from the Center for Legislative Archives:

> During the 1890s, the House of Representatives passed several resolutions proposing a constitutional amendment for the direct election of senators. Each time, however, the Senate refused to even take a vote. When it seemed unlikely that both houses of Congress would pass legislation proposing an amendment for direct election, many states changed strategies. Article V of the Constitution states that Congress must call a constitutional convention for proposing amendments when two-thirds of the state legislatures apply for one. Although the method had never previously been used, many states began sending Congress applications for conventions. As the number of applications neared the two-thirds bar, Congress finally acted.[22]

What is not quite revealed in this account is a feature that is crucial to the relevance of this story for our own time. The constitutional convention strategy was a good one, but it would never have succeeded in gaining the momentum it needed to impel Congress to act if it had not been part of a much larger movement of reform that reached far beyond the issue of how U.S. senators were elected. This brings us back to the earlier point emphasized by Maureen Flanagan: that the very multiplicity of arenas addressed by the reformers created a synergy that enhanced the prospects of many particular reforms beyond what they could have achieved singly.[23] That synergy was very evident in Montana in 1912, as indeed it was across the region so recently admitted to statehood.

In Montana, the memory of William A. Clark's bribery of enough Montana legislators to send him to Washington was still fresh enough to lead the 1911 legislative session to implement what amounted to the direct election of Montana's next U.S. senator by a clever circumvention of the Constitution. Adopting what had come to be called the "Oregon Method" of implementing direct election, the 1911 session put on the 1912 ballot a plebiscite that enabled Montanans to vote for their choice of U.S. senator and then required the next legislature to elect the candidate so chosen.[24] Democrat Thomas Walsh came out on top of the preference poll, and in January 1913 the newly installed legislature duly named Walsh as Montana's junior U.S. senator.[25] Then on January 30, Uncle Walter voted with a majority of his colleagues to make Montana the eleventh state to ratify the Seventeenth Amendment, providing for the direct election of U.S. senators by the people across the country.[26]

Walsh's election highlights one feature of the Progressive Era that should command our attention as we weigh the lessons that era of reform might hold for us now. Walsh was a Democrat, and while legislators with Uncle Walter's political heritage would certainly rather have voted for either a Progressive or a Republican to represent Montana in the U.S. Senate, his vote for Walsh reflected more than obedience to the 1912 plebiscite by which he and his colleagues felt themselves bound. It also reflected a recognition that Walsh (who would go on to play a key role in uncovering the Teapot Dome scandal during the Harding administration) was himself a reformer of some considerable conviction.[27] That same trans-partisan dynamic within the larger Progressive movement had played out in the 1912 presidential election when Woodrow Wilson, who had been nominated by the Democrats on the strength of his strong record of reform as governor of New Jersey, not only carried Montana but won a solid majority in the Electoral College, beating both the Progressive, Roosevelt, and the conservative Republican incumbent, William Howard Taft.[28]

The fact is that early twentieth-century democratic reform was very much a cross-partisan phenomenon. In this it can surely provide lessons for our own deeply partisan era. We have already encountered the likelihood that few if any of the major wounds and diseases now afflicting our body politic can be healed by any one political party—not least because excessive partisanship is one of the most serious of those diseases. In that regard, then, one feature of the story we have been considering in this chapter that bears special attention a century later is the deeply and broadly trans-partisan nature of that entire reform effort. That feature of the reform movement was almost certainly a reflection of the deeper phenomenon that we noted earlier: reform energy had arisen from multiple and varied dimensions of society—urban and rural, men and women; civil servants and factory workers. No one political party was at all likely to have claimed the allegiance of all these ways of being American, but because they all had a stake in making democracy work better, their democracy-healing work had to transcend ordinary partisanship.

As it turns out, Montana and its western neighbors supplied a footnote to one of the most striking instances of that transcendence of partisanship. By the mid-1920s, the Progressive movement was beginning to run out of steam, sapped in part by the overwhelming dynamics of the Great War.[29] But before succumbing terminally to Warren Harding's return to "normalcy," the movement made one last heroic effort, seeking to place a team of dynamic reformers in the White House. In the 1924 presidential election, Wisconsin's Robert La Follette ("Fighting Bob" to his friends), who had served as a Republican U.S senator and governor, chose as his running mate Montana's newest Democratic U.S. senator, Burton K. Wheeler ("Bolshevik Burt" to his enemies.)[30] The team ran third nationwide to Republican incumbent Calvin Coolidge and Democrat challenger John W. Davis.[31] La Follette and Wheeler garnered only Wisconsin's thirteen electoral votes, but they ran quite strongly in the West, where they finished second in eleven states.[32] That regional concentration of reforming energy had actually reached its crest about a decade earlier, and nowhere had it been more evident than in the women's suffrage movement.

The Nineteenth Amendment, finally ratified in 1920 after decades of intense struggle, had been presaged throughout the West by a series of state (and even territorial) adoptions of women's suffrage provisions. The territory of Wyoming had granted women full voting rights as early as 1869; it was followed by the territories of Utah in 1870, Washington in 1883, and Alaska in 1913.[33] As these western territories gained statehood, many of them began adding women's suffrage to their new state constitutions, in most cases well before ratification of the Nineteenth Amendment. Wyoming again took the lead, writing women's suffrage into its new state constitution in 1890.[34] Colorado followed suit in 1893, Utah and Idaho in 1896, Washington in 1910, California in 1911, Arizona, Kansas, and Oregon in 1912, and Montana and Nevada in 1914.[35] New York became the first state east of the Mississippi to adopt women's suffrage in 1917, just three years prior to the ratification of the Nineteenth Amendment.[36]

The strong, steady western push for women's suffrage had played a major role in persuading Theodore Roosevelt's Bull Moose party to include women's suffrage in its platform in the election of 1912.[37] In Montana, Progressive men like Uncle Walter voted to write women's suffrage into the state's constitution in 1914, six years before the ratification of the Nineteenth amendment.[38] That pioneering move was followed by an even more dramatic one in 1916, when the men and women of Montana combined to elect Jeannette Rankin as the first woman in the nation's history to take a seat in Congress.[39]

My point in recounting this concentration of reforming activity in the West is to invite us to think harder about how a similar kind of democratizing energy might be roused and sustained in our own time. What seems most telling about the widespread support for women's suffrage across the West in the late-nineteenth and early twentieth centuries was how fundamentally grassroots it all was—and that in a very nearly literal sense. As one commentator has put it, "While eastern society defined the ideal woman as being 'pious, pure, submissive, and domestic,' the harsh conditions of the West pushed women away from the traditional eastern stereotype and into new responsibilities and lifestyles. . . . It was in this context that women decided that they wanted a greater voice in the political process."[40]

In this sense, the successful push for women's suffrage can be understood as one crucial element in a much broader democratic movement—a movement that repeatedly drew its energy from—and built its success upon—the determination of ordinary people to assert or maintain effective control over the conditions of their own existence. In the harsh and demanding circumstances confronting settlers in the last American frontier outside Alaska, maintaining control over the conditions of their lives required an unusually demanding level of perseverance, ingenuity, and cooperation. It was in this setting that the "barn-building" culture of the frontier gained its greatest traction, alongside the celebration of "Yankee ingenuity," so evident in the seemingly inexhaustible ability of farmers to repair machinery whenever it broke down. That this level of self-determination under such challenging conditions could be accomplished by men alone was neither a conceptual nor a practical possibility. And in this situation where everyone was needed by everyone else, political institutions were held to the same standard of effectiveness as people held themselves and their machinery.

It was in this context, then, that new mechanisms of self-government were invented and spread across the landscape, while worn-out or dysfunctional machinery was laid aside. As a 2016 *New York Times* article put it, "The practice of statewide initiative and referendum gained traction among the populist movements of the Progressive Era, around the turn of the 20th century. Frustrated with the ineptitude of government and elected officials, these movements demanded a comprehensive program of reform that included women's suffrage, the direct election of United States senators, the recall mechanism, primary elections and the initiative and referendum process."[41] The *Times* article went on to note the frontier dominance of much of this activity:

> In 1898, South Dakota became the first state to adopt the process for statewide ballots, although Nebraska allowed local ballot measures the year before. Utah and Oregon implemented it in 1900 and 1902, respectively, and many others soon followed. All told, 26 states as well as the District of Columbia currently have some form of initiative or referendum, allowing citizens to directly engage in policy making.
>
> The process gained currency mainly in Western states, which, to this day, have an extraordinarily robust culture of direct democracy. More than 60 percent of all initiative activity has taken place in just six states: Arizona, California, Colorado, North Dakota, Oregon and Washington.[42]

A 2011 article in *High Country News* had made much the same point about the lasting impact of the old frontier's recourse to new democratic mechanisms:

> Nationwide, fewer than half the states allow citizens to make laws directly by gathering signatures on petitions and then having statewide votes. But every state in the West allows it, except for New Mexico and Hawaii. That's because Western states more or less took shape in the early 1900s, an era of populism and the progressive movement. Many people back

then were concerned about powerful corporations—railroads, banks, mining and steel—dominating legislatures. So they wrote citizen lawmaking into their state constitutions.[43]

With both women's suffrage and the direct election of U.S. senators, we can see what a crucial role the grit and determination of ordinary people had played in the long, difficult process of amending the national constitution. But those efforts would not have been likely to bear such hard-earned fruit if they had not been synergized by more local efforts to repair the machinery of democracy.

So it was that, in 1906, Montana voters had overwhelmingly approved an amendment to the state constitution that put their state among the small but growing number of jurisdictions giving their citizens the eminently democratic power to adopt legislation directly by initiative or referendum.[44] Then, on that same 1912 ballot that we have now encountered several times, Montana voters were asked to decide whether or not to approve a ballot initiative that would prohibit corporations from contributing to political campaigns.[45] The citizens of Montana approved the measure that fall, and the prohibition stood as the law of the state for exactly a century.[46] Its nullification in 2012 by the U.S. Supreme Court under the aegis of the 2010 *Citizens United* decision is part of the story of democratic decline that will occupy us through much of what follows here.[47]

This book was sparked in the first instance by my conviction that the *Citizens United* ruling was not only profoundly undemocratic, but that it could probably be put to rights only by citizens uniting in a movement of democratic renewal at least as powerful as the Progressive movement that had produced Montana's 1912 campaign finance law. As the book's focus broadened to take in some of the other wounds and diseases now afflicting our body politic, I found myself also paying attention to that broader range of democratic achievements that the Progressives had sown across the region and indeed across the nation. But given where I had started, I naturally kept in focus that one act of democratic self-determination embodied in the campaign finance law that Montana citizens adopted in 1912.

Our task today is certainly not to replicate the work of our ancestors, but perhaps we can find in their dogged democratic efforts some inspiration to help us take on and sustain the challenging work of revitalizing our own ailing democracy. Now, as then, the driving energy behind that work will come from ordinary people translating the way we live our lives into the resuscitation of our ailing body politic. Nothing more clearly exemplifies the need for that healing work than the Supreme Court's 2010 decision in *Citizens United v. Federal Election Commission*. I have personally drawn an extra surge of inspiration from the fact that the Supreme Court used *Citizens United* to strike down the most important provision of Montana's campaign finance law exactly a century after Uncle Walter, his Progressive colleagues, and their neighbors succeeded in making that citizen-enacted law a key component of their structure of self-government. How that reversal of democratic self-determination happened, how it fits into the larger picture of democratic decline in our time, and what we might now do about it will be the subject of the following chapters.

5   Campaign Finance

The Acid Test?

The Court's ruling threatens to undermine the integrity of elected institutions across the Nation. The path it has taken to reach its outcome will, I fear, do damage to this institution.

Essentially, five Justices were unhappy with the limited nature of the case before us, so they changed the case to give themselves an opportunity to change the law.

The Court operates with a sledge hammer rather than a scalpel when it strikes down one of Congress' most significant efforts to regulate the role that corporations and unions play in electoral politics. It compounds the offense by implicitly striking down a great many state laws as well.

> —*Justice John Paul Stevens, dissenting opinion*
> *in* Citizens United v. Federal Election Commission

On June 25, 2012, the U.S. Supreme Court issued what is called a per curium ruling in a case entitled *American Tradition Partnership v. Bullock.*[1] The plaintiff, originally known as Western Tradition Partnership (WTP), was a nonprofit corporation organized under the laws of Colorado but registered in Montana. Steve Bullock was at that time Montana's attorney general. The case had originated nearly two years earlier when, within months of the U.S. Supreme Court's decision in *Citizens United v. Federal Election Commission,* WTP and two other plaintiffs had filed suit in Montana district court asking that court to declare Montana's century-old law prohibiting corporate contributions to political candidates uncon-stitutional under the ruling of *Citizens United*. On October 19, 2010, state district court judge Jeffrey Sherlock had granted sum-mary judgement in WTP's favor, whereupon the attorney general's office appealed to the state supreme court. Steve Bullock person-ally argued the case to the state's high court, and on December 30, 2011, the Montana Supreme Court issued its decision in *Western Tradition Partnership v. Attorney General*.[2]

Writing on behalf of himself and four associate justices, Chief Justice Mike McGrath wrote that Judge Sherlock had "errone-ously construed and applied the *Citizens United* case."[3] Observing that "[w]hile *Citizens United* was decided under its facts or lack of facts, it applied the long-standing rule that restrictions upon speech are not per se unlawful, but rather may be upheld if the government demonstrates a sufficiently strong interest." McGrath went on to assert that "unlike *Citizens United*, this case concerns Montana law, Montana elections and it arises from Montana his-tory."[4] Noting that the history of "naked corporate manipulation of the very government (Governor and Legislature) of the State ulti-mately resulted in populist reforms that are still part of Montana law," McGrath went on to assert that the concerns of that earlier generation of Montanans were still valid in our time.[5] "The corpo-rate power that can be exerted with unlimited political spending is still a vital interest to the people of Montana," McGrath wrote. "The question then, is when in the last 99 years did Montana lose the power or interest sufficient to support the statute, if it ever did."[6] Reciting evidence from the trial record of ongoing corporate influence in the state, as well as unflagging determination among citizens to keep that influence in check, McGrath concluded, "Clearly Montana has unique and compelling interests to protect through preservation of this statute."[7] With that, he and four of his colleagues reversed the district court ruling and upheld the 1912 citizen-enacted statute.

The plaintiff organization, now calling itself American Tradition Partnership, appealed to the U.S. Supreme Court, a bare majority of whose members summarily overturned the Montana decision.[8] Devoting all of 190 words to the ruling that would nullify Mon-tana's century-old law, the majority wasted no time in coming to the heart of the matter. "In *Citizens United v. Federal Election Com-mission*, this Court struck down a similar federal law, holding that 'political speech does not lose First Amendment protection simply because its source is a corporation,'" the justices wrote.[9] "The question presented in this case is whether the holding of *Citizens United* applies to the Montana state law. There can be no serious doubt that it does."[10] With those few words, five Supreme Court justices abrogated one of the most crucial laws by which Montana citizens had governed themselves for exactly a century.

I remember hearing the outrage of many of my neighbors upon learning of this ruling. It seemed as if many of them had experienced it as an almost physical assault on the body politic of our state, inflicting a wound that was perhaps rendered especially painful by the richly democratic, citizen-driven genesis of the now euthanized law. I want to keep that raw sense of injury and democratic outrage in focus as we begin to examine what had led five Supreme Court justices to deliver this blow. If we are to draw any lasting inspiration for healing the body of democracy from the heritage that produced laws like Montana's, we will need at a minimum to become as clear as possible about both the causes and the contents of the cluster of judicial decisions that have overturned so many of those democratically enacted laws. That turns out to be a complex, multilayered matter. As we dig down through the layers, we will find two dimensions to each of them: (1) a presenting symptom of democratic damage, and (2) an accompanying reminder of the democratic strength or practice that has been both threatened by the rulings and that may at the same time prove crucial to accomplishing the work of renewal. We will need a few chapters to make our way through that analysis, but by the end I hope we will have produced not only a deeper understanding of the nature of the injuries that have been inflicted on the body of democracy but also the outlines of a set of practical lessons for how we might carry forward the labor of democratic restoration that we and our children are now challenged and privileged to undertake, not only in the arena of campaign finance but in response to all the other wounds and diseases now afflicting our body politic.

When the U.S. Supreme Court struck down Montana's century-old campaign finance law, the sense of violation that both I and so many of my neighbors felt surely had something to do with it being *our* law that was being wiped off the books. It was a law that had been duly enacted by our Montana ancestors, and it had helped to define who we understood ourselves to be as a self-governing people. But we were not the only state whose campaign finance laws were then being rewritten wholesale by the Supreme Court. Twenty-two other states had filed amicus briefs in the appeal of the Montana state court decision; for all of them, the eventual result would be the loss of statutory provisions that had been put in place by their own people or their democratically elected legislatures.[11]

Because the Supreme Court's *Citizens United* decision in January 2010 was chiefly responsible for this wholesale alteration of democratic enactments, and for the vast changes in the entire American electoral scene brought about by the decision, we begin by examining the genesis and content of that decision. While it may seem that the *Citizens United* decision appeared out of the blue in January 2010, that is very far from what happened. One step down the long, hard path of reversing the democratic damage caused by that decision is to understand at least a little about its historical antecedents. To that end, here is a very rough chronology of events that have contributed to the current, democratically deadly state of campaign finance law in America. This is by no means a comprehensive list of contributing events, and the relevance of some that are listed (including the first few) will only become apparent as the story unfolds.

> 1857: U.S. Supreme Court issues its decision in *Dred Scott v. Sandford*, ruling that no enslaved person—or indeed anyone of African descent—can be an American citizen, or entitled to any of the privileges of citizenship.[12]
>
> 1868: Fourteenth Amendment to the U.S. Constitution is ratified, reversing *Dred Scott* by declaring that "[a]ll persons born or naturalized in the United States, and subject to the jurisdiction thereof, are citizens of the United States and of the state wherein they reside. No state shall make or enforce any law which shall abridge the privileges or immunities of citizens of the United States; nor shall any state deprive any person of life, liberty, or property, without due process of law; nor deny to any person within its jurisdiction the equal protection of the laws."[13]
>
> 1880s: In a series of decisions known as the "railroad cases," the Supreme Court rules that corporations are "persons" within the meaning of the Fourteenth Amendment's guarantee of

due process—but explicitly states that they are not "citizens" protected by the privileges and immunities clause of that amendment.[14]

1890–1920: Progressive Era legislation prohibits corporate contributions to candidates for national and many state offices.[15] These laws survive for a century, until *Citizens United*. Meanwhile, though, the Supreme Court develops the doctrine of "substantive due process," using it to invalidate most of the Progressive Era (and later much of the New Deal) legislation enacted to protect workers against the worst abuses of corporate industrialism.

1937: Franklin Roosevelt's "court-packing" plan falls short of enactment, but a chastened Court drops its use of substantive due process to protect businesses against democratically enacted legislation.

1972: Watergate break-in and cover-up involves widespread abuse of campaign contributions.

1973: Lewis Powell writes a (private but eventually notorious) memo advising his client, the U.S. Chamber of Commerce, to employ more aggressive tactics in defense of business interests, including efforts to influence legislation and judicial decisions.[16] Later in 1973, Richard Nixon appoints Powell to the Supreme Court.[17]

1974: Nixon resigns in the face of impeachment.[18] Largely in response to Watergate abuses, Congress amends the Federal Election Campaign Act (FECA), imposing campaign contribution and spending limits and establishing a public-funding mechanism for presidential campaigns.[19]

1976: Supreme Court strikes down FECA's spending limits in *Buckley v. Valeo*.[20] In a decision supported by both liberal and conservative judges, the Court finds that the First Amendment protects both campaign contributions and expenditures. Legitimate concerns about corruption can justify limits on contributions, but those concerns do not apply to expenditures, which cannot therefore be restricted. This decision is often characterized as having established the First Amendment doctrine that "money is speech."

1978: Justice Powell writes majority opinion in *First National Bank of Boston v. Bellotti*, ruling that the due process clauses of the Fifth and Fourteenth Amendments bar states from prohibiting corporate contributions to ballot issue campaigns.[21] For now, bans or limitations on corporate contributions to candidates are not affected.

1990: Supreme Court rules in *Austin v. Michigan Chamber of Commerce* that a Michigan law prohibiting the use of corporate funds for independent expenditures to support or oppose candidates does not violate the Constitution.[22]

2002: Bipartisan Campaign Reform Act of 2002 (BCRA— popularly known as "McCain–Feingold" for its chief sponsors) prohibits "soft money" contributions to national parties which, since *Buckley*, had been widely used to circumvent still intact contribution limits.[23] The BCRA also prohibits corporate and labor union funding of "electioneering" communications.[24]

2003: In a 5–4 decision in *McConnell v. Federal Election Commission*, the Court rules that the "soft money" ban put in place by BCRA does not violate the Constitution, nor does its ban on the "use of corporate or union treasury funds to finance electioneering communications."[25]

2010: Another 5–4 decision, *Citizens United v. Federal Election Commission* overturns both *Austin* and *McConnell* and invalidates much of McCain-Feingold.[26] Later in 2010, the U.S. Court of Appeals for the D.C. Circuit rules in *Speechnow.org v. Federal Election Commission* that, under *Citizens United*, contributions to political action committees for "independent expenditures" in support of or opposition to candidates cannot be limited.[27] When the Supreme Court declines to review this decision, it becomes law; as a result, "super PACs" are born and spread across the political landscape. So do "social welfare organizations," which now begin spending millions from undisclosed sources on campaign ads masquerading as issue-advocacy messages.

2011–2012: Montana Supreme Court upholds century-old, citizen-initiated ban on corporate campaign contributions, but this is reversed by the five members of the *Citizens United* majority.[28]

2014: In yet another 5–4 decision, *McCutcheon v. Federal Election Commission*, the majority strikes down cumulative contribution limits, while further narrowing the "corruption" standard.[29]

2014: Senate Joint Resolution 19, seeking to overturn *Citizens United* by constitutional amendment, fails on a party-line vote to pass the Senate.[30]

With this very sparse historical context in mind, let's now look at the more immediate genesis of *Citizens United.*

In January 2008, as the battle between Hillary Rodham Clinton and Barack Obama for the Democratic presidential nomination entered an intense and prolonged primary season, a nonprofit corporation named Citizens United released a documentary video that was highly critical of Clinton.[31] (The conservative organization was not acting on behalf of the Obama campaign and certainly not at its behest. Seeing Clinton—as most observers then did—as the likely Democratic nominee, Citizens United was simply seeking to "soften her up" by launching its attacks on her early in the process.) Because its leaders and lawyers were concerned that the organization might be subject to either civil or criminal penalties for violating federal campaign finance law, they asked the U.S. District Court for the District of Columbia to enjoin the Federal Election Commission (FEC) from interfering with the distribution of the video.[32]

The organization was particularly fearful that the FEC would prohibit use of the video on the basis of Section 203 of BCRA.[33] That section prohibited corporations or labor unions from using their general treasury funds to make independent expenditures to advocate the election or defeat of a candidate for national office. In terms of its relevance to that 2008 primary season, the act defined an electioneering communication as "any broadcast, cable, or satellite communication" that "refers to a clearly identified candidate for Federal office" when that communication was made within thirty days of any given primary election.[34]

In its response to Citizens United's filing, the FEC asked the district court to enter summary judgment denying the requested preliminary injunction. After considering the parties' written and oral arguments, a three-judge panel of the district court granted the FEC's request.[35] That decision was appealed directly to the Supreme Court, which heard oral arguments on March 24, 2009.[36] (By that time, of course, both the primary and general election were history, but the Court has long followed a practice of deciding such cases after the fact for the benefit of potential future litigants.)

As the case was originally presented, Citizens United's lawyers had based their entire argument on grounds that neither asked for nor would have justified the Court in fashioning any new constitutional doctrines. The attorneys had argued that the campaign finance law was unconstitutional not on its face, not in general, not in principle, but simply *as applied* to this particular organization under these particular circumstances.[37] But a majority of the justices now ordered the parties to reargue the case, specifying that this time they were to address the far-reaching constitutional issues that the nonprofit's attorneys had not previously found it necessary (or, perhaps, plausible) to raise.

Anyone conversant with the history of the Supreme Court might have sensed at this point that the Court was entering into territory it had traversed before, with very unhappy results for itself and the nation at large. In 1856, when the *Dred Scott* case was first presented to the U.S. Supreme Court, there were ample factual and legal grounds for a sound ruling either in Scott's favor or to the contrary—grounds that would not have required the Court to enter into the constitutional issues of African American citizenship that would soon create such a furor. But a majority of the justices, having decided that they wanted to rule on those broader constitutional issues, requested that the case be reargued, with emphasis on its possible constitutional implications. That was exactly what the Court did again in 2009. In ordering a reargument, the justices who would become the *Citizens United* majority seemed clearly to be asking for ammunition to justify them in overturning key features of existing statutes as well as two previous decisions of the Court itself, and to do so with new and far-reaching constitutional doctrines.

In 2003, in *McConnell v. Federal Election Commission*, the Court had upheld McCain–Feingold's limits on electioneering communications.[38] That holding had rested substantially on a clear precedent set thirteen years earlier, in *Austin v. Michigan Chamber of Commerce*.[39] There, the Court had explicitly held that electioneering speech could be regulated based on the speaker's corporate identity. By the time that *Citizens United* was reargued, then, the *Austin* precedent was already two decades old and had been relied upon in *McConnell* to uphold the major effort at campaign finance reform represented by McCain–Feingold. The Court's majority now seemed to many observers determined to make new constitutional law even at the price of breaking one of the Court's most fundamental rules of jurisprudence.

That maxim holds that the Court should not rest a decision on constitutional grounds (and therefore not create new constitutional law) if there are other, narrower grounds on which the case can be decided. When the Roberts Court ordered *Citizens United* to be reargued specifically on constitutional grounds sufficient to justify overturning *Austin*, most court watchers were convinced that the majority had already made up its mind. In any event, the case was reargued on September 9, 2009, and the Court announced its 5–4 decision on January 21, 2010.[40]

Justice Kennedy wrote the majority opinion, which was supported by Chief Justice Roberts and Justices Alito, Scalia, and Thomas. Justice John Paul Stevens filed a dissent, joined by Justices Breyer, Ginsburg, and Sotomayor. The 5–4 decision did indeed overturn *Austin*, which had upheld the constitutionality of Section 441b of BCRA—the prohibition against corporations using their funds to support or oppose candidates.[41] The majority now held that this provision violated the First Amendment and could therefore no longer be enforced—even though the prohibition had, in one form or another, been a crucial part of federal election law since the Progressive Era.[42]

Not only would corporations henceforth be allowed to use their funds in election campaigns, but they could read the majority to be saying that, to the extent that they devoted those funds to "independent expenditures" rather than by making contributions to candidates themselves, there would now be no limit on how much they—or anyone else—could pour into these "independent" channels. That implication was explicitly confirmed two months later, when the U.S. Court of Appeals for the District of Columbia Circuit issued its decision in *Speechnow.org v. Federal Election Commission*.[43] Relying on the *Citizens United* decision to strike down statutory contribution limits to independent expenditure organizations, the circuit court (in a decision that the Supreme Court implicitly affirmed by declining even to review) thus opened the door to the creation of "super PACs," which immediately began to appear on (and to pour unprecedented amounts of money into) the American electoral scene.[44]

In fact, these two judicial decisions during the winter of 2010 transformed the nature of American elections overnight. Those super PACs, to which wealthy individuals and corporations could now contribute unlimited amounts of money, quickly became a key component of every serious campaign, not only for Congress and the presidency, but in gubernatorial, state legislative, and even judicial races.[45] The unprecedented floods of money that super PACs began dumping into those races was supplemented by another side effect of the *Citizens United* and *Speechnow* decisions: the now unlimited ability of so-called social welfare organizations to pour more millions (from sources that need not be disclosed) into election campaigns by employing the now ubiquitous ruse of pretending to be taking positions on issues when, in fact, they are attacking candidates.[46] Between these two sluice gates, opened wide by the *Citizens United* decision, American elections experienced an ever-rising tsunami of spending in the elections following the ruling.

Our primary interest here is to examine how the *Citizens United* decision and its progeny have operated to weaken American democracy and how citizens, uniting in defense of their democracy, might eventually respond to such injuries. There are various dimensions of the decision and its aftermath that especially deserve scrutiny from a democratic perspective. I summarize several of those dimensions here and then explore them more fully either later in this chapter or in subsequent ones.

- The most obvious and direct effect of the decision was the removal of democratically imposed limits on the role of money in elections. It may be too simplistic to say that either the people rule (as democracy would have it) or money rules, but at a bare minimum, any meaningful conception of democracy requires that the people must be able to decide what role money will play in their elections. Chapter 7 will examine more closely the crucial relationship of money to democracy.
- A meaningful conception of democracy also requires that the people must be able to decide what role corporations will play in their governing system and especially in their elections. Recognizing that the corporate form presented tremendous opportunities for national economic expansion, our ancestors also recognized (as chapter 6 will detail) that corporations presented substantial dangers, especially the

possibility of corporate wealth being deployed to influence elections. In a fundamental exercise of self-determination, the people had protected themselves from that danger by prohibiting corporate contributions to election campaigns. Now, in an equally fundamental exercise of undemocratic power, the Court's majority wiped out all the most crucial of those century-old protections.

- The Court's wounding of the body of democracy in cases like *Citizens United* has been further exacerbated by applying the rules emerging from such decisions to state as well as national law, rather than trusting the self-governing competence of individual states to determine their own basic rules of electioneering. By nationalizing so much of election law rather than permitting a more experimental (and truly federal) approach, the Court has undermined one of the founders' most basic instincts about the system of shared governance that they created. In the discussion of the Electoral College we have already encountered the case for a more vibrant federalism as a key component of a restored democracy, and later chapters will return to that theme.

- This brings us to a deeper layer of democratic injury accompanying the *Citizens United* decision, which might be characterized in terms of five judges with life tenure, none of whom had ever sought or been granted the people's mandate in any kind of election, deciding issues of ultimate significance to representative democracy and striking down countless state and federal rules enacted after thorough deliberation by thousands of legislators intimately familiar with the workings of democratic elections. The concept of judicial review implies, of course, the possibility of appellate judges occasionally overturning democratically enacted statutes. Historically, however, whenever a majority of the Court has this egregiously substituted its judgement for that of duly elected officials, the legitimacy of the Court has invariably suffered, and democracy has suffered even more at the hands of such unrestrained judicial activism.

- The leading example of that kind of judicially induced mayhem had been the 1857 *Dred Scott* decision. We will see that it is no accident that *Citizens United* has been repeatedly compared to that infamous rewriting of constitutional law. For now, it is worth noting that, in his dissent to the *Dred Scott* decision, Justice Benjamin Curtis wrote that the majority had allowed itself to make what he considered a mistake of historic proportions primarily by not recognizing when a particular issue constitutes "a legislative or political, not a judicial question."[47] This is a crucial, if inherently imprecise, way of delineating the boundary between democratic governance on the one hand and the appropriate (and appropriately restrained) exercise of judicial review on the other. At the beginning of this century, the Court had missed a significant opportunity to maintain its nonpartisan credibility by applying the "political question" doctrine in its 5–4 decision in *Bush v. Gore* in December 2000.[48] By the time the Court decided *Citizens United* a decade later, this very sound and serviceable instrument of judicial restraint seemed to have become a dead letter, and if so, its demise had exposed both the Court's credibility and the well-being of democracy to vast new dangers. (As we will see in a later chapter, the Roberts Court may have taken the first step toward resuscitating the political question doctrine in a 2019 reapportionment ruling.)[49]

- The primary vehicle for the Court's activism in the campaign finance arena has been an interpretation of the First Amendment, which I show in chapter 7 to be both fundamentally at odds with the republican intent of the founders and deeply injurious to the actual, day-to-day operation of the system of self-government that they created. In the course of making its own activist interpretation of the First Amendment the law of the land in a series of campaign finance rulings, the Court has contributed to a wider public amnesia about the reasons the founders considered free speech so crucial a component of republican elections and governing institutions. Recovering that more fundamental reason for protecting speech will be indispensable to any effort to reassert democratic control over our election laws.

- The diluted understanding of republican principles and practices that the Court's majority has brought to bear in its campaign finance rulings has led it to put inordinate weight on a concept of "corruption" that is itself a corruption of sound republican theory. As the Court's rulings have progressively narrowed the operative definition of corruption to something indistinguishable from outright bribery, the actual effect of those rulings has been a steadily more pervasive and insidious corruption of the tissue of American political life.

- One final, democratically damaging side effect of the *Citizens United* decision has been the deepening polarization of American political culture. This feature of the decision might at first have been obscured by the fact that Justice John Paul Stevens, a Republican appointee to the Court, wrote the very powerful dissent that is certain to play a key role in any future efforts to move the Court away from the democratically deadly jurisprudence of *Citizens United*.[50] Stevens, however, retired from the Court just five months after filing that dissent, and with his departure anything resembling a nonpartisan Supreme Court seemed to have vanished for the foreseeable future.[51] Beyond the steadily deepening politicization of the Court itself, the on-the-ground consequences of the *Citizens United* decision have immeasurably exacerbated the stranglehold of partisanship in American political life.

It is the nexus between these two factors—unlimited money and unrestrained partisanship—that constitutes the key challenge for democratic revitalization in our time. There are other significant threats to effective self-government, but they all cluster around the nucleus constituted by these two strong forces. Setting aside for a moment the possibility of making democracy work within the perimeters of these decisions (to which we will turn a skeptical eye in chapter 9), there seem to be two main ways of restoring democratic control over the role of money in elections. One would be by way of constitutional amendment; the second would depend on the Court itself, by a change in either its membership or its jurisprudence, receding from the most undemocratic features of its campaign finance jurisprudence.

What we will see is that the dominant role of partisanship has made either of these paths far more difficult than they would otherwise have been. But if we refuse to allow that to be the final word on the matter, how might we possibly work our way out of this trap? Either an empowered citizenry or a Supreme Court more committed to republican constitutional principles than to Republican Party ideology could contribute crucial components to such a solution. In either case, a return to democratic control of campaign finance law will depend on breathing new life into old tenets of republican theory. That will be a tall order, as we have already learned by walking down a couple of paths that have led back into the partisan quicksand. Let's turn first to the possibility that the Court itself might begin to depart from the line of campaign finance decisions that have so fundamentally altered the American electoral landscape.

For most of 2016, there had actually been reason to hope that the Supreme Court might begin repairing the damage it had inflicted on American elections with *Citizens United* and related decisions. That hope had been sparked in a most unfortunate way when Justice Antonin Scalia died suddenly and unexpectedly in February 2016. Since President Obama would now have the chance to appoint Scalia's successor, the 5–4 conservative majority that had prevailed in *Citizens United* and many other recent cases seemed likely to undergo a change of polarity. That expectation failed to materialize, however, first because Mitch McConnell, the leader of the Republican majority in the Senate, announced that he did not intend to allow the Senate to consider any nomination that Obama would make but would instead force the vacancy to remain open until a new president was inaugurated nearly a year after Scalia's death. When Republicans maintained McConnell's majority in the Senate that November, while Donald Trump secured a majority of Electoral College votes, the future of the Court took on a very different look. Not only would Scalia now be replaced by someone at least as conservative as he had been (and probably far younger), but with both the swing-voting Justice Kennedy and liberal Justice Ruth Bader Ginsburg already in their eighties, Trump and the Senate Republicans might well be in a position to give the Court a solidly conservative cast for decades into the future. Indeed, they appeared to have done just that in fairly short order, with the appointment and confirmation of Justices Neil Gorsuch and Brett Kavanaugh in the space of a few months of Trump's inauguration. Whatever else that might mean, it appeared to have terminated any hope that the Court itself might any time soon reverse the *Citizens United* cluster of rulings.

We will see, though, when we examine in the next chapter the history of the Court's treatment of corporations, that there is strong precedent for even a very conservative court backing away from a broadly unpopular line of jurisprudence when there are authentically conservative reasons to do so. One lesson that will suggest itself is that when the Court gets too far out of step with the people, it puts its own credibility and authority at risk. If popular discontent becomes acute, it can generate pressure for change in the structure or operation of the Court itself. This can be accomplished by changing the number of justices, limiting their tenure, or using arguments in subsequent cases to persuade a sufficient number of justices to alter their approach to the matters on which the divergence between the Court and the people has become most salient.

An element of institutional self-care has sometimes appeared to come into play in such situations during the Court's history. Given our tradition of naming eras in judicial history after the chief justice serving at the time, it is not surprising that it is they who have often seemed to be most alert to the reputation of the Court itself. There is reason to believe that some such legacy concern may have played a role in Chief Justice John Roberts' decision to affirm the constitutionality of the Affordable Care Act in 2012.[52] That legislation, which had been enacted on a strictly party-line vote in Congress, might well have been overturned by a Supreme Court majority of five Republican opposed by four Democratic appointees. Roberts' decision, not only to uphold the law but to assign the writing of the majority opinion to himself, may not have been motivated by concern about the growing public conviction that this was an excessively partisan Supreme Court, but there have certainly been worse motivations occasionally at work during the Court's history. It was this same element of institutional self-care that some Court watchers appeared to have in mind when the swing-voting Justice Anthony Kennedy retired in 2018. His departure led to immediate speculation that Chief Justice Roberts might begin to play that balancing role more deliberately himself, if only for the sake of husbanding the Court's credibility.[53]

Even apart from any such efforts to guard the Court's reputation, there are other paths by which a quite conservative Court might begin to lay the foundation for the softening, if not the reversal, of some of the most damaging of its campaign finance rulings.

That hope rests on the fact that some key components of conservative jurisprudence have been seriously undermined by those decisions. The thoroughly conservative concept of judicial restraint, for example, had for several decades been buttressed by the constraining influence of the "political question" doctrine. It may be significant that, in a 2019 decision in which Chief Justice Roberts again assigned himself the task of writing the majority opinion, the Court seemed to have resurrected the political question doctrine to justify not involving itself in a pair of partisan-imbued reapportionment cases.[54] Unlike the Affordable Care Act decision, Roberts was here aligned with the other Republican appointees, while the four Democratic appointees opposed Roberts's position. Although all of the liberal justices (and most of my liberal friends) supported Justice Elena Kagan's passionate dissent in *Rucho*, I would argue that any principled conservative return to the practice of judicial restraint (which this appeared to be) should be welcomed as a step down the path that might eventually lead to the reversal of those very elements of judicial activism that have enabled rulings like *Citizens United* to substitute the opinions of five Supreme Court justices for the considered enactments of thousands of elected representatives stretching across more than a century.

In addition to the revival of the political question doctrine, another eminently conservative pathway back to something resembling judicial deference would involve the reassertion of some of the key principles of federalism. While it was, as this book went to press, too early to discern all its possible implications, the 2019 decision in *Franchise Tax Board of California v. Hyatt*[55] seemed to open the door for some serious forays into the constitutional implications of federalism. In a key sentence of the majority opinion, Justice Thomas wrote, "The Constitution does not merely allow States to afford each other immunity as a matter of comity; it embeds interstate sovereign immunity within the constitutional design."[56] Liberal skeptics might be forgiven for suspecting that what the five conservative justices had really found embedded "within the constitutional design" was just one more way to expand sovereign immunity in order to hinder the activities of (mostly Democratic) trial lawyers. The same skeptics might have thought the sudden rediscovery of the "political question" doctrine in *Rucho* had less to do with applying judicial restraint to the issue of partisan reapportionment than to freeing state legislatures (mostly under Republican control) to gerrymander at will. I can more readily imagine than disprove any such hypotheses of unrestrained cynicism, but I do believe that it would be the height of folly for liberals (or anyone else concerned about the deeply undemocratic features of the Supreme Court's campaign finance decisions) to turn a blind eye to the possibility of a genuinely conservative juris-prudence eventually bringing more authentically republican prin-ciples to bear in that arena.

It would be even more foolish, though, for those of us who find the campaign finance rulings democratically devastating to put all our hopes (or even most of them) in the possibility of the Court itself modifying or overturning those decisions. This brings us, then, to the option of reasserting democratic control of this crucial feature of our elections by amending the Constitution. Here again, we find ourselves stumbling almost immediately into the familiar trap of partisan quicksand.

The *Citizens United* decision had provoked an immediate storm of outrage, erupting in op-ed pieces, blogs, and, more con-certedly, a flurry of city council resolutions, ballot issues, and calls for constitutional amendments. I will turn to the more grassroots or populist manifestations of that response soon, but first let's follow the constitutional amendment idea into its first encoun-ter with partisanship. The maelstrom of congressional resolutions calling for a constitutional amendment to overturn the *Citizens United* decision finally coalesced into one piece of legislation, Sen-ate Joint Resolution (SJR) 19, whose chief sponsor was Arizona senator Tom Udall.[57] The resolution, reflecting quite soberly the salient constitutional issues at stake, read as follows:

> Section 1. To advance democratic self-government and politi-cal equality, and to protect the integrity of government and the electoral process, Congress and the States may regulate and set reasonable limits on the raising and spending of money by candidates and others to influence elections.
> Section 2. Congress and the States shall have power to imple-ment and enforce this article by appropriate legislation, and may distinguish between natural persons and corporations or other artificial entities created by law, including by pro-hibiting such entities from spending money to influence elections.

Section 3. Nothing in this article shall be construed to grant Congress or the States the power to abridge the freedom of the press.[58]

Any such amendment could become part of the Constitution only after being approved by two-thirds votes in both houses of Congress and then being affirmed by at least thirty-eight state legislatures.[59] Viewed as the first step on that long and arduous journey, the Senate's consideration of SJR 19 in the autumn of 2014 might have been expected to unfold as a memorable moment in American constitutional history. Instead, it degenerated into a political charade of the kind to which Americans had by then all too wearily resigned themselves.

The Democrats, who then held a slender Senate majority, brought the resolution to the floor on a party-line vote in the Judiciary Committee.[60] The Republicans could have prevented any debate on the measure, as Senate minorities routinely did on almost any matter of substance, simply by threatening a filibuster. In this case, however, the Republican caucus chose to allow debate, for what most analysts saw as two reasons. One was to give some of their members (especially those up for re-election that fall) an opportunity to tell their constituents that they had voted to allow debate on an issue that obviously mattered very much to many of those constituents. The other reason behind the Republican decision to allow that first cloture vote to pass was that, by scheduling a debate on this issue just a few days before Congress recessed for the 2014 election, there would be no time left on the Senate calendar for the Democrats to force even cloture votes (let alone substantive debates) on any other issues on the Democratic agenda, such as raising the minimum wage or narrowing gender pay inequality.

For their part, the Democratic leaders were hardly less calculating in their decision to bring SJR 19 to the floor. They knew that there was never the slightest chance that the resolution would actually receive the sixty-seven votes required to send it on its journey, first to what was then the Republican-controlled House (where it stood even less of a chance) and then, if it miraculously surmounted these barriers, to the states. In fact, the Democratic leadership was doing what the Senate majority in these times mostly does: not actually attempting to pass legislation, which had become nearly impossible, but creating voting records for their own members to claim credit for supporting and for minority members to be attacked for opposing. In the end, SJR 19 was laid to rest on a straight party-line vote, and the senators left Washington for the culmination of what *Citizens United* had turned into far and away the most money-drenched midterm election in history to that point.

If this attempt to amend the Constitution to restore democratic control over campaign finance law had fallen so quickly into the mire of partisan quicksand, what about that solid ground of democratic citizenship that I have argued might provide some footing from which to rescue our floundering institutions? In chapter 3, I used stories from my own hometown of Missoula to illustrate the kind of grassroots citizenship that I believe can and will supply the musculature of an effective movement of democratic renewal. As we turn here to the specific challenge of reforming campaign finance law, it might be instructive to consider briefly what the citizens of Missoula brought to that task in the immediate wake of the *Citizens United* decision. We will see that they brought an ample ration of outrage over the injury they felt the decision had inflicted on the body of their democracy. There is little doubt that such passion will be an essential ingredient of any movement to restore that body to health, and slogans that encapsulate that passion will no doubt prove to be essential. We will see, though, that the ardor of my Missoula neighbors had not necessarily been matched by their understanding of the actual contents of the judicial decisions they opposed so vociferously. In particular, the slogan "corporations aren't people and money isn't speech," which proved so effective in mobilizing opposition to *Citizens United*, turns out to be a seriously misleading characterization of what the Court had actually said and done in that decision. Much of the remainder of this book rests on the conviction that getting clearer about hard historical realities (even when it requires moving beyond ideologically inspiring slogans) will prove crucial to any sustained movement of democratic reform. With that in mind, let's take a quick look at Missoula's (and Montana's) initial responses to the 2010 *Citizens United* decision.

On November 8, 2011, in the context of a city council election, Missoulians voted on a referendum that the sitting council had put on the ballot in response to *Citizens Untied*. Seventy-five percent of those voting on the issue opted "FOR urging our state and federal elected officials to amend the United States Constitution to state that corporations are not human beings." In this way, Missoula joined a growing list of cities (and eventually states) expressing their dismay at the *Citizens United* decision. That nationwide response was further exemplified here in Montana when, within months of the vote in Missoula, Montana citizens had begun gathering signatures on a statewide ballot proposition, directly addressing what its authors took to be the heart of the *Citizens United* ruling. By its own terms, "Ballot initiative I-166 establishes a state policy that corporations are not entitled to constitutional rights because they are not human beings, and [I-166] charges Montana elected and appointed officials, state and federal, to implement that policy."

By July 2012, the initiative's supporters had gathered enough signatures to qualify for the November ballot, where it secured a majority in every one of Montana's fifty-six counties and garnered the support of three out of four voters statewide. While a state district court (in a decision never appealed to the Montana Supreme Court) declared key provisions of I-166 to be unconstitutional, it had clearly served a major pulse-taking purpose by giving Montanans an opportunity to express their displeasure with the U.S. Supreme Court's *Citizens United* ruling—or at least with that presentation of the ruling encapsulated in the language of the initiative. In 2013, in a move fully faithful to that plebiscite, Senator Jon Tester joined a growing list of his colleagues by introducing into the U.S. Senate a resolution for an amendment to the U.S. Constitution aimed at overturning *Citizens United*. Tester's resolution adhered to the theme of the Montana ballot issue in declaring that "[t]he words people, person, or citizen as used in this Constitution do not include corporations."

Tester's constitutional amendment resolution was eventually subsumed in the more circumspectly worded SJR 19 discussed earlier. The wording of Montana's ballot initiative continued to play a role, however, appearing next in the context of Supreme Court appointments and confirmation hearings. In 2017, Tester's supporters cited that mandate in defending his vote against Neil Gorsuch's confirmation. As an op-ed piece written by a former executive director of the Montana Democratic Party (and featured on Tester's Senate website) put it, "Essentially, [the *Citizens United* decision] made corporations 'citizens' and ruled that their money was 'free speech' under the Constitution. Senator Tester's opposition to Gorsuch based on this is consistent with the position held by 75% of Montanans when they voted on these very questions on a ballot issue in 2012."

I fully understand the necessity, from a partisan perspective, of making exactly this kind of argument. At the same time, I want to raise here a possibility that we will examine in a later chapter: that of building and sustaining a powerful democracy lobby that would draw its strength not from partisan identification but from the widespread conviction that something is terribly amiss with our democracy. If we sought (as I argue we should) to make such a democracy lobby at least as potent as the gun lobby has been in recent decades, we might ask whether these potential members of a democracy lobby have anything like the Second Amendment to which the gun lobby has so readily and effectively appealed in pursuit of its cause. In the case of campaign finance reform, the need to identify those constitutional foundations is especially acute because, as we will see in later chapters, almost all the democratic damage that the Supreme Court has inflicted in this arena has been justified by a particular way of reading the Constitution.

With that in mind, we might consider confirmation hearings for judicial nominees in a new light. A visitor from another planet might find it odd that, in a nation that prides itself on being a "beacon of democracy," members of its Senate Judiciary Committee come to every Supreme Court confirmation hearing equipped with a finely honed battery of questions aimed at discovering the nominee's likely contribution to abortion law or gun rights but rarely with anything deeper than ideological slogans for probing this potential justice's understanding of (or commitment to) democratic principles and practices.

Given that the damage the Supreme Court has inflicted on campaign finance law has such deep and complex roots in constitutional history, it seems fairly obvious that this arena of constitutional jurisprudence, so crucial to democracy, cannot be meaningfully addressed in confirmation hearings or any other relevant venue solely by recourse to ideological posturing or sloganeering. A democracy lobby cannot, therefore, ever be as effective as it is going to need to be in such settings unless it is prepared to articulate fundamental democratic principles, backed by an authentic understanding of the underpinnings of those principles. Only then will a democracy lobby be in a position to maintain the steady support of millions of citizens for whom those principles are second nature, manifesting themselves in the way those citizens live their lives.

This is not to deny that clever slogans (like "Corporations aren't people and money isn't speech"), while remaining politically quite potent, can also serve as conceptual doorways into the more complex background that must eventually be recalled as we enter on the path to meaningful reform. Our analysis of the "money isn't speech" portion of the slogan, for example, will eventually help us uncover the most democratically misguided roots of the Court's campaign finance decisions. In the process of unearthing those roots, we will have an opportunity to recover some very valuable lessons about the genuinely and enduringly democratic significance of free speech.

By comparison to the amount of damage to our system of elections that has resulted from the Court's free speech rulings, the on-the-ground effect of its recent holdings on corporations and corporate personhood has actually been far less consequential. Yet, as we saw in examining the Missoula and Montana referenda in response to *Citizens United*, and even in Senator Tester's first version of a constitutional amendment, it was the "corporations aren't people" half of the slogan that initially moved Montanans to action. In fact, the outrage over the corporate issue is not a bad place to begin exploring, not only what the prevailing slogans conceal about *Citizens United* (which is a great deal) but also what they reveal about enduring democratic principles. Nowhere is the oversimplifying tendency of sloganeering clearer than in the pervasive misunderstanding about what the *Citizens United* Court had said (and done) about the electoral role of corporations.

What the Court has, in the course of its history, said and done about corporations and their role in our political system has been both far more complex and, in the end, even more damaging to democracy than the slogans indicate. The real story takes us back into some rather intriguing chapters of American history; it reminds us of how important it has always been for democracy to set the ground rules for corporate behavior and how the Supreme Court has occasionally needed to be reminded of that basic democratic principle. Until we are clear about all that, there is almost no chance that we will be able to correct the damage that the Court has actually inflicted.

6   Corporations and
the Body Politic

A corporation is an artificial being, invisible, intangible, and existing only in contemplation of law. Being the mere creature of law, it possesses only those properties which the charter of its creation confers upon it.

> —*Chief Justice John Marshall,*
> Dartmouth College v. Woodward *(1819)*

The question presented today, whether business corporations have a constitutionally protected liberty to engage in political activities, has never been squarely addressed by any previous decision of this Court. However, the General Court of the Commonwealth of Massachusetts, the Congress of the United States, and the legislatures of 30 other States of this Republic have considered the matter, and have concluded that restrictions upon the political activity of business corporations are both politically desirable and constitutionally permissible. The judgment of such a broad consensus of governmental bodies expressed over a period of many decades is entitled to considerable deference from this Court.

> —*Justice William Rehnquist, dissenting opinion*
> in First National Bank of Boston v. Bellotti *(1978)*

The State need not permit its own creation to consume it.

> —*Justice Byron White, dissenting opinion in* Bellotti

The argument of this chapter proceeds roughly as follows:

- What *Citizens United* did with regard to corporations, while certainly consequential in its impact on the electoral process, was quite different from the way the urban legend has portrayed it. In particular, the decision did not create the concept of corporate personhood.
- The judicial doctrine of corporate personhood arose in the late-nineteenth century, in a series of cases that provide some striking parallels to the corporate-empowering single-mindedness of the Roberts Court and more generally to a results-oriented jurisprudence that has been willing to abandon the most essential features of judicial restraint.
- *Citizens United* was thus part of an ongoing story, not yet completed, about the relationship of American democracy to corporations. In addition to creating the concept of corporate personhood, some of the previous episodes in this story also provide vivid reminders and frequent injunctions (often from conservative jurists) about the importance to democracy of maintaining human control of the social compact with corporations.
- The fact that solid conservatives have insisted that corporate activity must sometimes be restrained to protect democratic institutions should make it clear that enforcing the social compact with corporations is not synonymous with seeing corporations as inherently evil, or with wishing or advocating their abolition.
- Serious problems arise, however, when the social compact is ignored or blurred, as it was most injuriously in *Citizens United*.
- That injury has resulted primarily from the ardent pursuit of a pro-business agenda on the part of some conservatives, but it has also been buttressed by a civil libertarian interpretation of the First Amendment that has been as vigorously promoted by the American Civil Liberties Union (ACLU) as have business interests by the U.S. Chamber of Commerce.
- We won't succeed in reasserting democratic control of corporations until we recall and reclaim the republican roots of the Constitution, freeing them from both of these sets of ideological shackles.

DEMOCRACY AND THE SOCIAL COMPACT

The idea of social compacts has very deep roots in American political thought. When John Adams, for example, was assigned the task of drafting a new constitution for Massachusetts in 1779, the document he composed referred to itself as "a social compact by which the whole people covenants with each citizen and each citizen with the whole people that all shall be governed by certain laws for the common good."[1] That language may sound a bit archaic to our twenty-first century ears, but in late-eighteenth century America, it was the bread and butter of republican theory. Like Jefferson in drafting the Declaration of Independence three years earlier, Adams had been fundamentally influenced by John Locke and other English republicans' conviction that legitimate governments had to rest on something like a social compact. Such compacts do not necessarily have to be as formal as Adams's 1779 document; indeed, it was widely assumed even then that social compacts could, like the British constitution, be largely unwritten yet remain no less fundamental to the operation (indeed the very possibility) of self-government.

Deeply imbued with a sense of history in motion (what Jefferson called "the course of human events"), our republican founders took it for granted that a self-governing people must be able to respond to changing circumstances by reshaping their social compacts at need. A classic instance of such changing circumstances, and the challenges they presented to self-government, can be found in the impact of the Industrial Revolution on American life and society. Consider, for example, the appearance on the American scene, and then the spread across the continent, of railroads. As the "iron horse" became an increasingly important component of the Industrial Revolution, more and more manufacturing and commercial businesses wanted rail service. It soon became evident that few rail lines could be constructed, especially through developed areas, without access to the state's power of eminent domain. Some of the transcontinental lines received even more help in the form of land grants. In return for these and other public benefits, the railroads were required to abide by the rules governing "common carriers"—in effect, agreeing to carry any passengers or freight from any source that sought their services. This straightforward (and in this account certainly oversimplified) example of a social compact would very quickly devolve into a breathtaking complexity of legal details, but the point here is simply that, as this emerging technology presented the nation with new opportunities and challenges, a rough deal was struck between the railroad industry and society at large, acting through its institutions of self-government. As with any social compact, each side gained advantages from this bargain. The point that needs to be emphasized here is that without the ability to fashion such compacts for protecting or securing the common good, self-government in a complex and changing society would quickly be overwhelmed by ever-evolving social or economic forces.

In these terms, the story of America's social compact with railroads may be seen as one strand of the larger story of the compact with corporations in general. Railroads, like the steel mills or metal mines that were emerging at "industrial scale" during the nineteenth century, required the mobilization of capital at a corresponding magnitude, a scale beyond the reach of even the wealthiest individuals. The challenge of raising and effectively deploying that capital necessitated the invention of new business forms, or the transformation of old ones to new purposes. The most prominent of these was the for-profit business corporation.

The dramatic expansion in the number and size of business corporations during the nineteenth century, then, exemplified the dynamic nature of the Industrial Revolution as it (literally) gained full steam. This means of aggregating and deploying capital presented tremendous opportunities for economic expansion, but it quickly became clear that it also presented substantial challenges to the society seeking that economic growth. Since that society had organized itself on democratic lines, it was only to be expected that it would fashion a social compact to enable the society to reap the benefits while minimizing the dangers of this powerful mechanism of industrial capitalism.

At the heart of this emerging compact lay the inescapable fact that corporations of any kind are creatures of society, existing by its indulgence and of necessity subject to its rules. As Chief Justice John Marshall wrote in the 1819 *Dartmouth College* case, "A corporation is an artificial being, invisible, intangible, and existing only in contemplation of law. Being the mere creature of law, it possesses only those properties which the charter of its creation confers upon it."[2] Corporations, in other words, are a very specific form of human association authorized by the state and given certain privileges and advantages because of the contribution they are deemed to be capable of making to the well-being of the society.

It is society, for example, that has passed laws saying that when people associate in the particular form of a for-profit corporation, their individual assets will not be subject to attachment if the corporation injures someone. Only the assets belonging to the corporation itself are subject to legal actions for redress of such injuries. This concept of "limited liability" made it much easier to raise the kind of capital, and to raise it at the scale, that an enterprise like a new railroad required. Early railroads were as dangerous as they were expensive to build and maintain. The fires they often started, for example, could result in millions of dollars of property damage. Few individual investors would be willing to subject their personal assets to this kind of liability, but if the railroad's liability could be limited to the corporation's own assets, investment capital would become much easier to raise. Eager to facilitate the mobilization of capital at a scale that could fuel an exuberantly expanding economy, American society used the democratic institutions of state legislatures to put in place this key feature of the social compact with corporations.

Another privilege that society granted corporations is something called "perpetual existence." Whereas business partnerships have traditionally had to be dissolved or at least modified at the death of a partner, corporations have been freed from this connection to human mortality. Shareholders may die, but the corporation lives on and continues to engage in whatever business for which it was designed. Like limited liability, this social construct of perpetual existence contributes substantially to the efficiency and economic potency of business corporations. To garner those contributions to a robust economy, society has seen fit to grant this unusual privilege to those who invest in such corporations.

What is clear is that neither limited liability nor perpetual existence is some kind of God-given or otherwise inalienable right. Quite the contrary: they are major concessions that society makes to this particular form of association in return for certain expected benefits to society. The benefits have been substantial, playing a major role in propelling America to the global pinnacle of economic power that it had attained by the early twentieth century. In these terms, the compact with corporations has clearly benefited both corporations themselves and the larger society. This is why it is still entirely possible to insist on the protection of society's interest in the social compact without thereby becoming anticorporate, let alone seeking to do away with corporations. To the extent that the social compact with corporations enjoys a sense of democratic legitimacy, it is because we all (or at least a majority of us) still agree that society receives valuable economic benefits from granting gifts like limited liability or perpetual life to business corporations.

At the same time, it is important to note that it was precisely and solely for those *economic* benefits that this particular social compact was fashioned and is still maintained. We do not, for example, grant charters to for-profit corporations, nor do we give them the advantages of perpetual existence and limited liability because of the contribution we think they will make to the political process. On the contrary, we have long recognized that the economic advantages we choose to bestow on corporations automatically create a heightened danger of undermining democracy, simply because of the inherently corrupting nature of any large accumulation of capital. Given the built-in tendency of money to flow wherever its owners perceive value, and given the multitude of ways in which corporations can use their economic power to gain advantages from any of the three branches of government, it had to be expected that when society chose to give the corporate form extraordinary tools for amassing capital, it was simultaneously subjecting itself to a heightened likelihood that some of that capital would be invested in efforts to influence elected officials (or judges) to put in place policies or judicial doctrines calculated to protect or advance some given corporation's interests—or those of corporations in general.

This is precisely what happened "when, in the course of human events," railroad corporations persuaded the U.S. Supreme Court that certain constitutional provisions put in place after the Civil War to protect the rights of formerly enslaved humans should now protect the rights of railroads and other corporations. At first, this amendment to the social compact with corporations actually did very little to endanger democracy, by comparison to what corporations were then doing in the political arena. But the way the Supreme Court went about rewriting the social compact to benefit corporations in the 1880s would be replayed to democratically disastrous effect a century and more later, and its damage would reverberate from the doctrine of corporate personhood that the Gilded Age Court had spawned.

CORPORATE PERSONHOOD

The judicial doctrine of corporate personhood was introduced into American law not by the 2010 decision in *Citizens United* but well over a century earlier in a string of Supreme Court decisions that came to be known as the "Railroad Cases." In its initial form, the concept of corporate personhood was intended simply to make it clear that corporations could sue and be sued and, in the process, were entitled to due process and equal protection of the laws. Because little immediate harm resulted from this clarification of the law, few observers of the Court, until our time, have noticed or severely criticized the extremely unusual way in which the late-nineteenth-century Court inserted the concept of corporate personhood into constitutional law. But now that a later Court has used its own, very similar version of judicial activism to turn that doctrine into a democratically deadly poison, that earlier episode of high-handedness appears a little more sinister.

The background, as we have already seen, had been provided by the Industrial Revolution and its impact on nearly every dimension of nineteenth-century American life, including law and public policy. Railroads in particular were a source of almost constant litigation of one kind or another, keeping hundreds of lawyers (including, on occasion, Abraham Lincoln) employed for decades, either suing or defending the railroad corporations. In the 1880s, a number of these cases began to make their way to the Supreme Court. First in this series came *Santa Clara County v. Southern Pacific Railroad Co.*[3] The California legislature had enacted a statute requiring state revenue officials to determine the value of all property owned by railroads that operated in more than one county and then apportion the value to the various counties in proportion to the number of miles of track in each. When the officials made that assessment of the Southern Pacific Railroad's property, they included the value of the fences that had been built between the tracks and the neighboring landowners. The Southern Pacific contested this inclusion, and the matter made its way into the courts.

In the process, the railroad, now joined by other rail corporations, attempted to broaden the litigation considerably. They contested the entire structure of taxation, claiming that, as part of the continental system of railroads authorized and subsidized by Congress in the 1850s, the railroads should not be subject to state taxation at all. The consolidated cases made their way in due course to the U.S. Supreme Court.

The Court's opinion, delivered by Justice John Marshall Harlan, held that, since the appeal could be decided on the very narrow issue of the fences, the Court would not address the broader issues. It therefore would not venture into what Harlan called "a construction of the recent amendments to the national Constitution in their application to the constitution and the legislation of a state."[4] The "recent amendments," of course, were the post–Civil War amendments that had conclusively overturned the *Dred Scott* decision by abolishing slavery and guaranteeing voting and other civil rights to those who had been enslaved. In what can easily be seen as a kind of historical joke, the railroads had now asked the Court to extend to corporations the Fourteenth Amendment's due process and equal protection provisions written for people formerly enslaved. Although the Court would soon do just that, it declined to do it in *Southern Pacific* because, as Justice Harlan explained, this case could be disposed of on much narrower, nonconstitutional grounds.

In following this course, Harlan was applying an extremely important principle of judicial restraint, according to which the Court does not rest a decision on constitutional grounds (and therefore does not create new constitutional law) if there are other, narrower grounds on which the case can be decided. Here, Harlan wrote that if the case could be decided on the factual issue of whether or not the fences were properly assessed, "there will be no occasion to consider the grave questions of constitutional law upon which the case was determined below, for in that event the judgment can be affirmed upon the ground that the assessment cannot properly be the basis of a judgment against the defendant."[5]

Justice Harlan's opinion represents one of the last times, in the entire string of cases establishing and then expanding the concept of corporate personhood, in which the Court exercised anything resembling judicial restraint. From this point on, in case after case, culminating in *Citizens United*, the Court would inject itself into

*opposite of
¿ judicial restraint* "

the legislative realm by making law itself, or it would overturn
carefully worked out legislative solutions to various problems on
grounds that paid little or no attention to democratic principles
or practices. Justice Harlan maintained that boundary between the
judicial and legislative branches in his *Southern Pacific* opinion. But
in that same case, Chief Justice Waite, in a breathtaking breach of
judicial restraint and sound jurisprudence, laid the foundation on
which the entire edifice of corporate personhood would be erected.
He did not do it in the usual way, by writing his own opinion once
the case had been argued. Instead, he made an astonishing statement before the parties had even presented their arguments. "The
Court," Waite told the assembled attorneys, "does not wish to hear
argument on the question whether the provision in the Fourteenth
Amendment to the Constitution which forbids a state to deny to
any person within its jurisdiction the equal protection of the laws
applies to these corporations. We are all of opinion that it does."[6]

In a system of jurisprudence that relies fundamentally on
judges deciding cases only after each side to the controversy has
had a full and fair opportunity to "make its case," it is simply un-
heard of for an important principle to be established in this way.
The chief justice's edict might not have mattered if in a later case
the Court had ignored Waite's proclamation. But that is not what
happened. Instead, when in 1889 the Court held (in an actual
written opinion) that corporations are "persons" within the protection of the Fourteenth Amendment, it (astonishingly) cited *Santa
Clara* as precedent.

This second railroad case (*Minneapolis & St. Louis Railway Co.
v. Beckwith*) arose when three hogs, with a combined value of $24,
wandered onto the tracks in Kossuth County, Iowa, where they
were run over and killed by a locomotive.[7] This time, the Court
did allow the parties to argue the question of whether corporations could claim Fourteenth Amendment guarantees of due process and equal protection. The Court now held that corporations
were entitled to those protections, but it based that finding on the
flimsiest of foundations. "It is contended by counsel as the basis of
his argument," Justice Field wrote for the Court, "and we admit
the soundness of his position, that corporations are persons within
the meaning of the clause in question. It was so held in *Santa
Clara County v. Southern Pacific Railroad Co.* and the doctrine was
reasserted in *Pembina Mining Co. v. Pennsylvania*, 125 U.S. 181,
125 U.S. 189."[8] In fact, of course, it was not "so held" in *Santa*

Clara; it was simply declared out of the blue in an oral statement by the chief justice in a successful effort to prevent the issue from even being argued.

The second case cited in *Beckwith* was only slightly more valid as precedent. A year earlier, in *Pembina Mining Co. v. Pennsylvania*, the Court had addressed the question of whether or not corporations were entitled to the equal protection of law guaranteed by the Fourteenth Amendment.[9] In the end, the Court found that Pembina wasn't incorporated in Pennsylvania and therefore wasn't subject to its laws at all. Under those circumstances, the Court found, Pennsylvania could provide neither equal nor unequal protection of its laws, since those laws simply did not apply to the corporation. What matters here are not the details of the Court's holding but that the justices had now abandoned entirely the judicial restraint that Justice Harlan had exercised so conscientiously in *Santa Clara*. If there was no denial of equal protection, there was no need for the Court to apply the Equal Protection Clause of the Fourteenth Amendment, and therefore no need to decide whether or not corporations came within the reach of that clause. In *Pembina*, though, the Court declared that corporations were "persons" within the meaning of the Fourteenth Amendment and therefore entitled to the coverage of the Equal Protection Clause. For good measure, the Court also declared that corporations, as "persons," are covered by the Due Process Clause, even though no hint of a due process claim had been argued.

In one sense, none of this matters, since the Court was clearly determined to establish the doctrine of corporate personhood one way or another, and the end result would be the same, no matter which path the justices took to get there. What gives contemporary relevance to the Court's unorthodox route to that result is that it resembles so strongly the Roberts Court's route to its decision in *Citizens United*. From the moment that Chief Justice Waite had told the parties not to present arguments about corporate personhood because the Court had already made up its mind, it was clear that this doctrine would be adopted one way or another. Over a century later, the five-member majority in *Citizens United* would show the same studied determination to extend the doctrine of corporate personhood into the electoral arena. In doing so, those five justices also abandoned the last shred of judicial restraint bequeathed them by the corporate-friendly court of the 1880s. Before turning to modern developments in the saga of corporate personhood, however, it is worthwhile to note one important limit that the earlier court had placed on that concept.

In *Pembina*, the Court considered three possible constitutional grounds for striking down the Pennsylvania law in question: the Equal Protection, Interstate Commerce, and Privileges and Immunities Clauses. We have already seen that the Court had claimed a violation of only the Fourteenth Amendment's Equal Protection Clause after acknowledging that the case, in fact, presented no issue of equal protection. The Court fairly quickly rejected the claim (which is not directly relevant here in any case) that the Interstate Commerce Clause applied. Of far greater concern to us is the reason the Court gave for rejecting the third claim: that the corporation was covered by the clause in Article IV of the Constitution providing that "[T]he Citizens of each State shall be entitled to all Privileges and Immunities of Citizens in the several States."[10] Justice Field declared flatly that "[c]orporations are not citizens within the meaning of that clause."[11] Citing an earlier decision, he invoked the limited scope of corporate rights that the *Citizens United* court would essentially explode. "The term 'citizens,' as used in the [privileges and immunities] clause," Field wrote, "applies only to natural persons, members of the body politic owing allegiance to the state, not to artificial persons created by the legislature, and possessing only such attributes as the legislature has prescribed."[12]

Much as we might fault Field and his colleagues for casting judicial restraint aside in their determination to extend Fourteenth Amendment protections to corporations, they at least remained cognizant of the basic relationship between corporations and the body politic. They may have been overeager to expand the economic power of corporations by creating the legal fiction of corporate personhood so that corporations could sue or be sued, but those justices retained the awareness that corporations existed only because society allowed them to and that the privileges they had been granted lay solely within the economic, not the political, realm.

It was in the policy space left open by this exercise of judicial restraint that Congress and many state legislatures clarified the social compact during the Progressive Era by specifying boundaries to corporate involvement in democratic elections. While the social compact with corporations had clearly been created to facilitate the contribution that corporations could make to the nation's economy, not their contributions to election campaigns, it was a dead certainty that some of that capital would be put to such use unless democracy took steps to protect itself against such abuses. That protection is precisely what the people provided themselves a century ago when, as we saw in chapter 4, the power of Gilded Age corporations began to exercise a dangerous influence in politics. As part of the sweeping array of democratic reforms enacted at all levels during those years, many states outlawed corporate contributions to political campaigns. This was simply a further (and from the point of view of self-government a necessary) elaboration of the social compact with corporations. What the citizens in all these jurisdictions had said, in effect, was, "We have given you corporations certain privileges with regard to the way you may amass and deploy capital. That capital is to be used for economic purposes, not to influence our elections. They are and will remain *our* elections. You may not enter this arena." So spoke the citizenry of Montana, and of several other states, and so spoke the citizens of the United States through their elected representatives when, in 1907, Congress included in the Tillman Act a prohibition on corporate contributions to congressional and presidential election campaigns.[13] In doing so, they were acting squarely in accord with Justice Field's declaration that "[t]he term 'citizens,' as used in the [privileges and immunities] clause, applies only to natural persons, members of the body politic owing allegiance to the state, not to artificial persons created by the legislature, and possessing only such attributes as the legislature has prescribed."[14]

But if the Gilded Age Supreme Court continued to acknowledge this limitation on the role that the social compact allowed corporations to play, even while defining corporations as "persons" entitled to due process of the law, it now expanded the concept of "due process" itself in a way that would turn out to give corporations and other business entities overwhelming advantages against workers and others who sought to constrain the activities of those corporations.

SUBSTANTIVE DUE PROCESS

To the extent that the new doctrine of corporate personhood simply assured that corporations would be accorded the same rights to due process in the courts as individuals, there was nothing especially pernicious about the concept. Much more serious trouble arose, though, when the Supreme Court began to define due process itself in an entirely new way. The complex history of what came to be called "substantive due process" will have to be severely simplified here, with most of the emphasis focused on its salience to the intersection of democracy with business corporations. In a nutshell, the Supreme Court began, early in the twentieth century, to use the Due Process Clauses of the Fifth and Fourteenth Amendments to strike down a number of both national and state laws, especially those aimed at protecting workers from some of the most exploitative features of industrial capitalism.

The eponymous substantive due process case, eventually earning a reputation almost as dark as *Dred Scott*, was the 1905 decision in *Lochner v. New York*, which declared unconstitutional a New York law providing that no one working in a bakery could be required or permitted to work more than ten hours a day nor more than sixty hours a week.[15] On behalf of a narrow, five-member majority, Justice Peckham wrote that "[t]he general right to make a contract in relation to his business is part of the liberty of the individual protected by the Fourteenth Amendment of the Federal Constitution."[16] Citing that amendment's provision that "no State can deprive any person of life, liberty or property without due process of law," Peckham went on to articulate an understanding of the meaning of "due process" that reached far beyond the right to sue and be sued.[17] "The right to purchase or to sell labor is part of the liberty protected by this amendment unless there are circumstances which exclude the right," Peckham wrote.[18] The only credible candidate for such countervailing constitutional weight would be the "police power" of the state, by which all states protect the health and safety of their citizens through thousands of statutes and regulations.[19] Peckham and his four colleagues denied that New York's statute fell within the state's legitimate police power, a finding which he insisted "is not a question of substituting the judgment of the court for that of the legislature."[20]

That substitution, however, was exactly what the *Lochner* dissenters thought the majority had perpetrated. Writing for himself and Justices White and Day, Justice Harlan adhered to the same principles of judicial restraint that he had maintained in the railroad cases. Insisting that "the rule is universal that a legislative enactment, Federal or state, is never to be disregarded or held invalid unless it be, beyond question, plainly and palpably in excess of legislative power," Harlan went on to express much the same judicial attitude toward the democratic activity of legislation as Justice Curtis had articulated in his dissent in *Dred Scott.*[21] "If there be doubt as to the validity of the statute, that doubt must therefore be resolved in favor of its validity," Harlan wrote, "and the courts must keep their hands off, leaving the legislature to meet the responsibility for unwise legislation."[22]

It would be Justice Oliver Wendell Holmes Jr., however, who would provide the dissenting language that would be remembered when most everything else in *Lochner* had faded from our collective memory. "This case is decided upon an economic theory which a large part of the country does not entertain," Holmes wrote and then proceeded to state his view of how judges are to behave in a democratic society.[23] "If it were a question whether I agreed with that theory, I should desire to study it further and long before making up my mind. But I do not conceive that to be my duty, because I strongly believe that my agreement or disagreement has nothing to do with the right of a majority to embody their opinions in law."[24] Holmes reminded his colleagues that political jurisdictions restricted their citizens' freedom of action in countless ways and could not govern without doing so. "The liberty of the citizen to do as he likes so long as he does not interfere with the liberty of others to do the same, which has been a shibboleth for some well known writers," Holmes wrote, "is interfered with by school laws, by the Post Office, by every state or municipal institution which takes his money for purposes thought desirable, whether he likes it or not."[25] Then, referring to the book that had coined the term "survival of the fittest" in defense of a theory of raw social Darwinism, Holmes concluded that "[t]he Fourteenth Amendment does not enact Mr. Herbert Spencer's Social Statics."[26] A little less cryptically, he wrote that "a constitution is not intended to embody a particular economic theory, whether of paternalism and the organic relation of the citizen to the State or of *laissez faire.*"[27]

Holmes's defense of democratic self-determination against the judicial activism of the *Lochner* majority would eventually prevail but not until the doctrine of substantive due process had been used, three decades after *Lochner,* to overturn a whole series of New Deal statutes enacted by substantial congressional majorities.

The popular outrage at the Court's continued deployment of substantive due process on behalf of business interests led to Franklin Roosevelt's court-packing plan of 1937. While the Senate blocked that proposal, it had become clear that the Court had fallen dangerously out of step with the will of the people. In 1937, in what came to be called the "switch in time that saved nine," Justice Owen J. Roberts, who had been voting with the majority against the New Deal legislation, now voted to uphold a Washington state minimum wage law in *West Coast Hotel Co. v. Parrish*.[28] The decision is generally seen as marking the end of the *Lochner* era, as the Court from that point on steadily declined to invoke substantive due process to protect business interests against democratic majorities. It would have been strange, though, if those interests had simply given up the effort to bring constitutional interpretations to bear on their behalf, and indeed they did not. The next major episodes in this story will put us on the path to the major rewriting of the social compact in *Citizens United*.

THE POWELL MEMO AND *BELLOTTI*

This part of the story might be seen as beginning with a lengthy memo that a Virginia attorney named Lewis Powell prepared in 1971 for his client, the U.S. Chamber of Commerce.[29] The memo laid out in brilliantly strategic detail a multifront, long-term plan for moving American law and society toward ever greater protection of the business interests that constituted the core of his client's concerns. Powell began his memo with an account of how, in his opinion, liberal ideas and constituencies had come to dominate so much of American life and law, and the strategy he outlined focused single-mindedly on reversing this trend. Powell counselled business leaders to bring to bear on American politics and policy the same skills and techniques that they had used to such remarkable effect to achieve economic success. "It is time for American business—which has demonstrated the greatest capacity in all history to produce and to influence consumer decisions—to apply their great talents vigorously to the preservation of the system itself," he wrote.[30]

Of particular interest to us here was what Powell called a "neglected opportunity in the courts."[31] "American business and the enterprise system have been affected as much by the courts as by the executive and legislative branches of government," he wrote.[32] "Under our constitutional system, especially with an activist-minded Supreme Court, the judiciary may be the most important instrument for social, economic and political change,"[33] Powell argued. He continued, "Other organizations and groups, recognizing this, have been far more astute in exploiting judicial action than American business. Perhaps the most active exploiters of the judicial system have been groups ranging in political orientation from 'liberal' to the far left."[34]

Thus the "activist-minded Supreme Court" that concerned Powell was the one that had been led by Earl Warren and then Warren Berger to expand civil and criminal rights. But Powell provided a vision of a very different kind of judicial activism. Having already argued that business interests should sponsor speakers' bureaus and seek, where appropriate, to influence academic appointments, Powell turned to the previously unrealized opportunity to play the kind of role in judicial proceedings that groups like the ACLU had been performing for decades. "This is a vast area of opportunity for the Chamber, if it is willing to undertake the role of spokesman for American business and if, in turn, business is willing to provide the funds," Powell suggested. "As with respect to scholars and speakers, the Chamber would need a highly competent staff of lawyers. In special situations it should be authorized to engage, to appear as counsel amicus in the Supreme Court, lawyers of national standing and reputation."[35]

In the decades following the preparation of Powell's memo, an impressive number of his recommendations were pursued and realized. The memo has often been identified as a significant contributing influence behind the emergence, in the 1980s and beyond, of the extensive infrastructure of conservative think tanks and publications that have played such a major role in generating and sustaining the conservative resurgence in American politics. Organizations like the Heritage Foundation, the American Legislative Exchange Council, and the Federalist Society may well have emerged even if Powell had never written his memo, but they have all contributed notably to the shaping of American politics, policy, and law in ways fully consistent with Powell's recommendations.

The theme that concerns us here was Powell's strategy for expanding the legal protection of business, and especially corporate interests. Much of Powell's agenda, even on the legal side, has been accomplished without invoking constitutional protection. The effort to open American elections to direct corporate influence, however, would require the removal of several explicit statutory prohibitions, and (in the case of *Citizens United*) it would require overturning clear and long-standing precedents. Not coincidentally, it was Powell himself who had begun this process of opening the previously barred door of American elections to direct corporate involvement.

Lewis Powell did that not as counsel to the Chamber of Commerce but as an associate justice of the U.S. Supreme Court. It happened that, during that summer of 1971, while Powell was drafting his memo for the chamber leadership, Justice Hugo Black fell ill and retired from the Court. Richard Nixon, who had hoped to appoint Powell to the Court two years earlier, now persuaded him to reconsider his earlier refusal to be appointed. Readily confirmed, Powell was presented seven years later with an opportunity to reshape corporate law in a way fully consistent with what he had advocated in that 1971 memo.

Massachusetts had enacted a statute prohibiting business corporations from making contributions or expenditures "for the purpose of . . . influencing or affecting the vote on any question submitted to the voters, other than one materially affecting any of the property, business or assets of the corporation."[36] The First National Bank of Boston and other corporations, wishing to spend money to influence a vote on a proposed amendment to the Massachusetts constitution, sought to have this statute declared unconstitutional. When the Massachusetts Supreme Judicial Court rejected the challenge to the statute, *First National Bank of Boston v. Bellotti* was appealed to the U.S. Supreme Court.

Presenting the majority opinion on behalf of himself and four of his fellow justices, Powell wrote that the state court "viewed the principal question as 'whether business corporations, such as [appellants], have First Amendment rights coextensive with those of natural persons or associations of natural persons.' The court found its answer in the contours of a corporation's constitutional right, as a 'person' under the Fourteenth Amendment, not to be deprived of property without due process of law."[37] What Powell did at this point was so subtle as to be almost undetectable, yet the eventual impact of his maneuver on American politics would be incalculable.

Like a magician distracting the audience's attention with one hand, he pulled his former corporate clients firmly into the arena of electoral politics with the other. Here is the magical paragraph:

> The court below framed the principal question in this case as whether and to what extent corporations have First Amendment rights. We believe that the court posed the wrong question. The Constitution often protects interests broader than those of the party seeking their vindication. The First Amendment, in particular, serves significant societal interests. The proper question therefore is not whether corporations "have" First Amendment rights and, if so, whether they are coextensive with those of natural persons. Instead, the question must be whether [Section] 8 abridges expression that the First Amendment was meant to protect. We hold that it does.[38]

Powell was arguing that what the First Amendment protected was not so much the rights of corporations as the process of democracy itself—and that it did so by making sure that voters were fully informed. The fact that some of their information might come from corporations really had nothing to do with the First Amendment rights of corporations, Powell maintained; those rights were merely the wispy side effect of his sturdy defense of the truly consequential rights of democratic citizens. "We thus find no support in the First or Fourteenth Amendment, or in the decisions of this Court," Powell concluded, "for the proposition that speech that otherwise would be within the protection of the First Amendment loses that protection simply because its source is a corporation. . . ."[39] If speech in an electoral setting is protected exclusively because of who hears it rather than who utters it, then it surely would follow that neither Massachusetts nor any other state could prohibit or limit speech in that setting simply because it was a corporation that was doing the speaking. It was precisely on this conceptual foundation that the *Citizens United* majority would, thirty-two years after *Bellotti*, rely explicitly on that decision to rule that contributions to candidates could not be prohibited nor expenditures on those candidates' behalf be limited "because their source is a corporation."[40]

Four of Powell's colleagues vigorously disagreed with both his reasoning in *Bellotti* and his conclusion. Justice Byron White, writing for himself and Justices William Brennan and Thurgood Marshall, observed the following:

> By holding that Massachusetts may not prohibit corporate expenditures or contributions made in connection with referenda involving issues having no material connection with the corporate business, the Court not only invalidates a statute which has been on the books in one form or another for many years, but also casts considerable doubt upon the constitutionality of legislation passed by some 31 States restricting corporate political activity, as well as upon the Federal Corrupt Practices Act.[41]

The dissent then proceeded to identify precisely the crux of the relationship between a self-governing people and the corporations they chartered that lay at the foundation of all that state and national legislation:

> Corporations are artificial entities created by law for the purpose of furthering certain economic goals. In order to facilitate the achievement of such ends, special rules relating to such matters as limited liability, perpetual life, and the accumulation, distribution, and taxation of assets are normally applied to them. States have provided corporations with such attributes in order to increase their economic viability, and thus strengthen the economy generally. It has long been recognized, however, that the special status of corporations has placed them in a position to control vast amounts of economic power which may, if not regulated, dominate not only the economy, but also the very heart of our democracy, the electoral process.[42]

Finally, White got to the heart of the matter in one brief sentence: "The State need not permit its own creation to consume it."[43]

White, Brennan, and Marshall were all Democratic appointees to the Court and generally liberal in their jurisprudence. Neither of those features characterized the fourth dissenter in *Bellotti*. Richard Nixon had appointed William Rehnquist to the Court in the same month that he submitted Powell's nomination, and with the same hopes for a more conservative jurisprudence. But Rehnquist's conservatism had been focused far less decisively than Powell's on advancing the cause of business interests. Indeed, Rehnquist opened his *Bellotti* dissent with a glancing criticism of the judicial sloppiness of the post–Civil War majority that had created the doctrine of corporate personhood:

> This Court decided at an early date, with neither argument nor discussion, that a business corporation is a "person" entitled to the protection of the Equal Protection Clause of the Fourteenth Amendment. *Santa Clara County v. Southern Pacific R. Co.* . . . (1886). Likewise, it soon became accepted that the property of a corporation was protected under the Due Process Clause of that same Amendment. . . . Nevertheless, we concluded soon thereafter that the liberty protected by that Amendment "is the liberty of natural, not artificial, persons." *Northwestern Nat. Life Ins. Co. v. Riggs* . . . (1906).[44]

Rehnquist then proceeded to put this constrained understanding of corporate personhood in its ensuing political context:

> The question presented today, whether business corporations have a constitutionally protected liberty to engage in political activities, has never been squarely addressed by any previous decision of this Court. However, the General Court of the Commonwealth of Massachusetts, the Congress of the United States, and the legislatures of 30 other States of this Republic have considered the matter, and have concluded that restrictions upon the political activity of business corporations are both politically desirable and constitutionally permissible. The judgment of such a broad consensus of governmental bodies expressed over a period of many decades is entitled to considerable deference from this Court.[45]

Citing John Marshall's ringing statement in the *Dartmouth College* case that "[a] corporation is an artificial being, invisible, intangible, and existing only in contemplation of law," and that "[b]eing the mere creature of law, it possesses only those properties which the charter of creation confers upon it," Rehnquist went on to state his own conviction: "A State grants to a business corporation the blessings of potentially perpetual life and limited liability to enhance its efficiency as an economic entity. It might reasonably be concluded that those properties, so beneficial in the economic sphere, pose special dangers in the political sphere."[46] Massachusetts' concern about those dangers was more than reason enough to justify the adoption of its statute, Rehnquist concluded.

Finally, the future chief justice addressed Powell's solicitude for the rights of democratic citizens. "The free flow of information is in no way diminished by the Commonwealth's decision to permit the operation of business corporations with limited rights of political expression," he wrote, concluding with his own very trenchant comparison of corporations and human beings: "All natural persons, who owe their existence to a higher sovereign than the Commonwealth, remain as free as before to engage in political activity."[47] That was clearly the voice of an older conservatism, sounding strains of Edmund Burke himself. Rehnquist was in the minority in *Bellotti*, however, and it would be the ideology of Justice Powell (and of the Powell memo) that would come fully into its own three decades later when the Roberts majority ordered reargument of the *Citizens United* case.

A UNION OF OPPOSITES

Paradoxically, Powell's pro-business agenda as set forth in his memo to the Chamber of Commerce was, by the time of *Citizens United*, being substantially abetted by some of the very liberals whose influence Powell had sought to counter. If, as Jeffrey Clements argues in *Corporations Are Not People*, the *Citizens United* decision represented the culmination of success for Powell's strategy, it was a success that could not have been achieved without the assistance of some of the same liberals that Powell opposed.[48]

Powell had singled out the ACLU for special attention in his analysis of how American jurisprudence had been led astray. Having suggested that "the most active exploiters of the judicial system have been groups ranging in political orientation from 'liberal' to the far left," Powell continued: "The American Civil Liberties Union is one example. It initiates or intervenes in scores of cases each year, and it files briefs *amicus curiae* in the Supreme Court in a number of cases during each term of that court."[49] Now, nearly forty years after Powell wrote these lines, the ACLU had filed just such an amicus brief in the reargument of the *Citizens United* case.

Lewis Powell might have been surprised but would certainly have been delighted with what the ACLU told the Court: "The broad prohibition on 'electioneering communications' set forth in §203 of the Bipartisan Campaign Reform Act of 2002 (BCRA) . . . violates the First Amendment. . . . Accordingly, the Court should strike down § 203 as facially unconstitutional and overrule that portion of *McConnell* that holds otherwise."[50]

What we see in the *Citizens United* decision, in fact, is the confluence of two streams of constitutional activism and advocacy, one flowing into the decision from the left and one from the right. From the right flowed the stream of cases unfolding the aggressive pro-business philosophy of Lewis Powell's memo to the Chamber of Commerce. It now joined another stream that Powell had in general found inimical to his client's interests, the stream that Mary Ann Glendon had identified so clearly in her 1990 book about what she called "rights talk."[51]

For decades, liberal groups and their attorneys had pressed for the expansion of constitutionally protected individual rights into one after another arena of American life, from race relations to contraception and abortion. Indeed, in the latter two arenas, some conservatives would argue that liberals had talked the Supreme Court into embracing a whole new strain of substantive due process. Each of these expansions of individual rights could be defended on credible intellectual grounds, and most of them resulted in substantial improvements in our society. What almost no one except Glendon noticed, however, was that this expansion of individual rights had acquired a momentum of its own, with almost no constraints to protect democratic principles and practices if the extension of individual rights should begin to threaten democracy itself. We will examine that danger much more closely in the next chapter.

For now, it is sufficient to observe that, powerful as the pro-business stream of jurisprudence had become by 2010, there is good reason to doubt that it would have emboldened five Supreme Court justices to reverse the Court's own settled precedent and overturn a popular, bipartisan congressional enactment, had the civil libertarian stream not lain so close at hand. In particular, Justice Anthony Kennedy, who had often been the swing vote on the Roberts Court, was known for his single-minded devotion to the protection of individual liberty. Absent a strong argument based on that principle, Kennedy might well have exercised the judicial restraint he also cherished, thus joining the four dissenting justices in refusing to overturn both precedent and a duly enacted statute. The amicus brief of the ACLU could only have made it easier for Kennedy to join the other conservative justices in taking that activist course. In the end, it was Kennedy who wrote the majority opinion in *Citizens United*.

Potent as these two very different ideological strains were in dredging the channel for the *Citizens United* decision, though, that democratically destructive act still would not have occurred without the assistance of what we might think of as two dogs that did not bark in the night. As Sherlock Holmes did in Arthur Conan Doyle's "Silver Blaze," we have to pay special attention to what didn't happen in our story.[52] One dog that didn't stir was the buried memory of the social compact with corporations; the other was the slumbering awareness of the fundamental needs of democracy itself.

As to the social compact, one thing that has become unmistakably clear since the *Citizens United* decision is that we cannot maintain that compact in a democratically workable way unless we keep in focus the very particular kind of entity that a business corporation represents. It was precisely the blurring of that focus, however, that enabled the *Citizens United* majority to reach its democratically deadly conclusion. And that blurring occurred at the intersection of the pro-business with the individual liberty strains of constitutional jurisprudence. It was at the urging of the ACLU that the Court chose to treat corporations simply as "associations" of individuals and therefore endowed with all the constitutional protections afforded individuals. This way of treating corporations constitutes an almost willful ignoring or occlusion of the democratically crucial construct of the social compact. In fact, to all intents and purposes, it treats the compact as if it didn't exist. That is a deeply antidemocratic act, since, as we have seen, social compacts are one of the major mechanisms by which a self-governing people maintains control over the circumstances that most fundamentally affect it.

The Court's ignoring of the social compact manifested itself most tellingly in Kennedy's failure to distinguish between nonprofit and for-profit corporations. Citizens United, the organization that had launched the litigation, was of course a nonprofit corporation. By contrast with the situation in *Bellotti*, there were no for-profit business corporations involved in the *Citizens United* case. If the Court had paid even the slightest attention to the all-important social compacts with various kinds of corporations, it would have restricted its ruling to the kind of corporation that stood before it. It is only by refusing to acknowledge either the existence or the democratic significance of those compacts that any court could lump all corporations together as nothing more than associations of individuals and therefore endowed with all the constitutional rights of those individuals. That act of willful ignoring swept aside in one motion more than a century of painstaking democratic activity.

With both for-profit and nonprofit corporations, America's democratic society had quite deliberately enabled accumulated wealth to be deployed in new and more potent ways, and in both cases, it had circumscribed those permissions with sidebars that protected democratic institutions from being damaged by these structures. We have already examined some of the key features of the compact with for-profit corporations, both the economically empowering features, like limited liability and perpetual existence, and the restraining features, like prohibitions on corporate contributions to election campaigns.

Meanwhile, with tax-exempt nonprofit corporations, that democratic society had entered into an entirely different kind of social compact. It had said, in effect, "We will allow people to associate for certain societally beneficial purposes, and we will not tax the portion of individual or corporate income that is contributed to the support of these associations. But we will maintain strict limits on the extent to which those associations may seek to influence political processes, and if any of them step over those bounds, they will lose their tax-exempt status." This has been a straightforward, all but universally accepted compact between society at large and the particular kind of association that we call nonprofits. This social compact is similar in form to that between society and its for-profit creatures. In both cases, society has granted the corporations certain substantial privileges in the expectation that they will produce specific kinds of social good. In both cases, the society has set limits on the political activities of these associations, to prevent their using their privileged status to undermine the operation of democracy.

This all seems obvious enough in terms of democracy protecting itself against injuries from the corporate forms (both for-profit and nonprofit) that it has authorized and privileged. But the simple clarity that exists when the picture is viewed from this perspective suddenly blurs beyond recognition when corporations of all kinds are viewed simply as associations of individuals. They are associations, of course, but that is not all that they are; it has never been all that they are, and to act as if they are indistinguishable from one another or from other associations of individuals is to amputate from the democratic body politic one of its most crucial organs of self-determination: the social compact.

We will examine in a later chapter some of the details of the compact that both enabled and constrained the accumulation of capital for charitable purposes. For now, the important point is that by ignoring the concept of social compacts altogether, and instead treating all corporations as nothing more than "associations" of individuals, the Court created sweeping new constitutional rights for business corporations in a case that only involved nonprofits, and in the process swept aside some of the most basic features of both compacts. This was a grievous blow to the body of democracy, but democracy had long ceased to be of major concern to most members of the Supreme Court. It is to that much bigger problem that we need to turn next.

7   We Must Disenthrall Ourselves

The occasion is piled high with difficulty, and we must rise with the occasion. As our case is new, so we must think anew and act anew. We must disenthrall ourselves, and then we shall save our country.

—*Abraham Lincoln, 1862*

The previous chapter provided a foray into one set of democratically destructive consequences of the *Citizens United* decision. We found that, contrary to the prevailing myth, the concept of corporate personhood had not made its first appearance in *Citizens United* but had actually antedated that decision by well over a century. We also recalled, however, the even deeper roots of a crucial social compact, built on the awareness that the same economic potency that makes corporations so valuable to a prospering society also requires any democratic society to maintain firm mastery of the privileges granted to corporations. More than once in our history, the Supreme Court has loosened that leash in ways that have threatened the viability of democracy itself. As the latest, and perhaps the most damaging, chapter in that story, the majority opinion in *Citizens United* now challenges our democracy to reassert, simultaneously, its proper relationship with corporations and with the third branch of our own government.

One lesson from the last chapter is that whenever the Court gets too far out of step with the consistently expressed will of the

people, it begins to undermine its authority and to generate increased popular pressure for change in the structure or operation
of the Court itself. For that reason, I have argued that the possibility of the Court coming more closely into alignment with the will
of the people has to be seen as one potential path to revising the
deeply undemocratic doctrines that the Court's majority has imposed on our elections. If that happens at all, though, it will occur
while efforts are ongoing to reverse the most damaging campaign
finance rulings by way of constitutional amendment.

Whether the wounds the Court has inflicted on the body of
democracy in this arena end up being healed by the Court or by
the people, we can only benefit from understanding more clearly
what is so democratically damaging about this cluster of decisions. In the process, we have an opportunity to remind ourselves
of some of the too-often taken-for-granted principles that enable
a democratic republic to operate at all. Among other things, this
deeper dive into campaign finance jurisprudence will expose to
view the genuinely republican roots of the First Amendment. That
republican source, in turn, is the foundation on which any potential democracy lobby might stand as securely as the gun lobby
has stood on the Second Amendment. But getting there will take
some digging into constitutional history and democratic theory as
well as the removal of some misleading overburden.

I want to emphasize at the outset that the Supreme Court's
privileging of corporations over democratic legislatures has by no
means been the worst injury that its campaign finance activism
has inflicted on our body politic. To bring into focus those much
more grievous wounds, we might profitably turn our attention to
the second half of the anti-*Citizens United* slogan: "money isn't
speech." Here again, we find a substantial amount of truth underlying the catch phrase, but once more we will see that the truth
is both more complex and, in the long run, more consequential
than any slogan. As with corporate personhood, the Court did not
invent the "money as speech" concept in 2010. And as with the
story of the Court and corporations, we will be looking not only
for the nature of the wounds the Court has inflicted but also for
how that wounding might remind us of core principles of democratic vitality. Once again, we have to reach back to some of the
judicial history underlying the *Citizens United* decision. This time
we will go back not a full century but a few decades to an episode

we skipped over in the last chapter as not being directly relevant to the tale of the Court's treatment of corporations.

Barely two months after Richard Nixon's resignation from the presidency in August 1974, his successor, Gerald Ford, signed into law a sweeping set of amendments to the Federal Election Campaign Act.[1] President Ford summed up the legislation in a few words that now sound like the height of naivete, if not like an *Onion* parody. "By removing whatever influence big money and special interests may have on our Federal electoral process," Ford said, "this bill should stand as a landmark of campaign reform legislation."[2] In fact, if the legislation had been allowed to stand as Congress wrote and Ford signed it, it might not quite have removed the influence of big money and special interests altogether, as Ford predicted, but it would certainly have provided a landmark of democratic self-care on a par with the best efforts of the Progressive Era. As the legislation began its journey toward judicial dismemberment, the D.C. Circuit Court of Appeals would call the act "by far the most comprehensive reform legislation [ever] passed by Congress concerning the election of the President, Vice-President, and members of Congress."[3] Within a few months of its passage, however, the legislation was decimated by the U.S. Supreme Court in a decision that would open the door to the *Bellotti* ruling that we encountered in the last chapter and ultimately to the democratically disastrous decision in *Citizens United*. We must, therefore, take a close look at that seminal 1976 decision.

The Federal Election Campaign Act, as amended and strengthened in 1974 in the immediate wake of the Watergate scandal, placed limits on campaign contributions of all kinds, including those from the candidates themselves. The act, which also limited overall expenditures in particular campaigns, faced an immediate court challenge. The plaintiffs, a bizarre mix of outliers from both ends of the political spectrum, included *National Review* founder William F. Buckley's brother, James L. Buckley, who had been elected on the Conservative Party ticket as a U.S. senator from New York, as well as Eugene McCarthy, the liberal Minnesota Democrat whose 1968 challenge to Lyndon Johnson had helped drive Johnson into retirement. What united them here was a conviction that some of the provisions that Congress had just enacted could make it more difficult for unconventional candidates like themselves to challenge established incumbents. Reflecting the barbell-like balancing of these plaintiffs, their litigation was supported by amicus briefs from both the Conservative Party of New York and the New York Civil Liberties Union.

While it could scarcely have been foreseen at the time, this conjunction of appeals from opposite extremes of the American political spectrum was going to spell trouble—and deepening trouble—on down the road. The appeals engendered a set of constitutional doctrines that may have carried a certain theoretical cogency on their surface but that were, in combination, to prove both unstable and deeply corrosive of fundamental republican principles and practices. In the hands of a later Supreme Court majority that had come to embody the aspirations of the Powell memo noted in the previous chapter, these constitutional doctrines would be used in *Citizens United* and *McCutcheon* to annihilate the remaining self-governing vestiges of democratically enacted campaign finance law.[4]

After the D.C. Circuit Court of Appeals had sustained the bulk of the 1974 legislation, that decision was appealed to the Supreme Court.[5] In a complex, multi-opinion ruling, released at the very end of 1976, the Court invoked the free speech clause of the First Amendment to invalidate the act's most important campaign expenditure limits. While it upheld some of the contribution limits that Congress had put in place, the Court eradicated altogether the limits on candidates' contributions to their own campaigns, as well as limits on "independent expenditures." It was in striking down these provisions on free speech grounds that the Court first invoked what would come to be known as the "money is speech" concept.

Like many other critics of the Court's rulings on campaign finance, I had long assumed that the core problem with *Buckley* was the close connection that the majority forged between money (in the form of campaign contributions and expenditures) and speech. I have finally concluded, though, that this does not accurately identify the heart of the problem in *Buckley*. What the majority opinion in *Buckley* actually said was that "virtually every means of communicating ideas in today's mass society requires the expenditure of money."[6] Bringing this inescapable fact squarely into the electoral arena, the Court observed that "[t]he electorate's increasing dependence on television, radio, and other mass media for news and information has made these expensive modes of communication indispensable instruments of effective political speech."[7]

In seeking to reverse the deeply undemocratic effects of *Buckley* and its progeny, we have to acknowledge that the Court was absolutely correct in this foundational statement of fact. This is not by any means to deny that money can be and is a very significant problem in democratic elections. In fact, since *Citizens United*, it has become the major problem in that arena, and the *Buckley* decision has been a substantial contributor to that malady. The injury to the body politic does not derive from the equation of money with speech, however, as much as from a more deep-seated—and more complex—set of conceptual ingredients that the Court has unintentionally turned into a democratically deadly concoction.

While the Court has been the chief actor in this process, and while the resulting effect on our elections has been deeply and broadly unpopular, some of the main ingredients of this toxic brew have been all too consistent with broader trends in American culture. To the extent that we, the people, are thus complicit in the poisoning of our democratic well, we have abundant motivation to understand how that could have happened and what we can now do about it.

To gain an initial understanding of how this set of circumstances has emerged and evolved in the campaign finance arena, let's focus for a moment on one important element of the *Buckley* decision: its elimination of the limits that Congress had imposed on presidential and congressional candidates' contributions to their own campaigns. While the Court's intervention on this subject was not to prove the most democratically damaging holding in *Buckley*, it does serve as a very revealing window into the core of the Court's reasoning and the cascade of injuries that have followed from it. In brief, Congress had, in its post-Watergate legislation, imposed ceilings on how much candidates in federal elections could contribute to or expend on their own campaigns. Presidential or vice-presidential candidates could contribute up to $50,000; senatorial candidates were limited to $35,000 and House candidates to $25,000.[8] This was clearly an effort to maintain some semblance of equality in the electoral arena by preventing wealthy individuals from gaining an unfair advantage over those of more modest means. That we have now grown so accustomed to millionaires and billionaires gaining exactly that kind of advantage is a sorry reminder both of what Congress attempted to accomplish in 1974 and what the Court prevented our elected representatives from doing in our name.

It was inescapable, of course, that abolishing limits on direct candidate expenditures was going to give rich candidates a gigantic advantage (very often a decisive advantage) over less-wealthy candidates. On the face of it, that simply isn't fair, which is why every democratic nerve in our body politic cries out against it. Still, we have to identify as clearly as we can what was actually wrong with the *Buckley* court's abolition of limits on direct candidate expenditures. Surely campaign speech is protected by the First Amendment, so if we accept the Court's conclusion that campaign speech necessarily costs money (as I have suggested we must), then why shouldn't candidates be able to spend as much of their own money on such communication as they choose? Isn't that what free speech is all about? In effect, all the difficulties that have come to plague our elections under *Buckley* and *Citizens United* can be traced to the various answers that have been given to this question. So let's look a little more closely at the Court's justification for eliminating statutory limits on direct candidate expenditures.

The Court's abolition of those democratically imposed limits was based on the assumption that it was the free speech rights of candidates themselves that the Constitution protected and the statutory limits infringed. On its face, this seems too obvious to deserve notice, let alone refutation. But the seeming obviousness of this assumption actually masks the way in which fundamental principles of democracy have been forgotten as judicial revision of campaign finance law has proceeded, from *Buckley* through *Citizens United*. What is too easily overlooked is that, in using its reading of the free speech clause to strike down democratically enacted campaign finance rules, the *Buckley* Court was providing one more instance of a much broader shift in constitutional jurisprudence that has been underway for several decades now and seems not yet to have run its course. The essence of that shift is the change of focus of constitutional interpretation from guaranteeing the healthy operation of republican self-government to an almost exclusive focus on protecting the rights of individuals. In this case, the consequences for the republic have been dire indeed.

This shift in constitutional focus was perhaps most clearly articulated by Mary Ann Glendon in her 1991 book, *Rights Talk*. "At least until the 1950's," Glendon wrote, "the principal focus of constitutional law was not on personal liberty, as such, but on the division of authority between the states and the federal government, and the allocation of powers among the branches of the central government."[9] By the time Glendon wrote her book, however, the focus of constitutional jurisprudence had shifted dramatically. "Today," she wrote, "the bulk of the Court's constitutional work involves claims that individual rights have been violated."[10]

This is not to suggest—nor does Glendon herself argue—that the Court (or the society at large) should have ignored individual rights. The crucial point here is that the now nearly exclusive focus of our constitutional attention on individual rights has come at the expense of an understanding of (and care for) core republican principles, such as the needs of voters to have information presented in ways that enable them to fulfill their civic duties. The 1976 *Buckley* decision very clearly lay within (and added considerable momentum of its own to) this historical development.

To understand how the Court's reasoning about campaign finance law has so badly failed the cause of self-government, we need to remind ourselves of some of the fundamentals of representative democracy and of its role in our larger democratic ecosystem.[11] We start with the recognition that representation is by no means the only form of democracy occupying our political landscape. We have already encountered the kind of direct democracy characterized by the mechanisms of initiative and referendum that many states and localities adopted a century or so ago, while a much older and very different version of direct democracy is alive and well in those New England communities that continue to use the town meeting as an essential component of their self-government. In our jury system, we have even retained a form of democracy familiar to the ancient Greeks: the selection of a key set of decision makers by lot. But from colonial times to the present, these forms of face-to-face democracy have been supplemented by a representative form of government largely borrowed from England. In that version of self-government, public decisions are made by a small number of people chosen by a much larger number through the mechanism of election.

This representative form of governance only makes sense if certain assumptions are valid and can work only if certain conditions are in place. Those assumptions and conditions have emerged slowly over time and have evolved as circumstances have changed "in the course of human events." As we saw in the previous chapter, for example, the nineteenth-century emergence of corporations as dominant economic actors generated the social compact that kept those artifacts of human manufacture in bounds—and most emphatically kept them out of elections. Other preconditions for representative democracy have been in operation over longer historical stretches. As we will examine in more detail later, for example, we have known and insisted from at least the time of the English Bill of Rights that elected representatives have to be free to speak their minds if they are to do their job of governing on behalf of the people.

Another key assumption that has held steady over several centuries is that even citizens who don't want to make public policy decisions themselves, or otherwise to engage in governing directly, are nevertheless capable of selecting good people to do that governing on their behalf. Even that circumstance is not exactly a given, though. It might depend on the voters having been educated about how representative government works, and it certainly depends on them having enough reliable information about the candidates to make intelligent choices. That information might conceivably come from different sources (including, crucially, from the candidates themselves), but no matter who supplies it, the voters' ability to choose wisely remains the bedrock concern of any well-functioning representative democracy. It was precisely this core republican premise, however, that the *Buckley* majority overlooked in its elimination of democratically enacted limits on how much candidates could contribute to their own campaigns.

One way of understanding how that happened is to recognize that, at exactly the point of candidates deciding how much to invest in their own campaigns, republican principles run head-on into a stubborn if not inescapable real-world fact. Regardless of the democratically crucial interest of citizens in having an election campaign inform them so they can do their job well, the most salient interest of candidates will always be of a different kind. Their focus is (and can only be) on garnering enough votes to win the election. Having been a candidate several times myself, I have certainly been prey to the assumption that "this is all about me"— that the tremendous amount of time and energy devoted by my supporters and me to each campaign had one single end: to get me elected. It would be the height of naivete to expect any candidate to approach any campaign with a different attitude. It may be that this inescapable focus on the candidate has ineluctably lent itself to shifting our legal focus from the democratically crucial rights of voters to what we have instead privileged (and what the *Buckley* majority explicitly privileged) as the rights of the candidates themselves. But the basic premise of representative democracy remains unaltered: that elections and election campaigns exist not to serve the candidates themselves but solely to enable citizens to fulfill their democratic role of choosing the best leaders.

In fact, it is precisely in the service of this crucial citizen role that a well-functioning democracy will insist on protecting the speech of candidates. We protect it absolutely, in the sense that we enable candidates to present their records, their plans, or their guiding principles in their own terms, with no prior constraints on the content of their presentation. If they misrepresent any of this, it is up to citizens to find ways of correcting the record, but here, as in other democratic settings, we remain steadfast in imposing no prior limitations on the content of speech. It is emphatically not for the candidates' sake that we adhere so firmly to this principle, however, but because we have learned over centuries of democratic experience that speech unfettered as to its content is indispensable to the voters' capacity to make wise choices among candidates.

It was at just this point that the *Buckley* Court made the move that Mary Ann Glendon identified as characterizing so much constitutional jurisprudence at that time. While focusing on what it simply assumed to be the controlling First Amendment rights of the candidates themselves, the Court took a big step in the direction of eviscerating the vastly more consequential stake of democratic citizens in being meaningfully informed about the choice they were about to make among candidates. Because the Court had a lens called "individual rights" readily available to it, while the lens called "republican self-government" had seemingly been mislaid, individual rights had decisively trumped a key principle of republican self-government. In these terms, it is no surprise that the extremes of the political spectrum, represented by the *Buckley* plaintiffs and amici, played such a large role in contributing to this shift in focus from republican principles to individual rights. Both political and civil libertarians were primarily concerned about

individual rights, and in the absence of any lively concern for republican principles being advanced by anyone else, what Glendon
would call "rights talk" carried the day. The price we have subse-
quently paid, in terms of the thorough corruption of our electoral
system, might now finally recall us to those core (but largely forgotten) principles of republican self-government.

In particular, we need to get much clearer than we have generally been about why free speech is so important to all forms of
democracy. It turns out that freedom of speech matters to democracy far less because of individual rights than because of how crucial it is to our ability to govern ourselves. The wholesale shift of
constitutional emphasis from the basic principles of republican
self-government to the rights of individuals has made it considerably more difficult for us to read the Bill of Rights with the eyes of
the kind of self-governing citizens who wrote and adopted those
guarantees. As we will see, they brought to the work of constitution writing an acute and hard-won awareness that effective democratic citizenship absolutely depends on free speech. But now,
when most of us think about the First Amendment's guarantee
of free speech, we are far more likely to think of it in terms of
the protection of individual self-expression than of the necessary
ground of democratic citizenship. If we picture the Bill of Rights
as a mirror, and imagine ourselves looking into that mirror, what
we see there are not likely to be democratic citizens but private
individuals, each clothed in those individual rights. That is what
the Supreme Court has seen there, too. But until we reclaim our
citizen identity within the Bill of Rights, we have little chance of
rescuing our elections from the deadly doctrines that the Court
has (with far too much of our own complicity) imposed on them.

Indeed, the historical gravity of this situation is reminiscent of
the one Abraham Lincoln sought to transcend in his second annual address to Congress in 1862. His topic was emancipation, but
he argued that it was not only those bound in actual human slavery who needed to be emancipated. He thought the whole country had become enslaved to a view of reality that now had to be
discarded. "The dogmas of the quiet past are inadequate to the
stormy present," Lincoln wrote. "The occasion is piled high with
difficulty, and we must rise with the occasion. As our case is new,
so we must think anew and act anew. We must disenthrall ourselves, and then we shall save our country."[12]

So too, in our time, the first necessary step toward citizens uniting to remove the threat to democracy that so many perceive in the wake of *Citizens United* is to disenthrall ourselves from deeply embedded but fundamentally false doctrines of the role of free speech in a democracy and replace them with equally emphatic but far more reliable principles of the actual contribution of free speech to self-government. We cannot free our democracy from the shackles that now bind it unless we can first free ourselves from what amounts to the same misconception that has anchored the Court's reasoning. It is not too much to say that the fate of our democratic republic turns on our accomplishing this act of disenthrallment. The good news is that this same process will return us much more closely to the original principles of the Constitution than the Supreme Court's recent activism has done.

Indeed, millennia of republican experience (with which many of the founders of our republic were deeply familiar) had demonstrated that self-government had always been fundamentally dependent on speech being unconstrained as to its content. This is true primarily because of the too-often taken-for-granted fact that a fundamental strength of democracy as a form of governance lies in the way it contributes to a society's capacity to solve problems and pursue opportunities. Democracy provides this advantage over other forms of government by mobilizing not just individual but collective experience and intelligence. That outcome, however, is utterly dependent not only on the human capacity for speech but on the principled practice of making sure that every plausible idea about how to solve the problem or seize the opportunity is allowed to be articulated and considered. Without that principle and that practice, democracy is both unthinkable and unachievable. This capacity for deliberative problem solving is the deepest and most consequential foundation of free speech in any democratic society. Because we have so thoroughly (and so disastrously) lost track of this central justification of free speech, it will be worth taking some time to explore the roots of this connection between free speech and effective self-government.

In one of history's most compelling speeches about the nature and value of democracy, Pericles claimed, some 2,500 years ago, "We Athenians do not think that there is an incompatibility between words and deeds; the worst thing is to rush into action before the consequences have been properly debated."[13] Here lie the deepest roots of the reverence for freedom of speech within a democratic society. Pericles did not argue that freedom of speech is a god-given right but that Athens' well-being depended on the polis getting clear about things before acting, and that such clarity, in turn, depended on viewing the matter from every plausible perspective. That could not happen unless everyone with a point of view to offer was given the opportunity to explain that perspective.

Skipping ahead many centuries, we find an expanded version of this argument in the writing of the seventeenth-century English philosopher John Locke, who exercised a decisive influence on the thinking of America's founders:

> We are all short-sighted, and very often see but one side of a matter; our views are not extended to all that has a connexion with it. From this defect, I think no man is free. We see but in part, and we know but in part, and therefore it is no wonder we conclude not right from our partial views. This might instruct the proudest esteemer of his own parts, how useful it is to talk and consult with others, even such as come short of him in capacity, quickness, and penetration: for, since no one sees all, and we generally have different prospects of the same thing, according to our different, as I may say, positions to it; it is not incongruous to think, nor beneath any man to try, whether another may not have notions of things, which have escaped him, and which his reason would make use of, if they came into his mind.[14]

This same pairing of open dialogue with open minds in the search for what is true and reliable reverberates throughout John Stuart Mill's 1859 essay, *On Liberty*, a work that has deeply influenced both liberals and libertarians ever since. We can never be sure of the soundness of our ideas, Mill argued, unless we are willing to subject them to challenge from every quarter, including those quarters from which we least expect worthy criticisms or better ideas to emerge. When we do engage in that kind of intellectually courageous and honest dialogue, we come to the soundest and most reliable judgments within our reach.

> The beliefs which we have most warrant for, have no safeguard to rest on, but a standing invitation to the whole world

to prove them unfounded. If the challenge is not accepted, or is accepted and the attempt fails, we are far enough from certainty still; but we have done the best that the existing state of human reason admits of; we have neglected nothing that could give the truth a chance of reaching us: if the lists are kept open, we may hope that if there be a better truth, it will be found when the human mind is capable of receiving it: and in the mean time we may rely on having attained such approach to truth, as is possible in our own day. This is the amount of certainty attainable by a fallible being, and this is the sole way of attaining it.[15]

The importance of this deliberately open-minded approach to democracy should be as evident to us as it was to Pericles, Locke, and Mill. It is the fearless testing of ideas and points of view in open debate and dialogue that provides assurance that democratic decisions will be as sound and reliable as possible. If this strain of thought has influenced classical liberals of all stripes, including both civil and conservative libertarians, then we might expect that a lawsuit like the one that produced the *Buckley* decision (a lawsuit brought by exactly that cross-ideological mix of John Stuart Mill's heirs) would have soundly supported the practice of democracy that this entire tradition proclaims. Instead, the decision set us on a path that would not only profoundly undermine democratic practice but do it precisely in the name of free speech. How could this have happened? It happened for the very reason that Mary Ann Glendon identified: because of a shift of focus from core principles of republican self-government to a nearly exclusive focus on individual rights.

If our historical tour of the arguments of Pericles, Locke, and Mill has succeeded in reminding us of the inherent value of unconstrained speech to the republican theory of self-government, it also provides access to the roots of the First Amendment in that same republican soil. With a Supreme Court that, following the 2016 election, had become solidly conservative and seemed likely to remain so for many years, we might expect even greater weight to be accorded to the original principles underlying the Constitution. Whether that happens or not, the cause of democracy surely calls us as citizens to gain as clear an understanding of those republican foundations as possible. Because so much of our judicially constructed campaign finance law has hinged on the First Amendment guarantee of free speech, we will pay special attention to the republican foundations of that constitutional provision.

Since the English Bill of Rights had such a direct influence on the founders, we begin by noting that the 1689 English document did, in fact, contain its own version of a free speech clause. Parliament declared and the Crown consented to the declaration, "That the freedom of speech and debates or proceedings in Parliament ought not to be impeached or questioned in any court or place out of Parliament."[16] This protection of free speech within the halls of Parliament may seem too narrow an application of the right to have any real bearing on the much more inclusive guarantee in our First Amendment. But a closer look will help us to see what we have so thoroughly lost sight of in our own constitutionally protected right of free speech. Profoundly influenced by their contemporary, John Locke, the drafters of the English Bill of Rights were saying (and saying with deep conviction rooted in bitter experience) that they could not be the self-governing people they were now determined to be unless the deliberations within their primary arena of self-determination were free of royal or judicial constraint. The key here is not the narrowness of this protection but its deep foundation in the very bedrock of self-determination. What Parliament was saying, in effect, was that "unless we can say whatever needs to be said in the process of coming to agreement about the laws we enact, we cannot be sure enough of their soundness to fulfill our obligation as the representatives of the people of England."[17]

The framers of the U.S. Constitution would borrow the language of the English Bill of Rights almost verbatim when they provided in Article I Section 6 that "for any Speech or Debate in either House, [Members of Congress] shall not be questioned in any other Place."[18] A decade earlier in 1779, John Adams had incorporated in the Massachusetts Declaration of Rights a provision similar to the English article. Just returned from his wartime negotiations in Paris, Adams had been elected to the state's constitutional convention and designated as what he called "a sub-subcommittee of one" to prepare a draft of Massachusetts' governing document.[19] Adams had there made explicit the democratic foundation of the free speech protection that Parliament had given itself a century earlier and that the framers would later provide to Congress. "The freedom of deliberation, speech, and debate, in either house of the legislature, is so essential to the rights of the people," Adams had written, "that it cannot be the foundation of any accusation or prosecution, action or complaint, in any other court or place whatsoever."[20]

But Adams went far beyond protecting free speech within the Massachusetts legislature. Article 4 of his Declaration of Rights proclaimed that "[t]he people of this commonwealth have the sole and exclusive right of governing themselves as a free, sovereign, and independent State."[21] Within that emphatically articulated context of republican self-government, the Declaration enumerated rights to free elections, the "liberty of the press," the "right to keep and to bear arms for the common defence," and "a right, in an orderly and peaceable manner, to assemble to consult upon the common good; give instructions to their representatives, and to request of the legislative body, by the way of addresses, petitions, or remonstrances, redress of the wrongs done them, and of the grievances they suffer."[22]

This close connection between self-government and the protection of rights was not Adams's invention. It had been a leitmotif in most of the constitutional drafting that the colonies-becoming-states had carried out at the time of the Revolution. The 1776 Pennsylvania constitutional convention, for example, where Benjamin Franklin presided, had guaranteed freedom of speech and of the press but had also acknowledged the democratic context of those rights when it declared, "That the people have a right to assemble together, to consult for their common good, to instruct their representatives, and to apply to the legislature for redress of grievances, by address, petition, or remonstrance."[23] Just as neither Parliament nor Congress could do their representative business unless their members were free to speak their minds, so citizens could not effectively "assemble together, to consult for their common good" unless they, too, were free to speak their minds. The intimate relationship of such rights to self-government had also been clearly articulated in 1776 by the citizens of Virginia in what they called "[a] declaration of rights made by the representatives of the good people of Virginia, assembled in full and free convention; which rights do pertain to them and their posterity, *as the basis and foundation of government.*"(Emphasis added)[24]

It would have been very strange indeed if James Madison (who had been a delegate to that 1776 Virginia convention) had forgotten the connection of fundamental rights to self-government when he was persuaded a decade or so later to propose the amendments to the new U.S. Constitution that would come to be known as the Bill of Rights. In fact, that dominant republican strain runs throughout the Bill of Rights. It is unmistakably present in the guarantee of citizens' right to petition their representatives and in the right to assemble. These are clearly public or civic, not private, rights. But it is precisely the public dimension of those amendments that has slowly and disastrously faded from sight, as the crucial rights of self-governing citizens have been overshadowed by a nearly exclusive focus on the rights of private individuals.

If Madison had used the language of the Pennsylvania constitution and had referred (as that document did) to the right of citizens "to assemble together, to consult for their common good," perhaps the public dimension of the First Amendment's "freedom of speech, or of the press" would not so thoroughly have faded from sight. As we have known since the creation of the republic, a democratic people cannot effectively assemble and consult for their common good unless they are informed by a free press and unless their consultation is open to all points of view. Yet we have almost entirely lost sight of this crucial public dimension of the freedoms of speech and press. In place of democratic citizens assembling under the umbrella of these sacred rights "to consult for their common good," we now view those guarantees almost exclusively as protecting individuals.

This might put us in mind of the story of Benjamin Franklin, who was said to have been approached by a citizen of Philadelphia as he left Independence Hall after signing the newly drafted Constitution for the United States. "Well Doctor, what have we got: a republic or a monarchy?" this citizen inquired. "A republic—if you can keep it," Franklin supposedly replied.[25] After the heroic toil of the previous four months through the muggy Philadelphia summer, Franklin might well have recalled an early passage of the Aeneid, written as Virgil, witnessing the demise of the Roman republic, sought to remind his readers "how hard and huge a task it was to found the Roman people."[26] Founding the American republic had been about as hard, and keeping it, as Franklin implied, would be no walk in the park either.

If the present danger to our republic arises to any significant extent from what Mary Ann Glendon identified as a shift from focusing on the needs of the republic to the rights of individuals, that danger had actually been predicted in sweeping (and chilling) terms nearly two centuries ago, in the observations of that always incisive analyst of American democracy, Alexis de Tocqueville. Most of what Tocqueville identified with such enduring penetration in *Democracy in America* had to do with the subtle features of American society that had equipped its citizens to be especially skilled at self-government. But he was also concerned that there were cultural forces at work here that might eventually undermine democracy in America. He was convinced that this danger existed, but he struggled to put his finger on it:

> I think, therefore, that the kind of oppression with which democratic peoples are threatened will resemble nothing that has preceded it in the world; our contemporaries would not find its image in their memories. I myself seek in vain an expression that exactly reproduces the idea that I form of it for myself and that contains it; the old words despotism and tyranny are not suitable. The thing is new, therefore I must try to define it, since I cannot name it.[27]

What Tocqueville then offered looked less like a definition than a nightmare: the nightmare of unrestrained individualism eroding the precious capacity for citizenship that had so impressed him:

> I want to imagine with what new features despotism could be produced in the world: I see an innumerable crowd of like and equal men who revolve on themselves without repose, procuring the small and vulgar pleasures with which they fill their souls. Each of them, withdrawn and apart, is like a stranger to the destiny of all the others: his children and his particular friends form the whole human species for him; he exists only in himself and for himself alone, and if a family still remains for him, one can at least say that he no longer has a native country.[28]

Few of us would fully identify ourselves or our fellow citizens in this picture, but it does capture with eerie prescience the slide into an individualistic mindset that, among other things, has now rendered us almost entirely incapable of shaping our own

elections according to anything even remotely resembling republican principles.

One fairly subtle but telling clue to how this loss of republican
focus has occurred can be found in the language that the *Buckley*
Court used in striking down the congressionally imposed limits on
direct candidate expenditures. In the key sentence in this part of
its opinion, the *Buckley* Court held that "the ceiling on personal
expenditures by candidates on their own behalf . . . imposes a substantial restraint on the ability of persons to engage in protected
First Amendment *expression*." (Emphasis added) [29] The choice of
the word "expression" may seem totally unsurprising, especially
because that is how we have come, almost universally, to refer to
what the free speech clause protects. In fact, though, this ubiquitous equation of free speech with free expression lies very close
to the heart of how it is that the Court's campaign finance rulings
have become so democratically toxic.

Among the kinds of human speech that might be protected
by instruments like constitutions, there are three categories that
are particularly relevant: deliberative, informative, and expressive speech.[30] Most of what we encountered earlier in our historical journey from Athens to Philadelphia would have fallen in
the deliberative category, where leaving speech unconstrained as
to its content has long been acknowledged as a baseline necessity if people are to have any chance of governing themselves effectively. When we focus on elections (as we must in discussing
campaign finance law), it is not the deliberative but the informative dimension of speech that matters most. Here again, though, if
citizens are to receive the information they require to fulfill their
civic task of choosing able governors, that information must be
unconstrained as to content. If the Supreme Court was going to
apply the First Amendment's protection of speech to the electoral content, it is on this informative dimension of speech that we
might have expected it to focus. Instead, the Court invoked the
free speech rights of the candidates themselves, and in the process,
shifted the focus from the democratically crucial informational
dimension of speech to the right of individual candidates to "express" themselves.

This is certainly not to deny that democracy can sometimes be
advanced by pure expression: of anger, of pride, of solidarity, and
so on. This is why we diligently defend the right to assemble in

protests, parades, or rallies. Nevertheless, the core value of speech in a democracy arises not from occasional acts of self-expression but because self-government cannot occur without reliable information and open deliberation, both of which depend on the freedom to say what some might rather not hear. Yet the occlusion of these crucial public dimensions of free speech and their replacement by the private right of "expression" has come to dominate if not to subsume our understanding of the First Amendment. This narrowing of judicial attention to the expressive dimension of speech is, of course, just one more indicator of the shift from a constitutional concern for republican principles to a nearly exclusive concern with individual rights.

Unfortunately, this is not a problem that can be laid at the door of the Supreme Court alone, any more than it is likely to be a problem that the Court alone is going to solve. It is remarkable how widespread and unquestioned this view of the Bill of Rights in general and of the free speech clause in particular have become. For most of us there is quite simply no other way of thinking about free speech except in terms of self-expression. However, as we have already seen, the constitutional protection of speech originally had far more to do with buttressing citizenship than with enabling individual self-expression. In spite of that history, it has become increasingly difficult for us to read the words of the First Amendment with the eyes of citizens rather than those of separate, private individuals.

This by itself might still leave the shift in emphasis fairly harmless in its effect were it not for one very unfortunate side effect of this move—namely, an insidious absolutizing of the application of this individual right. Mary Ann Glendon saw quite clearly how that dynamic was playing out across a broad swath of constitutional concerns. Comparing American discourse about rights to that of many other democracies, Glendon wrote, "American rights talk is set apart by the way that rights, in our standard formulations, tend to be presented as absolute, individual and independent of any necessary relation to responsibilities."[31] In the context of free speech, this absolutizing dynamic has coincided with the equation of speech with "expression" and the ignoring or obscuring of the deliberative and informative dimensions (and values) of speech.

The unworkability of absolutist doctrines and the necessity of limitations is perhaps clearest in the arena of democratic deliberation. Our historical review reminded us of the crucial importance of protecting deliberative speech against prior constraints in any context where several people are attempting to reach the wisest solution to a difficult (and therefore usually contentious) problem. What we have paid far less attention to in our own time is that, while effective deliberation depends on there being no prior constraints on the *content* of speech, democratic deliberation is equally dependent on reasonable regulations on the *amount* of "air time" any individual speaker can claim. It is our recognition of the intrinsically social or relational nature of deliberation that enables us to understand that here the right of free speech simply cannot be applied as an absolute. Free speech in a deliberative setting is inherently bounded precisely because it is not an individual right but a right that belongs to the deliberating body. The first step toward recognizing that is to understand that it is not the self-expressive but the deliberative dimension of speech that we are protecting in those settings.

One of the most clear-sighted examinations of this crucial but often overlooked feature of democratic speech was provided by Alexander Meiklejohn in his 1948 masterpiece, *Free Speech and Its Relation to Self-Government*. Meiklejohn launched his examination of that relationship by examining the New England town meeting, which he called "self-government in its simplest, most obvious form." He proceeded to set forth the seeming paradox of free speech in this setting:

> In the town meeting the people of a community assemble to discuss and to act upon matters of public interest—roads, schools, poorhouses, health, external defense and the like. . . . They meet as political equals. Each has a right and a duty to think his own thoughts, to express them and to listen to the arguments of others. The basic principle is that the freedom of speech shall be unabridged. And yet the meeting cannot even be opened unless, by common consent, speech is abridged. . . . The moderator assumes, or arranges, that in the conduct of the business, certain rules of order will be observed. . . . The meeting has assembled, not primarily to talk, but primarily by means of talking to get business done. And the talking must be regulated and abridged as the doing of the business under actual conditions may require. . . . The

town meeting, as it seeks for freedom of public discussion of public problems, would be wholly ineffectual unless speech were thus abridged. . . . *It is not a dialectical free-for-all. It is self-government.* (Emphasis added)[32]

Meiklejohn has here articulated the key dynamic between freedom and constraint that makes democracy itself possible. Recalling how familiar we are with that dynamic in the myriad settings where we practice democracy every day will remind us both of the pervasiveness of democratic practice in our everyday lives and the core value of free speech within such practices.

In fact, it is not only in nongovernmental settings like a nonprofit board meeting, or in face-to-face town hall meetings, that productive deliberations depend both on speech being free and on there being some reasonable limits on speech. The Supreme Court itself imposes ironclad time limits on attorneys presenting cases, and it almost certainly observes well-established rules of deliberation when its members meet to discuss a case. With such a small body as the Court, as with my condominium association or your nonprofit board, the rules of deliberation can mostly remain unwritten. Congress, a much larger decision-making body, has to write down more of its rules of debate, but rules there certainly are, and their overriding purpose is to enable Congress to perform its decision-making role. Congress seems progressively less able to perform that function, but it is still clear that, like any other decision-making body, Congress could not operate at all if it did not impose on its members strict limits on when and for how long they may speak.

Even if we can agree that reasonable restrictions on speech are necessary in settings where people are exercising face-to-face democracy, however, we seem to be far less clear about whether the same is true in the arena of representative democracy. Yes, when the actual decision makers are deliberating, there have to be rules that constrain speech, but is that really the case when citizens are engaged in the quite different process of choosing whom to empower with decision-making authority? What is no longer at all clear to us is that (1) self-expression is no more relevant in electoral than in deliberative settings, and (2) unlimited expression may actually be *less* informative (and therefore less helpful to voters) than a process that, while scrupulously leaving *content* unconstrained, would impose the equivalent of time limits on the *quantity* of political advertising. It is precisely the failure to make these distinctions, so clear in the arena of deliberation, that has led to the incredible (and incredibly destructive) conclusion that because it takes money to provide citizens with the information required to enable them to vote intelligently, therefore anyone should be allowed to spend as much money as they want (to "express themselves" at whatever length they choose) in election campaigns.

If, for example, one of my neighbors at our condo association meeting claimed that she should be allowed as much "air time" as she chose to use during our discussion about paving the parking lot and was still talking an hour later with no sign of concluding, we would find some way of letting her know that we couldn't get our work done under such a practice. No one would claim that there is anything fundamentally unfair about this restriction, and everyone would understand that the democratic process absolutely depends on some sensible constraints on individual freedom being in place.

Yet, in the name of protecting the right of individual free expression, we allow the public space of our elections to be inundated and dominated by those with the deepest pockets and therefore the loudest mouths.

The *Buckley* Court tried to establish "corruption" as the one permissible reason for limiting speech as the spending of money, but subsequent decisions have progressively undermined this barrier. More to the point, it is clear that the real corruption of our elections is what the Court itself has created. Once the right at issue was identified as a right of individual self-expression (that right being taken as very nearly absolute) the Court moved directly to the total abolition of limits on direct candidate and "independent" expenditures. One result has been an electoral arena that blatantly advantages wealthy people over the rest of us. With the sweeping aside of all limits on campaign expenditures, the further result has been such gigantic floods of money into election campaigns that the vast majority of Americans have come to hate the very elections that are supposed to be one of the highest manifestations of their cherished exercise of self-government.[33]

Clearly, if the people were in charge of designing the processes by which they conduct elections, the result would bear no resemblance to what we now endure. Campaigns would be far shorter, for example, and, with reasonable limitations on how much could be spent, the numbers of negative attack ads would be sharply reduced, since almost all the spending beyond what is needed to inform voters of the qualifications of one candidate is spent undermining the credibility of the other.

Are there some kind of technical barriers that would prevent us from designing elections to meet the needs of actual human beings? No, of course not. Several other nations that we would not hesitate to call democratic have adopted limits on the length and expense of campaigns.[34] Yet Americans, who have justifiably thought of theirs as among the most democratic of nations, are not even able to exercise enough self-determination to make their elections serve their most basic civic needs. Why? By far the greatest barrier to our exercising democratic control of our elections has been the Supreme Court's rewriting of democratically enacted campaign finance laws—first, by stepping outside the judicial, into the political realm; second, by applying an interpretation of the First Amendment that ignores and seriously undermines the republican foundations of the Constitution; and finally, by nationalizing the results of its judicial activism rather than allowing states any scope to fashion their own rules in this crucial arena of self-government. It is clearly time for some reassertion of judicial restraint, constitutional foundationalism, and federalism.

Beyond the Court's role in all this, however, lies our acquiescence in it because of our own confusion about the republican roots of free speech. We must, as Lincoln said, disenthrall ourselves, and then we will save our democracy. The next chapter will explore two promising arenas where that is already happening.

8 Money and Speech in the Service of Democracy

The relationship of money to democratic speech has been the determining dynamic throughout the entire span of campaign finance jurisprudence from *Buckley v. Valeo*[1] in 1976 through *Citizens United v. Federal Election Commission*[2] in 2010 and beyond. I have argued that the Supreme Court's misinterpretation of the constitutional nexus of money and speech has inflicted inestimable damage on our democratic institutions.

At the same time that these judicial injuries have been so seriously afflicting our body politic, though, other far less visible but vastly more hopeful developments have been establishing their presence and influence in our public life. This chapter explores two overlapping clusters of positive trends: one having to do primarily with money and the other with speech. I am not aiming at a systematic analysis of the democratic potential of these developments but merely indicating that we need not feel trapped by the democratically dysfunctional relationship of money to speech that has emerged from the Supreme Court's substitution of its judgement for that of most citizens.

THE REVIVAL OF DEMOCRATIC DELIBERATION

The previous chapter traced briefly the time-tested relationship between democratic deliberation on one hand and the protection of speech against prior constraint on the other. It bears remembering that Americans have always honored democratic deliberation, especially in our governing institutions. It's now a little hard to believe, but our ancestors took considerable pride in hearing the U.S. Senate referred to as "the greatest deliberative body in the world." Indeed, in the days when Daniel Webster, Henry Clay, and John C. Calhoun debated the nation's most pressing issues on the Senate floor, people packed the galleries to watch and listen. Unfortunately, those days are a distant and fading memory. However else we might describe the proceedings of the Senate these days, the word "deliberative" is not likely to come up.

Indeed, as the twenty-first century dawned, it sometimes seemed as if the power and effectiveness of democratic deliberation had entirely disappeared from the American political ecosystem. If nature indeed abhors a vacuum, however, it isn't surprising that this vacancy began to draw forth new life forms, very tentatively at first, and then with increasing urgency and vitality. Beginning in the early 1980s, organizations like Public Agenda and the Kettering Foundation began to experiment with new mechanisms such as the National Issues Forums to bring the power of citizen deliberation to bear on a variety of public issues.[3] Eventually, National Issues Forums was joined in this deliberative arena by Study Circles (now Everyday Democracy),[4] by James Fishkin's practice of deliberative polling,[5] and then by the *Journal of Public Deliberation*,[6] in a cascading emergence of deliberative templates and forums. Among them, these organizations have by now involved millions of Americans in discussions of important public issues with fellow citizens from widely varied backgrounds and perspectives. In fact, so many organizations are now doing such good work in this field that they have created a network of their own, the Deliberative Democracy Consortium. The mission of the consortium is "to build knowledge, strengthen networks, and forge collaborations among researchers, practitioners, funders, and public officials at all levels of government, in order to improve democratic practice and democratic governance."[7]

In October 2012, as the tsunami of negative campaign ads unleashed by *Citizens United* began to crest in that election cycle, I traveled to Seattle to attend the fifth National Conference on Dialogue and Deliberation. There I found hundreds of people from around the country who had gathered for an intense three days of sharing stories, lessons, and new ideas about how to engage steadily more Americans in meaningful democratic deliberation. Session topics ranged from "Making Wise Choices in Dialogue, Deliberation, and Public Engagement" to "When Governments Listen," with stops in between at "Bringing Deliberation into Public Budgeting" and "Expanding Liberal–Conservative Dialogue in America."[8] I was especially intrigued by one session's description and analysis of the Oregon Citizens' Initiative Review, a process that had been formally instituted by the Oregon legislature for convening a random sample of voters to deliberate for several days on a ballot initiative and then present written findings and recommendations in the official state voters' guide.[9] I also heard how citizens in Ohio had just the previous week employed a similar "citizens' jury" approach to inject a shining moment of genuine deliberation into that state's most hotly contested congressional race.[10]

At the very least, developments like these sustain the awareness among citizens that people of good will can almost always find more common ground when they engage in genuine deliberation than they might otherwise have expected. And activities of this kind also keep alive the memory of a fundamental fact of democratic deliberation that seems to have escaped the notice not only of the Supreme Court but of most of the rest of us. Decisions like *Buckley v. Valeo* and *Citizens United* have been too focused on the protection of free speech to notice that democratic deliberation is never merely a matter of *speaking*; it is also, crucially, a matter of *listening*. Without active, attentive, responsive listening, there is no such thing as deliberation, and therefore no opportunity for democracy to demonstrate its superlative problem-solving capacity. If our larger political culture has abetted the Supreme Court in forgetting that fundamental fact, the deliberative democracy movement has helped to revive that memory among the multitudes of citizens who have engaged in real deliberation under that movement's umbrella. That memory will prove vitally important as the work of democratic revitalization gathers steam. It has been cultivated even more actively by deliberative democracy's sister: the collaborative democracy movement.

COLLABORATIVE DEMOCRACY

At roughly the same time that citizen-focused deliberative practices were gaining historical momentum and establishing a presence in our self-governing ecosystem, a related democratic life form began to emerge in the open spaces left by the increasing dysfunction of older, established forms of representative, procedural, and direct democracy. A phenomenon often called "multiparty collaboration" seems to have arisen primarily as a response to some of the short- comings of the late-twentieth-century framework of procedural democracy. Whatever else public hearings might accomplish, they almost never create an opportunity for anything resembling dem- ocratic problem solving. Yet with increasing frequency, stakehold- ers who for decades had battled each other in public hearings have begun to engage in serious, face-to-face, problem-solving work.

What has moved so many people to take on this hard work of collaboration has been the widespread perception that, in all too many cases, the existing governing framework was proving it- self incapable of getting the job done. To put it bluntly, the prob- lems that people have expected the government to solve have all too seldom been addressed in a problem-solving way. Rather than simply complain about this situation, or resign themselves to it, increasing numbers of people have been stepping up, engaging their neighbors (especially those with whom they have had signifi- cant differences), and doing the problem solving themselves. This hands-on, citizen-driven, problem-solving species of democracy has appeared and gained strength all across the country, around all kinds of issues. I will use my own part of the country—the Ameri- can West—and, in particular, collaborative efforts around public land and natural resource issues to illustrate the genesis, the prom- ise, and some of the challenges of this collaboration movement.

Of the 2.27 billion acres of land in the United States, 28 per- cent is owned by the federal government and administered by a variety of agencies, most notably the U.S. Forest Service in the Department of Agriculture, and the Bureau of Land Manage- ment, National Park Service, and Fish and Wildlife Service, all in the Department of the Interior. This vast amount of public land is heavily concentrated in one region of the country. According to the Congressional Research Service, "62% of Alaska is feder- ally owned, as is 47% of the 11 coterminous western states. By contrast, the federal government owns only 4% of lands in the other states."[11] But while the reservation of millions of acres of forest and grasslands kept human habitation off those lands, it did not prohibit other human uses of the public lands. The prevailing public policy was succinctly stated by Gifford Pinchot, the first chief of the U.S. Forest Service, when he argued that the national forest reserves should be managed in such a way as to produce "the greatest good for the greatest number in the long run."[12] This formula eventually became enshrined in the national forest policy of "multiple use and sustained yield."[13] From the outset, this formula for public land management began to generate conflict between the conservationists, who had provided the initial impetus to the reservations, and the logging, mining, and grazing interests that were invited to multiply the uses of these lands. The Congressional Research Service's report on the concentration of public lands in the West continues with what to most westerners sounds like a study in understatement: "This western concentration has contributed to a higher degree of controversy over land ownership and use in that part of the country."[14] Conflict among competing interests is, of course, the raw material of democratic governance, and it is therefore not surprising that, in some ways, the "public lands West" became a case study both in a set of problems in democracy and in the emergence of some very promising democratic solutions.[15]

The problems have arisen in no small part because the decision-making system that Congress put in place as the governing framework for public lands is breathtakingly complex. Key components include the Multiple Use Sustained Yield Act, the National Forest Management Act, the Federal Land Policy and Management Act, the Endangered Species Act, the Wilderness Act, the National Environmental Policy Act, and the Federal Advisory Committee Act.[16] These statutes (and several others) are fleshed out by a corresponding and even more voluminous set of agency regulations, by multiple layers of administrative appeals and frequent recourse to federal courts, and by the case law emerging from all that litigation.

Over several decades, the relentless struggle of "multiple use" interests within this byzantine governing structure has produced a level of gridlock that could neither by denied nor, apparently, resolved. The increasing problems with this governing framework have been extensively noted and analyzed. Former secretary of the interior Cecil Andrus described the public land governance system as "the tangled web of overlapping and often contradictory laws and regulations under which our federal public lands are managed."[17] Congressman Scott McInnis, former chair of the House

Subcommittee on Forests and Forest Health, decried "a decision-making apparatus that is on the verge of collapsing under its own weight."[18] Former Forest Service chief Jack Ward Thomas simply called this governing framework "the blob."[19] In June 2002, Forest Service chief Dale Bosworth presented to Congress a report entitled, "The Process Predicament," describing the effects of regulatory and administrative gridlock on national forest management, resulting in what he and his colleagues were experiencing as the agency's increasing inability to fulfill its primary duties.[20]

To oversimplify a complex historical development, we might say that collaborative democracy has emerged slowly but insistently in this setting of governmental gridlock because increasing numbers of people with the most direct stakes in these landscapes have concluded that the existing decision system could not reconcile those competing stakes as effectively as could the stakeholders themselves, acting on their own initiative. It was against this background that the public lands West began to witness a steadily growing number of local agreements among environmentalists, ranchers, loggers, miners, and recreationists about how the public land or natural resources in their particular river drainage area or ecosystem should be managed. More and more westerners on both sides of the political fence have come to believe that they can do better by their communities, their economies, and their ecosystems by working together outside the established, centralized governing framework than by continuing to rely on the cumbersome, uncertain, underfunded, and increasingly irrelevant mechanisms of that old structure, which had only taught them how to be enemies.

Concentrated as it might have been in its early stages in one region of the country, with its natural focus on public land and resource issues, this emergent democratic practice of multiparty collaboration has been spreading steadily into other issue arenas across the country. In fact, I would argue that this kind of citizen-driven problem solving across deep ideological and interest group divides has become an important, but still emerging, form of democracy nationwide, at the same time that our larger governing institutions have become steadily more gridlocked and dysfunctional. How might we account for this almost totally unexpected phenomenon? The one thing that has contributed most significantly to the steady expansion of the use of collaborative problem solving is that, in so many circumstances, *it works*, and it works better than any of the other available democratic mechanisms. In evolutionary terms, this is a straightforward example of natural selection: what works well survives and thrives. This element of adaptiveness becomes more striking when we consider the myriad factors that militate against collaboration, including the following:

- Most of the parties to collaborative efforts have spent years using more adversarial means of dealing with the kinds of issues they now seek to address collaboratively. This is a new, unfamiliar, and often intimidating way of proceeding.
- Dealing in a new way with people you have spent years treating (and thinking of) as enemies requires learning.
- Those who make this leap are subjected to suspicion, if not outright hostility, from other members of their own "tribe."
- Successful collaborative efforts are almost always quite time-consuming.
- The established decision system rarely provides any space or encouragement for collaboration.
- Even highly productive collaborations are often resisted by the established system.

The survival, and indeed the spread of collaboration, against these barriers is a vivid testament to its effectiveness. And it is in the context of this harsh, putting-to-the-test environment that the democratic credentials of collaboration have been established. People only go to all the trouble that collaboration entails because they have a real and substantial stake in the matter at hand and presumably no better means of advancing their interests. Their work is therefore democratic in the most fundamental meaning of that word: it is the dead-serious, determined effort of people to shape the conditions under which they live, rather than leaving that shaping to someone else.

I will begin the transition to the other major topic of this chapter by noting that one of the clearest signs of the potency of multiparty collaboration is provided by the attention that philanthropists are now paying to this kind of interaction. While some grant makers have promoted and supported collaborative work in various fields for some time, the deep recession that began in 2008 led to a significant increase in that support. As the recession reduced most foundations' investment pools and their giving capacity, and as their favorite grantees simultaneously experienced both declining support from other sources and growing demand for their services, it became increasingly clear that the philanthropic and nonprofit sector was going to have to squeeze even more effectiveness out of its scarce resources. One of the most promising ways of doing that appeared to be to promote greater collaboration both among grant makers themselves, among their grantees, and between this entire "independent sector" and various levels of government.

It was during this period, for example, that the concept of "collective impact" became a byword in the philanthropic world. A seminal article in the *Stanford Social Innovation Review* concluded that "substantially greater progress could be made in alleviating many of our most serious and complex social problems if nonprofits, governments, businesses, and the public were brought together around a common agenda to create collective impact."[21] At the same time and in the same vein, the philanthropic sector took a hard look at how it could promote more effective collaboration among its grantees. In an article entitled "Working Better Together: Building Nonprofit Collaborative Capacity," Grantmakers for Effective Organizations (GEO) articulated one of the core principles of the collaboration movement: "When people reach across the lines that too often divide organizations and sectors, they tap into new ideas and new resources and create new partnerships that can help them achieve their goals."[22] Taking its analysis a step further, GEO identified some of the key civic skills that collaboration both depends on and instills in those who practice it: "Working effectively in partnerships takes humility and willingness to trade control and power for a higher level of impact. As a result, participants often have to look beyond the specific objectives of their own organizations toward bigger mission goals. In order to do this well, participants need negotiating skills, the ability to compromise and see the big picture, the ability to share credit and control, and openness to criticism and change."[23]

If we read that passage against the background of the often-deepening failures of so many of our governing institutions, it becomes strikingly clear how valuable a democratic asset the collaboration movement is becoming. As more and more people learn how to "look beyond the specific objectives of their own organizations," how to "compromise and see the big picture," and how to "share credit and control," those people, usually without recognizing it, are becoming steadily more capable democratic citizens. When the number of people who have partaken of this learning are added to those who have experienced one or more of the activities of the deliberative democracy movement explored earlier, we begin to see the emergence of a truly potent constituency for a democratic renewal movement. Since philanthropy has played a major role in advancing democratic revitalization in both of these cases, let's take a more focused look at the potential for philanthropy to assist in healing the body of our democracy.

PHILANTHROPY AND THE RENEWAL OF DEMOCRACY

This book dwells at some length on the variety of challenges that concentrated wealth has posed at various times to the health of American democracy, including the intensifying challenge that it has raised in our own time under the aegis of the Supreme Court's campaign finance rulings. Given the generally baleful effect of concentrated capital on democratic governance, it may at first seem a dubious proposition to suggest that some forms of wealth accumulation could be among the most promising tools available to us for strengthening our democracy. One kind of accumulated capital—the form of wealth concentrated in the field of organized philanthropy—clearly does have that potential, though, and many of those charged with the care and use of that capital are starting to think harder about how the resources they steward might be deployed more effectively in the service of democracy.

If we revert for a moment to the image of an Archimedean lever being employed to remove some of the most deeply entrenched barriers to effective self-government, philanthropy certainly qualifies as a substantial enough tool to command our attention. In 2014, the Foundation Center reported that there were 86,726 legally recognized foundations in America, with assets totaling over $865 *trillion*.[24] Using the income from those trillions in assets, foundations contributed over $60 billion that year to a great variety of nonprofit organizations. These are big numbers by any standards—certainly big enough to make a difference in many of the arenas, whether social, cultural, or environmental, to which organized philanthropy addresses itself.

There has recently been a sharpening awareness within the field of philanthropy, however, that substantial as these resources surely are, they can seldom effect the scale of change that their stewards seek to bring about unless they are significantly leveraged by other, even larger resources—especially public resources. And this, in turn, has contributed to a growing interest among philanthropists in addressing more directly the needs of democracy itself. This two-step development within the field of philanthropy deserves a closer look because of its potential to bring serious philanthropic resources to bear on the long-term work of revitalizing our democratic institutions.

I'm going to focus particular attention here on the kind of institutionalized philanthropy practiced by foundations, but we should always bear in mind that this cluster of philanthropic institutions operates within a much larger philanthropic ecosystem that includes the charitable giving of millions of Americans to all the thousands of causes for which they are willing to forego the personal enjoyment of their own resources. This sharing of charitable activities between institutionalized and citizen philanthropy becomes especially important when we turn to how philanthropy in all forms can be mobilized more effectively in the cause of strengthening democracy. At a minimum, we can confidently say that every time a foundation invests deliberately in some democracy-strengthening activity, the success of that investment is going to depend on how thoroughly it meshes with the aspirations and activities of citizens. This leads us to one arena where at least some philanthropists have been very intentional about promoting democratic practices.

Civic Engagement

In the last few years, growing numbers of philanthropists have been quite deliberately seeking to increase their effectiveness in an arena often referred to as "civic engagement." These particular promoters of democracy have created, and for several years worked cooperatively through, an organization straightforwardly named "Philanthropy for Active Civic Engagement" (PACE).[25] The organization describes itself as "a community of funders that invest in the sustaining elements of democracy and civic life in the United States."[26] This mission is driven by the belief, shared among PACE's members, that "broad and informed public participation is the bedrock of a free, democratic, and civil society."[27] That PACE has been focused on encouraging the philanthropic field to "step up its game" in strengthening democracy is evident in its stated intention to "increase the quantity and quality of philanthropic investment in civic engagement."[28] The pairing of philanthropic investment with the power of citizenship is evident in the organization's declaration that "PACE and its members share a belief that America will be more healthy, successful, resilient, and productive if democracy is strong and the office of citizen is treated as central to how it functions."[29] One particular dimension of this nurturing of citizenship opens another entire arena within which a second set of philanthropists (sometimes overlapping the civic engagement supporters) have been seeking to strengthen democracy.

Promotion of Diversity, Equity, and Inclusion

When PACE describes its own work, it often refers to the democratic value of diversity and inclusivity. The consortium seeks, for example, to "build a philanthropic network that encourages participation *and inclusion* in community, civic, and political life." (Emphasis added)[30] Indeed, much of the democracy-strengthening work of PACE members is aimed not just at increasing civic participation in general but more specifically at broadening and deepening participation on the part of groups and individuals that have traditionally been excluded or in various ways discouraged from such participation. This dimension of PACE's work has overlapped a deliberate effort within the philanthropic field "to help philanthropy become more diverse, equitable, and inclusive." Describing itself as "a growing collaboration of foundations large and small, individual donors, regional and national associations, and organizations that focus on diverse communities," the self-styled "D5 coalition" gave itself five years from its launch in 2010 to become "a powerful, national network with the potential to impact philanthropy at every level."[31] The coalition described its goals in terms that resound with democratic overtones:

1. *Advance the common good.* Those of us in philanthropy have dedicated ourselves to promoting the common good. Advancing diversity, equity, and inclusion (DEI) in our organizations and grantmaking helps us live up to our values.
2. *Increase effectiveness.* Diverse perspectives within foundations can help build better relationships with grantees, improve team problem-solving, and lead to better outcomes.
3. *Enhance impact.* Our constituencies, from the communities we serve to our partners in business and government, are becoming increasingly diverse. We need to understand and reflect this rich variety of perspectives in order to achieve greater impact.[32]

Improving "team problem solving" capacity in order "to achieve greater impact" in "promoting the common good" covers a good deal of the ground that we might expect to see addressed by any effort to strengthen democracy. What was especially interesting about the D5 initiative was its focus on nurturing these democratic strengths among the practitioners of philanthropy itself. This determination to change how philanthropy operates was driven both by a conviction that the values of diversity, equity, and inclusion are good in themselves and by a perception that if the field more fully embodied these values, it would be better positioned to nurture them in the broader society. The theory seems to be that the people who lead and staff philanthropic organizations will learn lessons from their own experience of working in more diverse and inclusive settings and that they can then apply those lessons in ways that will make them more effective at cultivating the principles and practices of diversity and inclusivity beyond their walls. Not surprisingly, one of the most promising means of propagating those principles and practices into the broader society is by means of changes in public policy—an arena that has gained steadily more philanthropic attention in recent years.

Public Policy Formulation and Advocacy

I had an opportunity to view these particular developments from a little closer vantage point than I might ordinarily have occupied when, for several years, I served on and then chaired the public policy committee of Philanthropy Northwest (PNW), a regional association of grant makers operating throughout the Pacific Northwest.[33] My role there gave me a term on the corresponding committee at the Council on Foundations, the largest national association of philanthropists. At both the national and regional scales, the committees were hearing from more and more of their respective association's members about their desire to leverage their philanthropic investments more powerfully by becoming increasingly skilled in public policy development and advocacy.

This member-driven demand became a major focus of PNW's public policy committee during what happened to be my tenure as chair of the committee. For several years before the Great Recession slammed into the American economy in 2008, many foundations had already concluded that philanthropic resources were almost never substantial enough to contribute more than marginally to the solution of major social problems. This had led many grant makers to conclude that the solution to those social problems was often going to depend on mobilizing public resources. And that, for growing numbers of foundations, meant that they had to learn how to help shape public policy to bring those resources to bear on the problems that most concerned them.

David Bley, the director of the Pacific Northwest Initiative at the Bill and Melinda Gates Foundation, offered a helpful framework for understanding why philanthropy should consider paying closer attention to public policy formulation and advocacy. Drawing on the Gates Foundation's international work to illustrate his point, Bley said, "Technical solutions—like a vaccine for polio—are essential and powerful, even in the absence of a functioning democracy. You can save lives."[34] Then he came to the heart of the matter: "You can save more lives, more quickly, if there are public institutions (i.e., public health and transportation infrastructure) capable of delivering vaccine to the people."[35] Bley concluded by referring to the "need to recapture government, strengthen it, and put it to work more effectively on behalf of community interests, measured by positive, meaningful impact on people."[36]

Indeed, beginning in 2008, the Great Recession had made this focus on public policy work both more important (because, for example, of the increased numbers of families thrown out of work and often into poverty) and more challenging (because now public resources had themselves shrunk). Public policy work, in all its dimensions, was thus becoming an increasingly important part of philanthropy's programmatic portfolio across the country. In fact, so many regional associations of grant makers were scrambling to respond to their members' request for public policy training that they created a national-scale "PolicyWorks" initiative to help the regions respond to member needs in this mushrooming field.[37]

The William and Flora Hewlett Foundation provided a good example of a foundation that had long devoted a substantial share of its grant making to policy work, for reasons that were concisely stated by Larry Kramer, the foundation's president, in a 2014 article in the *Stanford Social Innovation Review*.[38] "The resources available to the Hewlett Foundation, while substantial by many measures, are miniscule in relation to the problems we take on,"[39] Kramer wrote. "Success, for us, as for many foundations, depends on harnessing the aid of government to support best practices that show evidence of delivering effective solutions." But then Kramer added another dimension to this picture, as he asked, "What then if the political process becomes so dysfunctional that evidence and proven solutions no longer matter?"[40]

Democratic Reform

Kramer was voicing a concern that had begun to pop up throughout the field of philanthropy, as the sector-wide focus on leveraging philanthropic resources through public policy work began to morph into a kind of second-order leveraging discussion. A few philanthropists had begun asking whether those among them who were investing in public policy development and advocacy might also want to pay attention to the deepening dysfunction of the same governing institutions that they were counting on to adopt those policies. This new focus would eventually bring growing numbers of philanthropists face to face with the question of how their field might become more effective in strengthening democracy itself. Thus, for example, in an effort to get clearer about this emerging dimension of its own work, PNW, in cooperation with the Kettering Foundation, published in the spring of 2014 a monograph entitled *Philanthropy and the Renewal of Democracy: Is It Time to Step Up Our Game?*[41]

Meanwhile, the Hewlett Foundation had not only acknowledged the declining effectiveness of democratic institutions but had taken major steps to do something about it, as its president, Larry Kramer, explained in the article cited earlier. Having become convinced that "solving problems at scale has become nearly impossible now that political polarization has all but extinguished rational debate and smothered any ability to compromise," Kramer wrote that the leaders of the Hewlett Foundation had decided to respond to this worsening situation by redirecting some of the foundation's resources to these deeper problems now besetting democracy itself.[42] The goal of its newly launched "Madison Initiative" would be "to help strengthen the nation's representative institutions so they can address problems facing the country in ways that work for the American people."[43] More specifically, "this Initiative calls upon us to join forces with other funders, civic groups, and leaders, in and outside of government, to restore pragmatism and the spirit of compromise in Congress; to reform campaigns and elections so they set the stage for problem solving; and to promote an informed and active citizenry."[44]

The Madison Initiative provided a leading example of what was proving to be a growing interest among philanthropists in the sector's potential to direct more philanthropic resources to strengthening democratic practices and institutions. Hewlett focused its efforts on making Congress more effective, but clearly the work of revitalizing democracy could be fruitfully pursued in many other arenas as well. To keep track of philanthropic investment in this cause, the Foundation Center launched a site, "Foundation Funding for U.S. Democracy,"[45] devoted specifically to tracking democracy-focused funding. The Foundation Center broke its monitoring into four categories: (1) campaigns, elections, and voting; (2) civic participation; (3) government; and (4) media.

Philanthropy Northwest used a different taxonomy, but it covered similar territory. Seeking to provide a user-friendly introduction into the range of pathways by which philanthropists might begin to play a greater role in strengthening democracy, PNW highlighted several possible arenas of investment. These included: (1) supporting public policy formulation and advocacy; (2) enhancing civic engagement; (3) promoting diversity, equity, and inclusion; (4) nurturing deliberative and collaborative skills; and (5) supporting democratic reform efforts. This is by no means an exhaustive catalogue of democracy-strengthening opportunities for philanthropy. But what we find under each of these headings is not only that philanthropy has an opportunity to become more deliberate about revitalizing democracy but also, in every case, that the surest way to achieve that goal is to assist citizens in the great variety of ways that they are deepening their own democratic capacity.

This focus on citizens brings us squarely back to the defining theme of this book. In that light, let's consider just one of these democracy-strengthening categories from that dual philanthropist-and-citizen perspective. One anecdote might illustrate how philanthropic investment in public policy can strengthen the practice of self-government by enhancing democratic citizenship (without necessarily intending that result). This story starts close to home.

When my wife retired from active parish ministry, I was pretty sure that the person I sometimes address as "Citizen Jean" would continue to be engaged with the world in any number of constructive (if to me sometimes unpredictable) ways. I didn't at first expect that engagement to have anything to do with guns, but after Congress failed to take any action at all following the December 14, 2012, slaughter of twenty young children and six staff members at the Sandy Hook, Connecticut, elementary school, Jean began attending meetings of a group called Moms Demand Action for Gun Sense in America (hereafter MOMS).[46] Since then, her steadily more active involvement with both the local and the statewide organization has given me a ringside seat from which to view an impressive example of philanthropy strengthening democracy while actually focusing on other worthy aims. One incident will illustrate what I observed.

On March 24, 2018, hundreds of thousands of students around the country (including hundreds in Missoula) took to the streets in what they called a "March for Our Lives" to demand action from legislators and members of Congress to staunch the epidemic of school shootings that had recently taken seventeen more young lives in Florida. From overhearing Jean's end of countless phone conversations in the weeks preceding the march, I knew how determined the Missoula MOMS were that the event should belong to and be organized by its young participants—but I also knew that MOMS volunteers were offering their own very considerable organizing experience when the young people asked for help. As the *New York Times* reported, "the March for Our Lives demonstrations that unfolded on Saturday . . . ultimately represented twin triumphs: of organic, youthful grass-roots energy, and of sophisticated, experienced organizational muscle."[47]

My point here is not about gun violence or even about movement organizing, but about philanthropy . . . and democracy. In fact, the "sophisticated, experienced organizational muscle" referred to in the *Times* article had been carefully cultivated and supported by some very deliberate philanthropic investments.[48] The center of gravity had been a multimillion dollar investment by Bloomberg Philanthropies[49] in a cluster of organizations, including MOMS as well as Mayors Against Illegal Guns,[50] both operating under the umbrella of Everytown for Gun Safety.[51] In April 2014, former New York City mayor Michael Bloomberg had pledged $50 million to Everytown; then in 2017, in the wake of another mass shooting in Las Vegas, he made an open-ended promise to match anyone else's contribution to the organization. Even without Bloomberg's match offer, the philanthropic investment in gun safety organizing had by then grown far beyond his contributions, with many other foundations and individual philanthropists bringing substantial resources to bear on the effort.

So, what would it mean to view these philanthropic investments not through a gun safety but through a democracy lens? The primary aim of these grants, of course, was to influence public policy at the local, state, and national levels, which means that they constituted a direct engagement with our most prevalent form of self-government: representative democracy. But I would argue that the way that advocacy played out had even deeper and more far-reaching democratic implications. Above all, it was expanding and enhancing these volunteers' capacity to participate in representative government around any issue at all. As a former legislator myself, I was struck by the palpable strengthening over time of the MOMs volunteers' effectiveness in working with their state legislators. They would win some of their policy battles and lose others, but the gain in their political effectiveness was an unalloyed dividend to our democratic culture above and beyond the mission-directed policy aim of the philanthropic investment.

The importance of this dividend is further accentuated if we think for a moment about the youngsters in all those marches. If philanthropic investments end up making them safer, that will be a very good thing indeed and worthy of the noble name of philanthropy. But there is even more at stake here. We owe these students not only safe classrooms but a sound and effective democracy by means of which they can deal with all the challenges they will be facing in the course of their lives. The wounds, weaknesses, and diseases in our body politic that have made it so difficult to enact sensible gun laws have also stood in the way of enacting humanly enhancing policy on nearly every other social, economic, or environmental issue with which philanthropy concerns itself.

Viewing the gun safety work of a few philanthropists through the lens of these democratic challenges leads, then, to this question: if it is true that philanthropic investments in this advocacy work are producing unintended democratic dividends, are there opportunities to expand those dividends by being more deliberate about nurturing them? And what does this suggest in terms of other ways that philanthropy has been strengthening democracy and might be able to do it even more effectively? Let's keep these questions in mind as we consider a couple of much more general and almost entirely unintentional (but still very potent) ways in which philanthropy has an opportunity to help revitalize democracy.

Human-Scale Democracy

Quite apart from their democratically explicit focus on diversity, equity, and inclusion, or on civic engagement or public policy, the daily activities of philanthropists working in almost any field provide opportunities to strengthen democracy simply by helping people become more aware of the self-governing significance of that work in its very ordinariness. If any given philanthropic organization were to view its own daily work through a democratic lens, it would very likely discover that its board, for example, is itself a little democracy, bringing together people from diverse backgrounds and perspectives in a setting of board and committee meetings in which (without necessarily meaning to) they deepen their own problem-solving skills as they continue, meeting after meeting, to pursue the organization's mission.

Indeed, the skills they unconsciously hone in these settings turn out to be the same ones that any self-governing society must develop and nurture if it is to succeed in solving the problems and seizing the opportunities it faces. Most highly-functioning foundation staffs also cultivate internal practices that enable them to draw most effectively on their shared intelligence and commitment. This, again, is democratic practice in its most essential form. Most philanthropists have developed such practices to a fairly high level in the course of doing their everyday work. But few of them ever view their work in those terms. It is worth asking whether more awareness of this democratic dimension of everyday philanthropic activities might by itself leverage the capacity of philanthropy to strengthen democracy beyond its own borders.

Paying attention to the skills and practices that enable a foundation's board and staff to do good work might, for example, heighten these philanthropists' appreciation for how their grant making almost always (albeit unintentionally) nurtures the same kind of problem-solving capacity within their grantees' own board and staff structures. Here, I believe, lies one of the richest of all veins of democratic strength, a vein that philanthropy has been developing for decades without actually meaning to—and that it could strengthen far more effectively with only a little more intentionality. I will use another brief story from my home town to illustrate this point.

As part of a gathering of philanthropic leaders in Missoula a few years back, I had been asked to conduct a walking tour of our downtown riverfront, paying particular attention to some of the improvements that have been made there in the last couple of decades. I love taking people on this "Old Gray Mayor's Tour," primarily because I'm so proud of what the community has accomplished along the Clark Fork River. Almost all of those accomplishments have been the result of very active civic engagement, much of it involving public-private partnerships of the kind that have become increasingly ubiquitous in most of our communities. Without that thriving civic engagement and those productive partnerships, I wouldn't have been showing off the quite attractive affordable housing developments, the kayak wave in the heart of the city, the hand-carved carousel, the world-class skateboard park, or the whole complex of riverfront trails and parks, none of which had existed a few years back.

As I showed all this to my philanthropic friends that day, it occurred to me that Missoula owed far more to the field of philanthropy than I had ever quite realized before. Many of those projects had benefited directly from philanthropic contributions from foundations, businesses, or individuals. But beyond that direct contribution to particular projects or initiatives lay a much more subtle, wholly unintended philanthropic contribution to these community amenities. Many of the citizens who had conceived, planned, and brought to completion the projects I was bragging about were either staff or board members of Missoula's hundreds of nonprofit organizations. Much of the know-how and confidence that they brought to these public projects had been acquired or deepened in the course of the good work they had been doing for years on affordable housing, micro-enterprise development, arts events, or environmental advocacy.

Few philanthropists had set out to strengthen the civic capacity of our community when they made grants or donations to various community-based organizations or gave them technical assistance to build organizational capacity. Both they and their grantees had been motivated primarily by the particular social concerns that were reflected in the terms of the grants or the missions of the nonprofit organizations. But without the philanthropic support and nurturing of hundreds of these nonprofits over several decades, Missoula's civic capacity would have been a mere shadow of the thriving body politic that I have had the pleasure of participating in for so many years. Especially during my years as Missoula's mayor, I became acutely aware of what a tremendous public resource that vibrant civic capacity had become. It enabled public officials like me to leverage scarce public resources far beyond what city government could ever do on its own.

I have recounted this river-walk episode because I believe that every community in the country could tell its own version of this story. If the benefits that society derives from philanthropic investment come not just in measurable terms—more symphony concerts or more after-school programs, greater food security or less infant mortality—but also in terms of a far less measurable but still invaluable strengthening of civic capacity, and if philanthropic investments often produce these civic benefits unintentionally, might even more benefits be produced—even greater civic capacity be generated—if grantors and donors became more aware of this unintended side benefit and more deliberate about producing that civic good? What this invites us to consider once again, quite apart from the role of philanthropy, is the vast resource for democratic revitalization that has persisted in American communities even as our larger governing institutions have continued their slide toward polarization, gridlock, and dysfunction. The next chapter is meant as an invitation to begin imagining what could be accomplished by these millions of citizens uniting their remarkable democratic skills and experience in the work of healing our body politic.

9   We Can Do This

So let us not talk falsely now
The hour is getting late.

          —*Bob Dylan, "All Along the Watchtower"*

I have often had recourse in the preceding pages to the old image of the "body politic," sometimes encapsulating our current state of affairs by suggesting that our democratic body, afflicted by a variety of threatening diseases and serious wounds, has fallen on some very hard times. There is, for example, the deepening paralysis of governing institutions occasioned by unrelenting partisanship, a disease that is fed, in turn, by a viral form of polarization within the electorate itself. Equally debilitating have been the wounds inflicted by the Supreme Court on our democracy with a series of campaign finance rulings, culminating in the 2010 decision in *Citizens United v. Federal Election Commission*.

These wounds and infections in the body politic, along with several others we have examined, are problematic in two big ways. First, they have made it progressively more difficult for us to address some of the most pressing problems facing our society and, indeed, our world. Climate change, income disparity, gun violence, immigration, and racial conflict are among the challenges that we as a democratic people should be mobilizing our collective intelligence to address. But the weakened state of our democracy has left us less and less capable of doing anything about these or other problems. Meanwhile, the growing power of money, ideology, and partisanship in our politics leaves more and more citizens feeling either completely powerless or so alienated from politics and government that they choose not to exercise whatever power they might still have.

As individuals most of us have, at one time or another, recognized that we have let our health decline in one or a number of ways. What, then, do we do? We take a deep breath and call on our various internal resources to start getting ourselves in better shape: by exercising more, eating healthier food, maybe drinking less, perhaps doing yoga or meditating. These personal campaigns sometimes flag or even fail, of course, but often they do produce significant, even enduring, improvements in our well-being. In any case, as self-respecting individuals, we feel some obligation to do what we can to restore our bodies to health when we have to acknowledge how out of shape we are. As self-respecting citizens, we have no less obligation to do whatever we reasonably can to restore our body politic to as hearty a state of health possible.

One key to success in that enterprise is to pay at least as much attention to our democratic assets as we do to our all-too-obvious deficits. We need to remind ourselves of those settings where we continue to practice democracy effectively, or where we are actually improving that practice, so that we can begin to mobilize those assets in the cause of restoring democratic principles and practices to larger institutions of self-government. Earlier chapters have sought to remind us of some of those sources of strength. Chapter 8, for instance, examined some overlapping strains of democratic revitalization very much in play right now: an expanding and deepening practice of democratic deliberation and problem-solving collaboration on one hand, often supported on the other hand by a philanthropic sector newly committed to devoting resources to these and other forms of democratic renewal. Undergirding all of these hopeful phenomena is the enduring solid ground of democratic citizenship we encountered in chapter 3–that foundational form of democracy practiced every day in every community across the land, as people devote time, energy, and resources to caring for the communities they love, by serving in local offices or on boards or commissions or by supporting a great variety of humanly or ecologically nurturing organizations. These individuals, in fact, are the able democratic citizens who are going to bear the chief responsibility for restoring our body politic to health.

If there was ever a time in the years-long gestation of this book when I felt my democratic faith fundamentally shaken, it was at that moment late in the evening of November 8, 2016, when I had to acknowledge that a person I considered totally unqualified for the presidency, having lost the popular vote by a resounding margin, was yet going to be occupying the highest office in our nation. My own reaction to that stunning event is of no great significance, but what I saw around me in the following days and weeks provided me with new and unsuspected wellsprings of democratic hope.

The fact is that I had never, in four decades of involvement in public life, experienced such widespread and heartfelt determination to *do something* effective in the political arena as I witnessed repeatedly in the months (and then years) following the 2016 presidential election. I was especially impressed that almost none of these people seemed content simply to moan or rage a little and then get on with their lives. For some reason, they all seemed to feel a personal imperative to do something about the situation, rather than simply adapting to it. And this in itself seemed to me a democratically hopeful sign. Surely throughout most of human history, in a situation even remotely like this, the vast majority of people would simply assume that someone else (most likely someone in authority) would be responsible for responding—but not them. It is an indication of how deeply engrained the practice of democratic citizenship is in the fabric of our lives that so many of us feel that we, personally, have to do something about a situation like the one we encountered in November 2016.

Of course, I knew that few of the people I was hearing from would have framed their personal struggles in terms of their "practice of citizenship." I also know that most of us don't wake up in the morning thinking about how we can make history that day, nor am I suggesting that we should. Most of us wake up thinking about getting the coffee going, or what our aged parent or youngest child told us last night, or what awaits us at work in an hour or so. To the extent that we think about public matters, it is far more likely to be about climate change or business regulations, about racism, about the widening income gap or American jobs moving overseas, about women's health, gun violence, or the treatment of refugees or immigrants. To the extent that my friends and neighbors were engaging in personal soul searching following the 2016 election, most of them would have framed their search in terms of "what do I need to do right now to make sure that the issues I care most about are going to be addressed?" Very few of these people were asking what they should do to heal democracy. But in fact, democracy was sorely in need of healing (as indeed it had been for years before 2016), and these people, by their intense soul searching, were convincing me anew that they were exactly the ones—indeed the only ones—in a position to undertake that healing.

If this highly stressful moment in our political history held any promise of democratic regeneration, it would clearly require us to find some way of keeping this flame burning rather than letting it burn itself out as, for example, the Occupy movement had done a few years earlier. To avoid that kind of flame-out, we would need to attend closely to the fuel and oxygen supply for this bright—but surely vulnerable—flame. Furthermore, the passions of the moment will have to be directed beyond the next election and beyond any one or two of the important issues that we care so much about as individuals (and therefore believe that our representative institutions need to address.) Some portion of those passions has to be directed to the cause of democracy itself. Among the myriad ways that this might (and no doubt will) happen, I am going to suggest a couple of accessible mechanisms: a democracy tithe, lying within the reach of any of us individually, and a powerful democracy lobby that we can and should build together.

One way to sustain the personal determination to make a difference might be thought of as a democracy tithe or perhaps a democracy set-aside. The concept of tithing is generally associated with various organized religions that encourage their members to set aside a certain percentage of their income to support that religion's institutions and practices. More generally, though, a tithe might be thought of as the intentional dedication of some specified portion of one's income, resources, or time to a higher, broader, or longer-term purpose for which the rest of those assets are used. If we try to imagine how such a practice might operate in the arena of democratic revitalization, we could start by assuming that most people are going to continue devoting most of their civic resources where they do now—to their favorite charities, nonprofit organizations, or candidates. But if we became convinced that all of those investments are undermined or put at risk by the various wounds and weaknesses in our political culture, it would make sense to set aside some portion of our giving or volunteering specifically for the work of restoring democratic institutions and practices themselves. While the magnitude of the set-aside will almost certainly vary from one individual or group to another, many of us would clearly benefit from setting for ourselves some specified target or benchmark, if only because having such a standard in mind makes it more likely that the discipline of tithing will be maintained. So, let's say that you have decided to devote 10 percent of your total civic or political contributions to strengthening democracy itself. Where should you send your check?

I believe that the work we now face in restoring our body politic to health is going to require the emergence of a twenty-first century movement of democratic reform and renewal at a scale, breadth, and depth equivalent to that of the Progressive movement of a century ago. As that movement emerges, it will (almost by the definition of a movement) present a steadily expanding set of options for the investment of the time, energy, and resources of any citizen's democracy tithe. But we don't need to wait for something new to emerge before we start tithing. There are already many such options available, and investment in any of them now will almost certainly contribute to the proliferation of other, yet undreamt-of venues.

Some of the organizations that might be worthy of a twenty-first century democracy tithe investment actually have their roots in the Progressive movement itself. The National Civic League, for example, has been pursuing its democracy-strengthening vision since Theodore Roosevelt and its other founders created it as the National Municipal League in the 1890s.[1] The League of Women Voters has been dedicated to "making democracy work," as its motto declares, since its founding in 1920.[2] Common Cause has been doing patient, often highly effective work in this field since John Gardner founded what he called a "citizens' lobby" in 1970.[3] Gardner, a "Rockefeller Republican," had served as Lyndon Johnson's secretary of health, education, and welfare until his disenchantment with Johnson's Vietnam policies led to his resignation from the cabinet.[4] Dismayed by the prevalence of special interests and what he saw as the relative lack of advocacy for the common good, Gardner launched the organization that is still a major player in the arena of democratic revitalization, particularly on the subject of campaign finance.[5]

Alongside these democracy-nurturing pioneers, scores of newer organizations devote themselves diligently to the care and nurture and, indeed, the revitalization of democratic practices. Many of them, like FairVote and American Promise, are entirely focused on some of the specific reform efforts that we will examine later in this chapter. The citizens-uniting.org website associated with this book will point out and link to other reform initiatives and organizations as they emerge on the scene, and it will also link to other sites performing that same kind of networking function. One of my favorite nodes, for example, was created by the former *New York Times* reporter (and Pulitzer Prize winner) Hedrick Smith. Naming his site "Reclaim the American Dream," Smith proclaimed, "Our political system is broken. . . . It's time for us to take action. . . . We get it, but we're not sure where to begin. People worry that reform is impossible. Not true. It's already happening in many places. . . . Working together in our home states and communities, We the People can reclaim the American Dream."[6] Supporting this very fertile site, or FairVote, American Promise, Common Cause, or any of the democratic renewal efforts that have not yet been launched but will be in the coming years, is what I mean by a democracy tithe. Meanwhile, and even more concretely, citizens desiring to apply some portion of their civic time, energy, or money to the larger work of restoring democracy, have a steadily expanding menu of reform efforts from which to choose. To stimulate our democratic imagination, let's take a quick tour of the reform ecosystem as it appeared at the end of the decade of the "twenty-teens." We already took a warm-up look at Electoral College reform in chapter 1. To broaden the options for investing in democratic revitalization, consider the prospects for citizens uniting to restore democratic principles to campaign finance law.

CAMPAIGN FINANCE REFORM

Both the title and the structure of this book reflect my belief that reclaiming democratic control over the crucial arena of campaign finance must lie very near the heart of the larger project of restoring democracy. The "good news" side of this situation is that the

Supreme Court assault on that democratic control in the form of its *Citizens United* decision instantly fanned the flames of reform—as nothing else had done for decades—to the point that a critical mass of citizens may now be ripe for uniting into a sustained and effective movement of reform, not only in the arena of campaign finance but across the field of democratic activity. It is in that larger context that we will here examine the challenge of campaign finance reform.

As we saw in chapter 1 with Electoral College reform, and as we will encounter here in examining other reforms, the effort to reassert democratic control over campaign finance law can and indeed must unfold on a number of fronts simultaneously. Probably the most remote possibility, but one that can't be ignored and will therefore be examined briefly later, is the scenario whereby the Supreme Court itself changes course by deciding that it should, in fact, allow the people to exercise democratic dominion in this crucial arena. Rather than count on that fairly slender possibility, efforts to rescind *Buckley v. Valeo* and *Citizens United* by way of constitutional amendment must and will continue. Meanwhile, we have seen a proliferation of efforts to reclaim as much democratic control of campaign finance law as may be possible within the confines of the Supreme Court's rulings on this subject. We will start there.

Those efforts include both new disclosure requirements and some very creative new public campaign financing initiatives. Voters in New York City, for example, have steadily strengthened and broadened a public financing program that has existed there since 1988.[7] In 2013, for the first time in the program's history, a participating candidate was elected mayor of New York, and by 2016, this pioneering program had been expanded to match with $6 in public funds each dollar (up to $175) that a New York City resident contributes to a municipal election campaign, for a maximum of $1,050 in public funds per contributor.[8]

Across the continent, meanwhile, Seattle citizens approved in the 2016 general election a program under which Seattle voters receive four $25 "democracy vouchers" apiece to give to the municipal candidate or candidates of their choice. The program made its election debut in the 2017 city council elections.[9] As the *Seattle Times* reported in a story on two key races that fall, "Taxpayer-funded 'democracy vouchers' figured prominently in both council races. [Jon] Grant and [Teresa] Mosqueda each collected the $300,000 maximum in vouchers from Seattle voters."[10]

If, as I believe, a robust program of public financing of campaigns will be an important component of any future, truly democratic system of elections, then the kinds of experiments that New York City and Seattle have undertaken will be of great value in shaping that scenario. In the meantime, though, there is strong reason to doubt whether initiatives like this, however innovative, can by themselves have more than a marginal effect in ameliorating the damage that the Supreme Court has inflicted on our elections with its sweeping campaign finance rulings. In particular, it seems extremely unlikely that any city councils or state legislatures (let alone Congress) are going to be willing to devote the magnitude of public funding to such mechanisms that would be required before we could even come close to balancing the floods of money from wealthy individuals and from nonprofit and for-profit corporations that the Court has allowed to inundate our electoral landscape.

Even before Seattle's first primary election under its new "democracy voucher" program, for example, the *Seattle Times* had concluded in a headline that "Seattle's democracy vouchers haven't kept big money out of primary election."[11] As an example of the post–*Citizens United* reality in play, the newspaper noted that "Amazon dumped $250,000 into the political action committee (PAC) of the Seattle Metropolitan Chamber of Commerce this month, part of the $667,728 the PAC has amassed in advance of Tuesday's primary election."[12] Some observers worried that there could be even worse to come. As the *Seattle Times* reported, "Bob Mahon, a former chairman of the watchdog Seattle Ethics and Elections Commission . . . said it's not likely money will be squeezed out of politics by I-122, 'but will be driven to less transparent forms of expenditures including IEs [independent expenditures].'"[13] This is exactly what occurred in the next municipal election. As the *New York Times* reported on October 30, 2019, "Thanks in large part to the hometown tech giant Amazon, independent groups that receive bulk donations have already spent more money—$4.1 million—on next week's City Council elections than they spent in the previous two decades of elections combined, according to campaign finance data."[14]

I am not arguing that reforms like Seattle's democracy voucher program are a waste of time and energy—far from it. At a minimum, as I mentioned in chapter 1 when discussing various efforts at Electoral College reform, whether any given reform succeeds by its own terms or not, any well-conceived and vigorously pursued reform effort has the potential to contribute in less tangible ways to the larger, longer-term work of democratic revitalization. The amount of organizing activity that is required to get something like the democracy voucher program adopted can be thought of not only in terms of the mechanism itself but perhaps even more important in terms of the democratic muscles that are being strengthened in the process. That musculature will prove indispensable if (as I would predict) the battle to reclaim democratic control over campaign finance law has to move outside the range permissible under Supreme Court rulings into an effort to change those rulings themselves.

Turning briefly, then, to the possibility of persuading a majority of the Court to reverse course on campaign finance, we should note that there is no bright line separating that approach from the one we have just been observing. Efforts to make things work in as democratic a way as possible within the narrow policy space that the Supreme Court has left open may sometimes, either intentionally or not, push the limits of that policy space and may then create just the kind of litigation that will eventually have to be provoked if the Court were ever to reconsider some of the doctrines that have done so much damage to the democratic process. In fact, Seattle's democracy voucher program was already in court by the time of the municipal elections in November 2017.[15] That same month, the King County Superior Court dismissed the challenge, but the conservative Pacific Legal Foundation vowed to appeal the ruling.[16] Whether that case itself ever comes before the U.S. Supreme Court or not, both it and the public financing program that occasioned the litigation stand as an example of how reform activity may eventually provide that tribunal with the opportunity to begin (if it were so inclined) to retreat from its existing chain of campaign finance rulings.

Given the trajectory of the Court's decisions in this arena over the past few decades, an intelligent betting person would probably predict that any imminent decisions are likely to move further from rather than closer to democratic principles. At the time of Donald Trump's appointment of Neil Gorsuch to replace Antonin Scalia, and then of Brett Kavanaugh to replace Anthony Kennedy,

the stage seemed as well set as it was ever likely to be for an effort
to have contribution limits themselves ruled unconstitutional. The
chances of persuading a majority of justices to move the needle
in the opposite direction seemed slender indeed. Under those circumstances, it is reasonable to ask why any effort should be ex-
pended on a likely losing cause.

On the one hand, as I suggested earlier, there is too much at
stake for us to overlook any feasible path to bringing democratic
principles to bear once again in the campaign finance arena. Courts
do sometimes reverse themselves (as the Roberts Court had indeed done when it overturned decades-old precedent with *Citizens
United*). As we have seen, the majority opinion in *Citizens United*
was so conceptually slipshod that even a modicum of intellectual
honesty on the part of a single conservative justice could be enough
to open avenues to a more rationally sound jurisprudence. In fact,
many of the very substantial gaps in Justice Kennedy's reasoning
could be filled with eminently conservative principles that would
be far more consistent with our republican roots than what the
Court has decreed to be the law.

This leads us finally to the threshold of what must surely become the core work of campaign finance reform. Valuable as various creative efforts to make elections work within the confines of
the Supreme Court's rulings may prove, it is simply not going to
be possible to restore anything resembling genuine democracy to
the crucial arena of elections without reversing those rulings. As
I argued in chapter 7, the entire thrust of the Court's decisions,
beginning in 1976 with *Buckley v. Valeo*, has been based on fundamentally undemocratic foundations. Until campaign finance law
is once again allowed to be shaped by (and to serve) democratic
principles and practices, the voice of the people will continue to
be overwhelmed by the power of money and special interests.
This is why, at the same time that we should be pursuing all feasible paths of campaign finance reform within the narrow limits
left standing by the Supreme Court, and at the same time that we
should do everything possible to leverage those reforms into opportunities for the Court to modify its democratically disastrous
rulings, we must also be pursuing the one clear option for democratic renewal that "we the people" wrote into our Constitution:
namely, a constitutional amendment to take back the control of
our elections by reversing *Buckley* and *Citizens United*.

That is the path that John Paul Stevens advocated when he retired from the Court six months after filing his seminal dissent in *Citizens United*. In his 2014 book, *Six Amendments: How and Why We Should Change the Constitution*, Stevens summarized his objections to both *Citizens United* and *Buckley* in one sentence: "Unlimited expenditures by nonvoters in election campaigns—whether made by nonresidents in state elections or by Canadian citizens, by corporations, by unions, or by trade associations in federal elections—impairs the process of democratic self-government by making successful candidates more beholden to the nonvoters who supported them than to the voters who elected them."[17]

Based on this democratic principle of opposition to the Court's key rulings on campaign finance, Stevens proposed this amendment to the Constitution:

> Neither the First Amendment nor any other provision of this Constitution shall be construed to prohibit the Congress or any state from imposing reasonable limits on the amount of money that candidates for public office, or their supporters, may spend in election campaigns.[18]

Long before Stevens' book appeared, the outrage stirred by the *Citizens United* decision had generated a number of resistance efforts, mobilizing a variety of constituencies around as broad a variety of messages and strategies. An organization calling itself "Move to Amend" offered Americans the opportunity to proclaim, "We, the People of the United States of America, reject the U.S. Supreme Court's ruling in *Citizens United* and other related cases, and move to amend our Constitution to firmly establish that **money is not speech**, and that **human beings, not corporations, are persons entitled to constitutional rights**." (Move to Amend's emphasis)[19]

A little later, the resistance to *Citizens United* gave voice to a somewhat broader constituency with the creation in 2016 of American Promise, which aimed to be "leading the charge to win the 28th Amendment so We the People—not big money, not corporations, not unions, not special interests—govern the United States of America."[20] This effort attracted the endorsement of a number of widely known citizens and former officeholders, ranging from ice cream magnate Ben Cohen to author Doris Kearns

Goodwin and including former U.S. senators Olympia Snowe and Alan Simpson and former Massachusetts governor Mike Dukakis.[21]

The very deliberate bipartisanship of American Promise stood in marked contrast to the effort at constitutional revision represented by End Citizens United, as that organization made clear on its website:

> The Supreme Court's 2010 decision in Citizens United v. F.E.C. completely changed the landscape of American elections. It further established the legal basis for the idea that 'corporations are people' and opened the door for billionaires and special interests to spend unlimited, untraceable money in America's elections. . . . It's time to fight back. Established March 1st, 2015, End Citizens United is a Political Action Committee funded by grassroots donors. We are dedicated to countering the disastrous effects of Citizens United and reforming our campaign finance system.[22]

In fact, End Citizens United was, to all intents and purposes, an extension of the Democratic Party, committed to electing Democrats to House and Senate seats and characterizing itself on its website masthead as "Democrats Fighting for Reform."[23] As the Open Secrets organization reported, contributions from End Citizens United to federal candidates during the 2016 reporting cycle had totaled $689,000, 100 percent of which had gone to Democrats.[24] This is not to suggest that this partisan organization is either misguided or insincere in its commitment to reforming campaign finance law, nor would I argue that a "democracy tithe" contribution to the organization would be misplaced. The point here is simply that in this context, as in many other reform efforts, partisanship has worked its way deeply into the body of democratic renewal. On one level, this may well bear beneficial fruit. If the Democratic Party is successful in parlaying opposition to Citizens United into electoral victories for any substantial number of its candidates, that will undoubtedly contribute to the momentum of campaign finance reform, and it may well persuade some Republican candidates to take similar stands. But that possibility only underscores that one party by itself cannot be the vehicle for democratic restoration. There are three commanding reasons for that conclusion.

The first is that parties are by their nature driven to oversimplify what are often very complex matters, as End Citizens United did in claiming that the decision it seeks to overcome "established the legal basis for the idea that 'corporations are people.'" We saw in chapter 6 what a distortion of constitutional history that urban legend represents. This is not necessarily a criticism of party speak, however; there are often good, practical reasons to "keep it simple, stupid." But however valuable oversimplifications may sometimes prove to be in election campaigns, they rarely contribute anything useful to the solution of complex problems. The deep and complex roots in constitutional history that have underlain the damage the Supreme Court has inflicted on campaign finance law are going to have to be addressed in their own complex terms, not by ideological posturing or sloganeering.

The second reason that no one party can substitute for the kind of transpartisan, reform-focused democracy lobby we will soon turn to is that many of the problems requiring reform are also going to require the action of supermajorities that no one party is ever likely to command. That is certainly the case with campaign finance reform, especially if meaningful reform in that arena can be accomplished only by a constitutional amendment.

The third (and primary) reason that ever-more-refined partisan strategies and mechanisms cannot by themselves reverse *Citizens United* or in any other way restore health to the body of democracy is simply that excessive partisanship is itself one of the major diseases afflicting that body. Reform efforts aimed at ameliorating excessive partisanship are therefore at least as worthy of support as those seeking campaign finance reform.

INITIATIVES TO CONTAIN PARTISANSHIP

Next to the Supreme Court's substitution of its own law for democratically enacted efforts to govern campaign finance, the greatest threat to our democratic institutions today is certainly the excessive partisanship that so often precludes effective problem solving by those institutions. That infection within our body politic has called forth a variety of efforts to bring partisanship under control. These efforts reach across a broad spectrum, from the creation of specifically nonpartisan policy centers through reforms aimed at changing the way primary or even general elections are conducted.

Before turning to the efforts to break the grip of partisanship through structural changes to redistricting, or to primary or general elections, let's take a brief look at the emergence of important initiatives to soften or transcend partisan gridlock from another direction: that of policy formulation and advocacy. As the movement for democratic reform gathers momentum, we might expect these bipartisan initiatives to gain supporters and to proliferate in number and variety of approaches. For now, the genre is well enough established that it can be delineated by a few key examples.

In the early 1990s, as many thoughtful citizens were becoming alarmed by the fallout of the increasing partisanship in Washington, in particular by the way that this polarization was blocking the development of effective fiscal policy, former senators Warren Rudman (R-NH) and Paul Tsongas (D-MA) joined Richard Nixon's secretary of commerce, Peter G. Peterson, in launching the Concord Coalition.[25] This assertively bipartisan organization is still playing a major role in developing and advocating policy options in the vexed arena of the national debt and deficit. When Tsongas succumbed to cancer in 1997, former senator Sam Nunn (D-TN) joined Rudman in co-chairing the organization.[26]

The bipartisan efforts of the Concord Coalition have been echoed in the more recent emergence of policy initiatives reaching beyond the fiscal arena. As partisan gridlock tightened within our governing institutions in the early years of this century, efforts to transcend it continued to proliferate outside government. For example, No Labels, created in 2010, explained that "[w]hile many outside political groups are working to push our leaders apart, No Labels was the first organization to call on our leaders to come together to focus on fixing America's most pressing problems."[27]

Former officeholders, and especially former senators, have often played a key role in these bipartisan efforts, as they did and still do in the Concord Coalition. In 2007, for example, four former senate majority leaders, Howard Baker (R-TN), Tom Daschle (D-SD), Bob Dole (R-KN), and George Mitchell (D-ME), joined in the creation of the Bipartisan Policy Center. This organization describes itself as "a non-profit organization that combines the best ideas from both parties to promote health, security, and opportunity for all Americans."[28] From that stance, the organization has produced policy papers on a very broad range of subjects, from foreign policy to immigration, defense spending, and Wall Street regulation.

Turning now from these efforts to give bipartisanship a greater voice in policy formulation or advocacy, let's examine a few initiatives aimed at lessening the effect of partisanship by changing the way we conduct our elections. One example of an election reform strategy that has gained some traction in recent years is the effort to institutionalize a "top-two" or "blanket" primary. Unlike efforts to mandate nonpartisan elections (such as those the Progressives pursued successfully in many cities), this contemporary reform is not a direct attack on partisanship per se but an effort to contain the growing tendency toward electing ideologically extreme candidates to Congress and state legislatures.

We noted in chapter 2 the increasing tendency of party-controlled reapportionment processes to create "safe" districts for one party or the other. This, in turn, has contributed to the deepening ideological polarization both in Congress and in growing numbers of state houses. In a safe Democratic district, for example, if the seat is to be contested at all, the action will be in the Democratic primary election because the winner of that primary is all but guaranteed to win the general election. (That's what makes it a "safe" seat.) Since primary election turnout is almost always considerably lower than in a general election, the most committed or most readily mobilized voters will be the ones making the choice of the party's candidate.[29] In a Democratic primary, those will almost always be the most liberal voters, just as the most conservative voters will usually dominate a Republican primary. It was this dynamic that enabled a number of Tea Party candidates to unseat Republican incumbents or win against other more moderate candidates beginning in the 2010 election cycle. The corresponding dynamic on the Democratic side has resulted in congressional and legislative delegations more liberal than they would be if the district boundaries hadn't been drawn to guarantee Democratic victories—or if the primary election system could be re-engineered to lessen or short-circuit this polarizing dynamic. That is what the top-two primary system seeks to do.

The mechanism is simple enough. Instead of requiring voters to choose either a Democratic or Republican primary ballot, all candidates for a given office are listed on a single ballot (with their party affiliations still clearly indicated). The top two vote-getters (regardless of their party affiliation) then advance to the general election. The idea is that, in a heavily Democratic district, the most liberal candidate might still garner the most votes in a light-turnout primary, but it may well be that a more moderate Democrat would edge out any of the Republicans for second place. In that case, the general election would not be a race between a liberal who is guaranteed to win and a conservative sure to lose, but a choice in which moderation might have a chance of prevailing.

My intention here is not to make the case for this particular reform so much as to point out both its potential and the problems its critics see in it. There are strong arguments, for example, that third-party or independent candidates would have an even harder time than they now do in winning a general election, simply because they would rarely be among the top two vote getters in any primary. Another perfectly reasonable objection is that driving the electoral process toward the center is not necessarily the best strategy for producing sound public policy.

Concerns like these may have contributed to Oregon voters twice (in 2008 and 2014) rejecting the top-two primary system that Oregon's neighbors to the north and south had adopted.[30] In the 2014 vote, the electorate voted in keeping with the advice of the Oregon Citizens' Initiative Review Commission, a remarkable democratic innovation in its own right, which we examined briefly in chapter 8. That entirely nonpartisan body had criticized the proposed reform of the primary election system, citing the opposition of a broad coalition "including at least two election reform groups, as well as major and minor political parties."[31] The majority report from the review commission went on to say that "M90 limits the voice of minority voters, minor parties, and grassroots campaigns. A diverse electorate needs choice & diversity in the General Election."[32] In the end, Oregon voters rejected the proposed reform by more than a 2–1 margin.[33] This was all the more remarkable, given that supporters of the initiative had vastly outspent opponents ($9,144,516.96 to $1,553,638.09).[34] John Arnold, a Houston investor and philanthropist, for example, contributed $2,750,000.00 to the campaign, while another billionaire (and former New York mayor), Michael Bloomberg, gave $2,130,000.00.[35]

Given that level of commitment and interest, the results in Oregon were certainly a disappointment to the proponents (both in Oregon and beyond) of this form of electoral reform. It may be, though, as with a variety of other reform initiatives, that the real value of the efforts to implement a top-two primary will in the end lie less in the actual reform itself than in the building of reformation consciousness and more generalized reform skills. Those democratic capacities would then be available for other democratic reform efforts.

Beyond this muscle-building feature of any plausible reform effort, the varying fates of this particular reform in neighboring states is a potent reminder of the value of allowing the citizens of different states to take different approaches in the way they structure (or finance) their elections. In those terms, it is one more reminder of what a disservice to federalism the Supreme Court has inflicted with its one-size-fits-all legislating in the arena of campaign finance.

Meanwhile, for those citizens who are especially concerned about making elections more democratic, there are a number of other promising paths to reform. The "FairVote" organization, for example, serves as an advocate and clearinghouse for efforts to adopt ranked-choice voting (also called "instant runoff") and various approaches to proportional representation.[36] Ranked-choice voting is motivated by the perception that the prevailing system of plurality voting is a key factor in maintaining the stranglehold of the two-party system on American politics by discouraging third-party or independent candidacies.

In an instant runoff system, voters are allowed to rank candidates in their own personal order of preference. All voters' first choices are tabulated in a first round of vote counting, and if one candidate garners an absolute majority, that candidate is declared the winner and that is the end of the process. If no candidate for a given office garners a majority of first-choice votes, however, a series of runoffs are conducted digitally (and instantaneously) until someone wins a majority of the votes, in roughly the following way. After the first round, the candidate receiving the fewest first-choice votes is eliminated. The ballots are then counted again, with voters who ranked the newly eliminated candidate as their first choice now-having their second-choice votes added to the totals for that candidate. All other voters are again counted as supporting their top candidate, since that candidate still remains in the race. Round by digital round, then, the weakest candidates are eliminated in turn and, as their names drop off, those voters who had supported them now have their next choices tallied in the instant runoffs. This continues until a single candidate receives a majority of the votes in what will therefore be the last round of tabulation. Proponents of this reform contend that it allows voters to express support for dissenting views without harming the chances of their most preferred candidate by wasting their vote on a "spoiler" candidate.

In 2016, citizen groups in Maine secured enough signatures to place an instant runoff proposal on the November ballot. On November 8, by a margin of 52 to 48 percent, the citizens of Maine adopted this new way of conducting their elections.[37] While several local jurisdictions across the nation had previously adopted this mechanism, the 2016 election would have made Maine the first state to adopt it. Within months of the vote, however, the Maine Supreme Judicial Court declared the initiative contrary to a provision of the state constitution.[38] That ruling came in a form that was not legally binding, but it cast a dark shadow over what had at first appeared to be a groundbreaking reform. Still, after a series of partisan legislative maneuvers and more litigation, Maine used ranked-choice voting in its 2018 elections to the U.S. House and Senate.[39]

Here again, as with the top-two primary, there are pros and cons to this particular reform from a democratic perspective, but in both cases, there is the possibility of softening the stranglehold that the two major parties now have on our politics. Both of these reforms would achieve that objective in a fairly circuitous way. Other reforms would get there much more directly. Chief among them is a cluster of voting systems usually called "proportional representation" or "proportional voting." FairVote describes this reform approach (its favorite) as dividing up the seats in multi-member districts "according to the proportion of votes received by the various parties or groups running candidates. Thus, if the candidates of a party win 40% of the vote in a 10-member district, they receive four of the ten seats—or 40% of the seats. If another party wins 20% of the vote, they get two seats, and so on.[40] Proportional voting is the norm in most democracies around the world, but in this country it has been adopted only by a handful of jurisdictions—all of them local.

This electoral method, in one form or another, has proven crucial to the establishment and maintenance of a multiparty system of governance in many other countries, since third, fourth, or fifth parties that cannot win pluralities can nevertheless often garner a large enough proportion of the vote to capture at least a few seats in a local, provincial, or national legislative body. This is exactly why America's two parties have maintained implacable resistance to the spread of proportional representation systems. Seldom as they may agree on anything of substance in the public policy arena, the two parties have no difficulty in concurring on their opposition to this democratic reform. The flip side of this dynamic is fairly obvious: if immoderate partisanship is one of the most virulent diseases infecting our body politic, this well-tested means of loosening the grip of partisanship has to be on the menu of democratic reform. Meanwhile, another kind of reform is gaining real momentum as it takes on some of the most polarizing features of the two-party system.

REDISTRICTING REFORM

Introduced in chapter 2 as a major contributor to partisan quicksand and therefore one of the most serious afflictions besetting our body politic, gerrymandering has naturally become a focus of democratic reform. The heart of those reforms is almost always an effort to take control of redistricting out of the hands of state legislators and, one way or another, to establish a higher level of citizen control over this key democratic process.

This issue has a long and complex history, but we might take up its recent lineage in California, with Proposition 11—the so-called Voters FIRST Act—which qualified for the ballot in 2008.[41] This citizen initiative proposed the creation of a fourteen-member "Citizens Redistricting Commission" to oversee the redrawing of state legislative district boundaries. Sponsored by California Common Cause, the initiative was supported not only by the California League of Women Voters but by former governors Gray Davis (a Democrat) and his Republican successor, Arnold Schwarzenegger.[42] Endorsed by the *Los Angeles Times*, the *San Francisco Chronicle*, the *Sacramento Bee*, and a broad range of civic and business groups, the initiative was strongly opposed by both Senator Barbara Boxer and Congresswoman Nancy Pelosi, then Speaker of the U.S. House of Representatives, and opposed perhaps most tellingly by the

California Democratic Party.[43] The state party's opposition was succinctly summarized by Willie Brown, then serving as mayor of San Francisco after a long career as Speaker of the California assembly, where he and Democratic congressman Phillip Burton had in the 1980s made gerrymandering all but synonymous with California Democratic politics. "Let me assure you," Brown now told the California delegation to the 2008 Democratic National Convention in Denver, "whoever is drawing the lines will dictate the course of action of who gets elected." Ever the vote counter, Brown concluded his remarks in opposition to redistricting reform by telling the assembled Democrats, "We have got to make sure that the no vote on Prop 11 equals the yes vote for Barack Obama."[44]

As it turned out, that didn't happen. Obama carried California by a 61 percent landslide, but despite Brown's, Boxer's, Pelosi's, and the Democratic Party's opposition, voters narrowly approved Proposition 11.[45] In so doing, they took control of the redistricting process for legislative districts out of the hands of the legislature itself and gave it instead to a new fourteen-member commission. Any registered voter could apply to serve on the commission. From the resulting applicant pool, government auditors were required to select sixty names. Legislative leaders could then play their only remaining role by exercising a limited number of vetoes. From the remaining pool, the auditors were required to pick eight commission members by lottery; those commissioners would then pick six additional members for a total of fourteen.

Emboldened by this successful change in the process for drawing the state's legislative district lines, the reformers next sought to extend citizen control to California's fifty-three congressional districts—the nation's largest delegation. Hoping to enact that reform in time for the next round of reapportionment, the reform coalition went to work to secure enough signatures to put Proposition 20, the U.S. Congressional Redistricting Initiative, on the 2010 ballot.[46] At the same time, the opponents of the 2008 reform were also busy gathering signatures, and they secured enough of them to put another initiative on the ballot: one that would repeal Proposition 11. This time, the reformers won decisively on both fronts. Proposition 20 garnered 61.2 percent of the vote, while Proposition 27, the repeal initiative, lost by nearly the same lopsided margin. Redistricting reform was now an indisputable fact of life in California.[47]

The effects of the reform were already apparent in the 2012 election, the first to take place under the new system and the new maps. After years of universal reelection of incumbents, five congressional incumbents actually lost to challengers in 2012, along with three state legislative incumbents.[48] With many other factors at work as there always are, these results cannot confidently be attributed to the reapportionment reform, but if the unaccustomed vulnerability of incumbents persists through more election cycles, the effect of the citizen commission will be clearer. Meanwhile, this initiative is clearly another case of the muscle-strengthening and momentum-building dynamic of such reform activities. The difference in the 2008 and 2010 initiative results is evidence of that growing capacity. It may also be evidence of a settling-in of expectations among the broader electorate—an expanding and deepening determination to maintain citizen control over this key feature of representative democracy.

That certainly seemed to be the situation a few years later in Ohio. For decades, the state's highly partisan redistricting commission had drawn gerrymandered maps of mostly safe (that is, uncompetitive) congressional and legislative districts. After three previous efforts to reform that system had failed, a citizen-driven campaign, spearheaded by the Ohio chapters of Common Cause and the League of Women Voters, had persuaded a bipartisan majority of the Ohio legislature to put a reform proposal on the ballot. In November 2015, voters overwhelmingly approved the ballot measure to replace the old redistricting commission with one that would be required to reflect a partisan balance and to draw compact districts that were constitutionally prohibited from deliberately favoring either party.[49] That ballot measure applied only to legislative redistricting, but the citizen coalition that had supported it immediately launched a petition campaign to create a new ballot measure for an amendment to the state constitution extending the new system to congressional redistricting. In May of 2018, Ohio voters approved that amendment by a nearly 3–1 margin statewide, with at least 2–1 approval in every congressional district, Republican and Democrat seats alike.[50]

Meanwhile, the ability of citizens to enact reforms of this kind had received a boost from an unexpected quarter: the U.S. Supreme Court (or at least from five of its members.) In 2000, Arizona citizens had used their Progressive Era initiative mechanism to place on the November ballot a constitutional amendment to take the power of drawing legislative and congressional district lines from the Arizona legislature, handing it instead to an appointed redistricting commission.[51] Legislative leaders would still play the key role in appointing the commission, so this reform did not achieve as much citizen control as California would with Proposition 11, but the Arizona reform represented an important step away from the legislature directly drawing its own reapportionment maps. In November 2000, Arizona voters approved the measure by a resounding 56 to 44 percent margin.[52] The redistricting commission was duly appointed and proceeded to fulfill its responsibilities following the 2000 census.

After the 2010 census, a new commission was appointed and had proceeded once again to adjust congressional and legislative district boundaries when the Arizona legislature filed a lawsuit to prevent the commission from redrawing the congressional boundaries.[53] The legislators argued that the commission's authority to set those boundaries was barred by Article I, Section 4, of the U.S. Constitution, which provides that "the Times, Places and Manner of holding Elections for Senators and Representatives shall be prescribed in each State by the Legislature thereof."[54] Since Arizona's reapportionment commission had been created by citizen initiative, not by the legislature, that body now argued that the portion of the initiative relating to congressional redistricting should be struck down. When the U.S. district court upheld the commission's authority, the legislature appealed to the Supreme Court. On June 29, 2015, that court announced its decision, in an opinion written by Justice Ruth Bader Ginsburg.

"The people of Arizona turned to the initiative to curb the practice of gerrymandering and, thereby, to ensure that Members of Congress would have 'an habitual recollection of their dependence on the people,'" Ginsburg wrote. "In so acting, Arizona voters sought to restore 'the core principle of republican government,' namely, 'that the voters should choose their representatives, not the other way around.' The Elections Clause does not hinder that endeavor."[55] Specifically, the majority opinion interpreted the constitutional reference to "the Legislature" to encompass any legislative process approved by a state, including citizen initiatives. "Redistricting is a legislative function," Ginsburg wrote, "to be performed in accordance with the state's prescriptions for lawmaking, which may include the referendum and the governor's veto." Ginsburg was joined in this holding by Justices Breyer, Kagan, Sotomayor, and (crucially) Kennedy.

Not surprisingly, the Court's four most consistently conservative justices entered a strong dissent, written by Chief Justice Roberts, and focused on what the dissenters saw as the unambiguous language of the Constitution. When that document referred to "the Legislature," Roberts in effect wrote, it meant "the Legislature," not some form of legislating never dreamed of by the document's drafters.[56] Given such a forceful (and indeed plausible) dissent, there was good reason to suspect that, if either Kennedy or Ginsburg (the two oldest justices) were to be replaced during the Trump presidency, the ruling in the Arizona case might well not survive a challenge from some other state that had also reformed congressional redistricting by citizen initiative.

When Kennedy's retirement in 2018 was followed by Trump's appointment of Justice Kavanaugh, that possibility may have moved up a notch or two. Its likelihood remained purely speculative at the time of this writing; however, even if a new majority were to reverse the Arizona ruling, it would not constitute anything like a fatal blow to redistricting reform. For one thing, the language of the Constitution on which that ruling turned only applies to congressional districting; reform of the method of drawing state legislative boundaries would not be affected. And of course, the option of persuading state legislatures themselves to reform congressional redistricting would still be open under even the strictest reading of the constitutional language. In any event, any of these paths to reform will depend very substantially on citizen activism and will thus contribute to democratic body conditioning.

Because the Arizona case focused solely on the issue of who could set the rules for congressional redistricting, it did not require the Court to take up the issue of gerrymandering itself, or any other substantive feature of the redistricting process. But in a later case from North Carolina, gerrymandering did directly occupy the Court's attention. In its May 22, 2017, ruling in *Cooper v. Harris*, the Court held that North Carolina's legislature had unconstitutionally redrawn the boundaries of two legislative districts.[57] What made this redistricting unconstitutional was its racial dimension: the Court affirmed a trial court finding that the Republican legislature had intentionally drawn the boundaries of those districts in such a way as to concentrate black voters in as few districts as possible (thus leaving more districts free of that mostly Democratic influence). As Justice Kagan succinctly put the matter at the outset of her opinion on behalf of the majority, "The Constitution entrusts States with the job of designing congressional districts. But it also imposes an important constraint: A State may not use race as the predominant factor in drawing district lines unless it has a compelling reason."[58]

What is important about the holding for the purposes of this chapter is what it did not address. Important as the decision was in terms of racial equity, it was only in those terms that it confronted the issue of gerrymandering. The case was argued and decided on equal protection grounds, as any case attempting to challenge gerrymandering is likely to be. At that time, the draft of this chapter had noted that any Democratic voter in North Carolina might argue that Republican legislators had gerrymandered congressional districts in such a way as to reduce Democrats' voting power. It is that inequity, of course (whichever party inflicts it), that lies at the core of what is most objectionable in good government terms about gerrymandering because it is this partisan inequity that allows for the creation of "safe" districts. With the 2017 decision in *Cooper*, it became conceivable that the Supreme Court might someday find all such partisan gerrymandering to be unconstitutional.

In fact, just two years later, the Republican gerrymandering in North Carolina was back before the Court, along with an equally egregious Democratic gerrymander from Pennsylvania.[59] Race was not a factor in either of these cases; they were both straightforward, indeed brazen, partisan gerrymanders, and in a 5–4 decision, with Chief Justice Roberts writing for the majority, the Court held in effect that neither Democrats simply as Democrats nor Republicans as Republicans can invoke the same level of constitutional scrutiny of a redistricting map as can a member of a class (like African Americans) that has been historically subject to discrimination. Not only are Democrats and Republicans not the kind of protected class that can command the strictest equal protection scrutiny, but the majority held that their fundamentally political nature puts their purely partisan gerrymandering beyond the Court's jurisdiction. This was the feature of the *Rucho* decision that may eventually have the most profound implications for the issues of central concern to this book. For that reason, we need to examine the ruling a bit more closely.

What the conservative majority did in *Rucho* was to revive the political question doctrine that Justice Curtis had invoked in his *Dred Scott* dissent. Curtis' concern seemed to evaporate in this century as conservative majorities of justices stepped boldly into turbulent political waters in cases such as *Bush v. Gore* and *Citizens United*. Each of those cases presented what Justice Curtis had called (and what conservative jurisprudence might still call) "a legislative or political, not a judicial question."[60] Indeed, in *Rucho*, Chief Justice Roberts wrote, "The question here is whether there is an 'appropriate role for the Federal Judiciary' in remedying the problem of partisan gerrymandering—whether such claims are claims of *legal* right, resolvable according to *legal* principles, or political questions that must find their resolution elsewhere."[61] The majority unequivocally chose the latter option. "To hold that legislators cannot take partisan interests into account when drawing district lines would essentially countermand the Framers' decision to entrust districting to political entities."[62]

Justice Kagan, in a dissent joined by Justices Ginsburg, Breyer, and Sotomayor, took very strong exception:

> The partisan gerrymanders in these cases deprived citizens of the most fundamental of their constitutional rights: the rights to participate equally in the political process, to join with others to advance political beliefs, and to choose their political representatives. In so doing, the partisan gerrymanders here debased and dishonored our democracy, turning upside-down the core American idea that all governmental power derives from the people. These gerrymanders enabled politicians to entrench themselves in office as against voters' preferences. They promoted partisanship above respect for the popular will. They encouraged a politics of polarization and dysfunction. If left unchecked, gerrymanders like the ones here may irreparably damage our system of government.[63]

Kagan is applying here just the kind of "democracy lens" that I have argued was missing in the majority opinion in *Citizens United* and indeed throughout most of the Court's other campaign finance jurisprudence. If those rulings had shown even the slightest concern for the rights of citizens "to participate equally in the political process," they would not so readily have "debased and dishonored our democracy, turning upside-down the core American idea that all governmental power derives from the people," and would therefore not have been so prone to "irreparably damage our system of government" as they will have done and will continue to do if they are not rescinded. At the same time, though, the majority opinion in *Rucho* may prove to be more significant than the dissent in enabling the Court eventually to recede from the democratically most damaging of its campaign finance rulings. The revival of the political question doctrine, if it is given some real scope and staying power by the *Rucho* majority or other justices, could provide one of the most secure stepping-stones on the path toward an authentically conservative, and at the same time a genuinely democratic, exercise of judicial self-restraint.

Indeed, Roberts' invocation of the political question doctrine would be given greater force and weight if it were clothed in some of Kagan's stirring democratic language. And the doctrine should wear such garments. Much as I agree with Kagan about the damage that unrestrained partisan gerrymandering has done to the practice of democracy, I agree with Roberts that the courts are not the place to address that problem. With this issue, as with most of the problems afflicting our democracy, it is citizens themselves that will have to take up and carry to completion the work of healing democracy. It is above all citizen action that has already brought both Electoral College and redistricting reform as far as they have come to this point. To an even greater extent, it is democratic citizenship that will have to bring excessive partisanship under control. To that end, citizens are going to need to step up their game in various ways, including the reform mechanism that I will conclude with: a democracy lobby powerful enough to reclaim our republic.

CREATION AND MAINTENANCE OF
A POTENT DEMOCRACY LOBBY

In the introduction, I invoked the image of Archimedes's lever as a way of picturing how we might approach the exceptionally daunting enterprise of moving the heavy weight of embedded obstacles to democracy, such as the Electoral College, the role of unconstrained partisanship in our governing institutions, and the role of unlimited money in our elections. At a minimum, to reclaim the democratic potential of our governing institutions from the overburden of partisanship and plutocracy that now encrusts them, citizens will eventually need to deploy some kind of political action committee or lobbying organization capable of securing the support of elected officials for a range of contentious reforms. With the Electoral College, for example, no matter which of the multiple paths to reform we might consider—whether a constitutional amendment, an interstate compact, or more localized changes in how individual states allocate their electoral votes—on any of these paths, the fate of the reform will eventually hang on votes by state legislators or members of Congress, or on the signatures or vetoes of governors or presidents. Given the multiple forms of resistance that are guaranteed to confront any of these reforms, their success will depend on the exercise of credible and persistent pressure on those public officials.

While individual arenas of reform (like the Electoral College or campaign finance) will certainly have their own issue-specific advocacy organizations, there is also reason to believe that effective democratic reform will depend on some level of coordination among these arenas and that this will depend, in turn, on citizens uniting their energy and resources into some more coordinated way of holding elected officials accountable for democratic restoration generally. It is the mechanism for applying that pressure that is the focus of the remainder of this chapter. For now, let's just call this indispensable mechanism the "democracy lobby" while we begin to imagine some of its characteristics and its promise.

Like nearly everything else about the work of democratic restoration, the particulars of a democracy lobby are not amenable to up-front prescription. They will have to emerge organically from the circumstances they seek to mobilize and address. There will almost certainly come a time when someone will have to impose some design specifications on the emerging mechanism, but this chapter will not do that in any but the most sketchy and suggestive of ways. Our purpose here is only to begin to imagine the Archimedean lever we are calling a democracy lobby and to imagine how we might deploy it in the enterprise of restoring democracy.

A first step in that act of imagination might be to say that, at a minimum, this democracy lobby is going to have to be at least as powerful as the gun lobby and at least as effective in advancing the cause of democracy as the National Rifle Association (NRA) has been in pursuing its objectives. In fact, I am going to use the NRA as a kind of foil (if not as a model) for the democracy lobby. I should disclose at the outset that I am among the millions of Americans who believe that the NRA has too often succeeded in promoting harmful policies or blocking beneficial initiatives at all levels of our government and that its muscular (some might say strong-arm or even bullying) tactics have not infrequently contributed to the weakening of our democratic culture. Having claimed that bias, though, I want to make it clear that my purpose in bringing the NRA into this chapter's analysis is not to denigrate the activities of the NRA or the motives of any of its members. In fact, as I hope will become quite clear, I have used this example both because it has been a supremely effective lobby and because I believe its members' motivations can shed a helpful light on what might motivate and sustain an equally effective democracy lobby.

Saying that the democracy lobby has to be "at least as effective as the gun lobby" is primarily a way of illustrating the political muscularity that is called for. Other organizations would also offer instructive examples: the senior lobby, exemplified by the American Association of Retired Persons, or the Israel lobby, exercising its formidable power through the American Israel Public Affairs Committee. These and other impressively powerful lobbies should be carefully studied for lessons about how they have built and sustained their often-remarkable effectiveness. For now, it is enough to note some of their main features, as they might come to play a role in a democracy lobby.

Without something like a democracy lobby at least as powerful and persistent as these well-funded and superbly organized groups, there is no hope of persuading 67 U.S. senators, 290 members of the House, and 38 state legislatures to amend the Constitution to abolish the Electoral College or to overturn *Citizens United* and the other Supreme Court rulings that have so seriously undermined democratic control of our elections. That magnitude of reform, necessary as it may prove to be, simply won't happen without the kind of organized, relentless pressure that the NRA consistently brings to bear in the cause its members so fervently support. But if millions of citizens who are fed up with all the procedures and practices that have so weakened our capacity for self-government were to lend their support to a well-organized democracy lobby, none of these reforms would be beyond our reach.

How, then, could a democracy lobby with the necessary kind of political clout come to be? To begin with, as with any major, long-term advocacy effort, certain more or less technical elements will have to be put in place and maintained. Here are a few likely components of such an effort:

1. An effective democracy lobby will have to include mechanisms for monitoring and publicizing the variety of ways in which elected officials are already engaged in supporting or undermining democratic practices. At a minimum, this would entail creating, maintaining, and disseminating a scorecard where key votes on democratically significant issues are tabulated. Obvious examples would be any votes in either congressional chamber on resolutions proposing constitutional amendments addressing campaign finance. Short of that, both state and national legislation regulating campaign spending or aiming for greater transparency in that arena would be natural candidates for such a scorecard.

2. A democracy scorecard would reach beyond issues of campaign finance to embrace other key elements of the democratic reform agenda. Wherever state legislatures have an opportunity to depoliticize the redistricting process, the democracy lobby should be keeping score, and the same is true of any efforts to democratize the presidential election process.

3. As the democracy lobby matures, it would naturally begin to identify other issues that would become candidates for score keeping. And since nonincumbent candidates would not be subject to that kind of scoring, it would also be necessary to devise candidate questionnaires to put all candidates on record with regard to crucial issues on the reform agenda.

4. The results of both questionnaires and scorecards would then need to be disseminated in a form that enabled and encouraged voters to reward candidates with good records or supportive stances and to withhold support from those with poor democratic credentials.

5. This reference to disseminating information is a reminder that the democracy lobby will have to be digitized to a fault, with its own very informative and interactive website and a full range of social media options. I will have more to say about the content of these conversations later, but at a minimum they will have to provide a forum—a public space—where good democratic citizens and public servants can get to know each other better and begin to strategize and leverage their democratic capacity.

6. Finally, a political action committee would have to be established, with enough financial backing and political will to put the democracy lobby's money where its mouth is, by supporting candidates who are committed to the democratic reform agenda and opposing those who most significantly oppose or hinder it.

While we can learn valuable lessons from a number of powerful advocacy organizations, including the NRA, we might be inclined to conclude that the similarity would be limited to such mechanics. Beyond technique, however, lies the crucial issue of people. All these powerful advocacy organizations depend substantially on a large and highly motivated membership or support base. By definition, that will be at least as true of an effective democracy lobby. So, who are the people who will power that effort? Here, in particular, a closer look suggests that the gun lobby may have broader and deeper lessons to teach a democracy lobby than we would at first suspect.

It starts with empowerment and self-determination. Any kind of firearm is almost by definition an empowering instrument, and anyone who holds and shoots a rifle or a handgun experiences a very palpable form of empowerment. This is true regardless of the cultural, social, or political status of the one holding the gun. If any part of that background is disempowering, however—if the individual is poor or is marginalized in any other way, the power that individual holds in the form of a firearm is all but guaranteed to take some of the edge off that experience of disempowerment. It only makes sense, then, that the more dimensions of disempowerment there are at work in a person's life, the more welcome this tangible form of empowerment is likely to be.

Having less power than we might like is something almost all of us experience, at least occasionally. Since most of us feel that we inhabit a world that is largely beyond our control (and becoming steadily more so), we all compensate for that lack or loss of control in a number of ways. We might, for example, become annoying "control freaks" over some tiny corner of our universe whose contours we can determine. We might resort to various forms of escape from the discomfort of disempowerment, whether in drugs, computer games, sex, or even books. In this context, to the extent that owning guns is an expression of the deeply human need for self-determination in a complex and threatening world, it is only one response among many, and in its own terms, it is a perfectly sensible response.

But this particular form of self-empowerment carries with it some extra dimensions—let's just say some added firepower—that most others lack. If owning, holding, and shooting a gun is an empowering experience, that very tangible, physical sense of empowerment is leveraged remarkably when individual gun owners are given access to a form of political power that most of the rest of us never experience. To know, for example, that over 80 percent of your neighbors favor stronger background checks on gun purchasers but that you and your fellow NRA members hold in your hands the power to coerce the U.S. Senate into defying the clear wishes of such a large majority of their constituents in order to protect your passionately defended but minority position— that kind of political leverage is empowering in a way that firing a handgun or even an assault rifle can never match.[64]

When those two very different forms of power—the physical and the political—are blended in such a way as to become psychologically indistinguishable, the result is something quite astonishing. And when that power is surrounded and infused with the purported blessing of the U.S. Constitution itself, it assumes truly historic proportions. For the most remarkable dimension of the empowered gun lobby, of course, is that it comes equipped with its very own constitutional amendment. Those among us who fight back against disempowerment by becoming control freaks or exercise addicts have nothing even remotely comparable to that. Or so it might seem.

The fact is, though, that the potential participants in a democracy lobby do have something comparable to, and indeed something far more powerful than, the combination of the NRA with the Second Amendment. Millions of American citizens share an embodied practice of democratic problem solving that we deploy day after day to make our neighborhoods and our communities more humanly satisfying for ourselves and those who will follow us. We are effective at shaping our world in that way in no small part because we have taught ourselves to speak honestly and to listen openly to one another. Thus we bring the practice of democratic deliberation to bear every day, secure in the knowledge that our national and many of our state constitutions protect our deliberations, not so that we can express ourselves as individuals but so that we can continue to solve problems and realize opportunities together as citizens.

That work is rarely easy, and sometimes it is very difficult indeed. The hardest problems, the biggest challenges, the most vexing conundrums are the ones that put our democratic skills and our republican institutions to their greatest test. Sometimes we may even have to amend our constitutions themselves so we can continue to govern ourselves effectively. Our ancestors gave us that option (and exercised it themselves) because they knew that no truly self-governing people could do without it. If we now have to change our national Constitution to make the election of the president more democratic or to keep all of our elections free of the domination of great wealth, then we will do that because we are—and we are determined to remain—a self-governing people, fully capable of setting the rules under which we shape the conditions of our lives.

The sustaining article of faith behind this book is that we can do this. In fact, the restoration of our body politic to the kind of vigor we expect of it depends fundamentally on our knowing that we can do it. We might remind ourselves that there is simply no one else who can do it. It is, absolutely and inescapably, up to us. That is the practical truth, and the theoretical one comes to the same thing since the very concept of democracy rests on the assumption that we, the people, are capable of governing ourselves. If we ever come seriously to doubt that we possess that capacity, it will mean that our democracy has already expired. While some among us have no doubt (and understandably) reached that despairing conclusion, it hasn't by any means overtaken all of us—in large part because we continue to govern ourselves, imperfectly but effectively, close to home.

There is no denying, though, that we have gone through a long period of declining confidence in the effectiveness and indeed the legitimacy of our larger democratic institutions. Because those are *our* institutions—because they are precisely the instruments through which we govern ourselves—our loss of confidence in the responsiveness or effectiveness of those institutions means one of two things. Either it means that we have lost faith in our ability to govern ourselves—and are therefore no longer in any meaningful sense a self-governing people—or it means that it is time to get to work to heal the wounds and diseases that so seriously afflict our republic. There is really only one choice that a democratic people can make. This book arises from the conviction—and is dedicated to the proposition—that we can and will get this job done.

Epilogue

Democracy in America and America in the World

They [Americans] see that up to now, democratic institutions have prospered among them, while they have failed in the rest of the world; they therefore have an immense opinion of themselves, and they are not far from believing that they form a species apart from the human race.

Alexis de Tocqueville, Democracy in America

. . . a decent respect to the opinions of mankind . . .

—Thomas Jefferson, Declaration of Independence

In chapter 4, I recall how my great-uncle, Walter D. Kemmis, served a heroic role in my childhood, his legislative experience, reaching back to the Progressive Era, serving as an inspiration to my own lifelong love of politics. In those terms, Walter stood alongside another of my childhood heroes: Montana's own Mike Mansfield. First elected to the U.S. House of Representatives two years before I was born and then to the Senate, he became majority leader in 1961 and served the longest tenure in that office in American history. Upon Mansfield's retirement from the Senate in 1977, President Carter appointed him ambassador to Japan, where he continued to serve through all eight years of Ronald Reagan's administration. By then, his career-long interest in Asia had been carried over into the mission of the Mansfield Center,[1] established at the University of Montana in 1983.

It has been my good fortune to present guest lectures to many of the groups of international students that the Mansfield Center brings to Missoula, and those occasions nearly always draw my attention to various dimensions of democracy—local, national, and global. It was mostly my experience in local politics that has led the Mansfield Center staff to ask me to meet with these students. I have always spent some time discussing with the visitors what they have experienced of Missoula—especially the riverfront trails and parks and the other features of the community that I described in previous chapters. I'm always impressed with how eager the students are not only to learn about Missoula but to think about how my neighbors' experience of caring for this community might relate to the students' experiences in their own communities. The conversations become even more intense as we start to ask what we might learn, together, from these local experiences about our ability as human beings to govern ourselves and, in so doing, to address the problems we all agree that we face globally.

The nature of these discussions changed fairly substantially after Donald Trump assumed the presidency in 2017. With his unilateral withdrawal of the United States from the Paris Agreement on climate change and from the international agreement on Iranian nuclear containment, his open declaration of trade wars with both former adversaries and long-time allies, and his proclivity for replacing normal forms of diplomacy with bombastic messages on Twitter, it became, frankly, an embarrassment to speak of American democracy to these bright and globally engaged students. My one hope in that painful context was that the Trump debacle might, whenever it should end, create an opportunity for America to reposition itself in relation to the family of nations— and (in a truly democratic spirit) to bring our historically endowed blessings to bear on the global challenges confronting us all.

But that possibility, like so many of the prospects for democratic renewal examined in this book, would require us to recognize that, as bizarre and all-too-often dangerous (perhaps even impeachable) as Trump's words and deeds might be, they were not something totally apart from a longer history that would have to be engaged if America and the world were to move together toward a more fair, farsighted, and secure future. For, at the same time that American democracy is beset by major injuries that have seriously weakened our domestic problem-solving capacity, it has become clear that the global governance structure that emerged from World War II is itself no longer adequate to the multiplying challenges of our time. From climate change to nuclear-armed rogue states, from cyber espionage to global pandemics, we face a growing list of consequential and often confounding global problems. Given the inescapable fact that more and more human systems of survival are becoming globally integrated, this list of planetary challenges can only continue to expand. We have no choice, then, but to improve our global problem-solving capacity.

What that might look like is a subject far beyond the reach of both this book and its author. Whatever else might come to characterize a global structure for problem solving, though, we can be certain that most of the world will demand that it be in some fundamental way democratic. And in terms of global democracy, we might at a minimum say that whenever an issue of genuinely global concern presents itself, unilateral action by any one nation is inherently undemocratic both in principle and in practice. In terms of principle, democracy requires that all participants have a voice in the decisions made by a democratic body or institution. In terms of practice, one of the lasting values of democracy, as preceding chapters emphasize, is that many minds almost always make better, more sustainable decisions than any single actor can reliably attain—and this is as true among nations as among individual humans. It is the combination of this principle and this practice that has made democracy so widely appealing, and it is this combination that will continue to strengthen the demand for democratic practices within global settings and institutions.

Regrettably, for all its pride in being the "beacon of democracy," America has in the last few decades fallen into a dangerous presumption that this core incompatibility between democracy and unilateralism does not, for some reason, apply to us. And while we never quite say it, we seem to think that we alone are exempt. Which is to say that this deeply problematic penchant for unilateralism is closely associated with the ingrained idea of American exceptionalism. Whether in the hands of foreigners (like Tocqueville) or of Americans, the concept of American exceptionalism has always been far more fruitful and, frankly, more attractive when it takes the form of inquiry rather than assertion.[2] Asking why America has provided fertile soil for democracy is much more appealing and potentially more enlightening than shouting, "We're number one!"

Inattentive as this and other boorish forms of the claim of exceptionalism are to what Jefferson called the "opinions of mankind," however, this kind of flag-waving has done far less actual harm than the more studied claims of American exceptionalism that have assumed such a central role in our foreign policy since the end of the Cold War. And the truth is that Democrats and Republicans have contributed about equally to this refrain. Bill Clinton's secretary of state, Madeleine Albright, provided a memorable formulation in 1998. At a crisis point in international efforts to halt Iraq's development of nuclear weapons, Albright declared that the Clinton administration was prepared (and indeed preparing) to use force for that purpose. During an appearance on *The Today Show* on February 19, Albright said, "Let me say that we are doing everything possible so that American men and women in uniform do not have to go out there again. . . . But if we have to use force, it is because we are America; we are the indispensable nation."[3]

The "indispensable nation" phrase might have been taken with a grain of salt or seen as an incautious overstatement were it not that this is precisely how America seemed to see its role on the global stage in the years following the collapse of the Soviet empire. As the world's sole remaining superpower, America now clearly occupied a unique niche, but it was one that was inherently problematic in terms of anything like a democratic system of global governance.

With the election of George W. Bush to the presidency, official policy turned in a starkly undemocratic direction on the global stage while simultaneously expanding the claim that our policy sought to bring the blessings of democracy to more of the world. In 2002, a year after the attack on the World Trade Center, the Bush administration issued a new version of the National Security Strategy (NSS).[4] This document boldly proclaimed the exceptional position now occupied by the United States: "The United States possesses unprecedented—and unequaled—strength and influence in the world. Sustained by faith in the principles of liberty, and the value of a free society, this position comes with unparalleled responsibilities, obligations, and opportunity."[5] While the document voiced support for cooperation among nations, it left no doubt that America was prepared to use its exceptional power to advance its interests and objectives in ways that were themselves unprecedented. Secure in its hegemonic position, America now declared its willingness not only to use its overwhelming power to repel attacks but even to use that power preemptively. "The greater the threat, the greater is the risk of inaction—and the more compelling the case for taking anticipatory action to defend ourselves, even if uncertainty remains as to the time and place of the enemy's attack. To forestall or prevent such hostile acts by our adversaries, the United States will, if necessary, act preemptively."[6]

Having persuaded a majority of the American people and their congressional representatives that Iraq was bristling with weapons of mass destruction, the Bush administration proceeded to act on the basis of its new policy, attacking Iraq in force without provocation. When the American occupation of a conquered Iraq revealed none of the weapons that had supposedly justified the invasion, the administration began to argue that our real mission was to democratize Iraq.[7]

That belated statement of our objective never carried much credibility. But if we view the invasion against the background of the 2002 NSS, a much more credible and considerably more sinister objective presents itself. At its core, that version of the NSS proclaimed American hegemony, not only as a fact but as a deliberate policy. The world order that it envisioned was one in which the United States, as the sole remaining superpower, would exercise its own will whenever and wherever it chose, whether provoked or not. Viewed in that light, the "shock and awe" occasioned by our assault on Iraq might be hoped to be felt in Beijing as well as Baghdad.

Whatever the precise intention of the blustering language of the NSS may have been, the period from its publication in September 2002 through President Bush's appearance in a flight jacket under a "mission accomplished" banner on the deck of the USS *Abraham Lincoln* in May of the following year marked the flood stage of that particularly swaggering strain of American exceptionalism. But it certainly was not the last instance, and the next would come from another Democratic president.

The context was the protracted civil war in Syria, which had itself emerged from the democratically inspired "Arab Spring" of 2011. The Obama administration, while calling for the ouster of the Syrian dictator Bashar el-Assad, had resisted all pleas from the rebels and their supporters for America to take an active role in the civil war. In August 2012, however, Obama made a unilateral declaration in America's name that would set the stage for the next year's crisis. Rejecting once again the calls for a more direct American involvement in the civil war, Obama nevertheless went on to say, "We have been very clear to the Assad regime, but also to other players on the ground, that a red line for us is [if] we start seeing a whole bunch of chemical weapons moving around or being utilized. That would change my calculus. That would change my equation."[8]

A year later, in August 2013, an attack on a Damascus neighborhood by chemically armed rockets killed over one thousand people, many of them children. While Assad claimed that it was the rebels who had launched the attack, Obama, convinced with good reason that Assad's forces were responsible, declared his intention to order a limited but consequential American military response.[9] The American public's reaction to this threat was mixed at best, and the international response was even less enthusiastic. When Prime Minister David Cameron, for example, sought parliamentary approval for the United Kingdom's participation in the threatened American action, Parliament simply refused.[10] Paul Flynn, a Labour member of Parliament, caught the historical essence of the matter when he asked, "Is not the real reason we are here today . . . a result of the American president having foolishly drawn a red line, so that he is now in the position of either having to attack or face humiliation?"[11]

It was, in other words, not the threat of force itself but the unilateralism of the American policy that was so problematic. And here, once again, American unilateralism was justified by invoking American exceptionalism. "America is not the world's policeman," Obama asserted.[12] "Terrible things happen across the globe, and it is beyond our means to right every wrong. But when, with modest effort and risk, we can stop children from being gassed to death, and thereby make our own children safer over the long run, I believe we should act. That's what makes America different. That's what makes us exceptional. With humility, but with resolve, let us never lose sight of that essential truth."[13]

It isn't very difficult to imagine people in other countries or continents asking if Americans think they are the only people who care about children being gassed to death. Here is an instance where "a decent respect for the opinions of mankind" or perhaps some of the humility that Obama invoked in his next breath might have been in order. Whatever he meant by his claim to exceptionalism, Obama had opened himself and his country to an all-too-obvious rejoinder, and Vladimir Putin lost no time in delivering it. In a remarkable diplomatic move, Putin spoke over the head of America's president, addressing American citizens directly in an op-ed in the *New York Times*.[14]

Putin concluded his essay by observing that he had "carefully studied [Obama's] address to the nation on Tuesday. And I would rather disagree with a case he made on American exceptionalism, stating that the United States' policy is 'what makes America different. It's what makes us exceptional.' It is extremely dangerous to encourage people to see themselves as exceptional, whatever the motivation. There are big countries and small countries, rich and poor, those with long democratic traditions and those still finding their way to democracy. Their policies differ, too. We are all different, but when we ask for the Lord's blessings, we must not forget that God created us equal."[15]

The profound cynicism of Putin's rhetoric was overshadowed by its brilliance and its laser-like effectiveness in probing the weakness in the American position. Here was the famously manipulative president of Russia (of all people) lecturing the American people, with unimpeachable justification, on what it means to act democratically on the global stage. He told us what almost none of our elected leaders ever dared to say: that "it is extremely dangerous to encourage people to see themselves as exceptional." Of course it is, and furthermore, such an attitude makes it much more difficult for that people to play a constructive role in global self-determination. Putin topped this off by reminding us of the language Jefferson had employed in our greatest democratic document!

We might have expected that this would be the last of President Obama's invocation of American exceptionalism, at least for a while. But remarkably, within a fortnight, he used very similar language, this time in an address to the United Nations itself. "I believe America must remain engaged for our own security," he told the assembled nations, "I believe the world is better for it. Some may disagree, but I believe that America is exceptional—in part because we have shown a willingness, through the sacrifice of blood and treasure, to stand up not only for our own narrow self-interest, but for the interests of all."[16]

By this point, American exceptionalism had begun to look like a concept in search of a rationale. How, for example, was Obama's claim that America was exceptional because it was willing to sacrifice "for the interests of all" supposed to sound to the scores of nations that have, over the years, faithfully provided soldiers for United Nations peacekeeping forces—thousands of whom have been killed or wounded "for the interests of all?" That way of justifying unilateral action only obscures the real (and much more legitimate) reason that America repeatedly decides that it has to act on its own (to act exactly like the world's policeman), which is simply because the existing structure of global governance is not adequate to the planetary challenges of our age.

In fact, beyond the diplomatic gamesmanship of the Syrian crisis, both Russia and America recognized (at least implicitly) the dangerously dysfunctional nature of the existing international system. In his *New York Times* column, President Putin asserted that "[n]o one wants the United Nations to suffer the fate of the League of Nations, which collapsed because it lacked real leverage."[17] A few days later, President Obama expressed his own concern about the United Nations. Referring to the "profound challenges" arising in the global arena, Obama asked "whether we possess the wisdom and the courage, as nation-states and members of an international community, to squarely meet those challenges; whether the United Nations can meet the tests of our time."[18]

On one level, Obama and Putin were setting one another up to be blamed for the failures of the international system. Putin wrote that the United Nations could "suffer the fate of the League of Nations . . . if influential countries bypass the United Nations and take military action without Security Council authorization,"[19] while Obama's concern that the Security Council might not force Syria to comply with its resolution was clearly an allusion to Russia's ability, if not propensity, to veto such coercive steps. But perhaps what mattered more than this maneuvering to put the other at fault was the implicit recognition by both parties that this key feature of the global governance system was fragile at best and at worst "incapable of enforcing the most basic of international laws."[20]

This is not the place to examine in any detail the reforms that will be required to prepare our global institutions to deal effectively with the steadily growing list of planetary challenges. What is clear is that the world has outgrown the governance system that was put in place by the victors in World War II (the five permanent, veto-wielding members of the Security Council).

The situation is remarkably similar to that confronting the new American nation soon after its war of independence. The governing structure that the rebelling colonies had cobbled together to enable them to fight a war soon revealed its inadequacy for the ongoing challenges of self-government. In a very similar vein, the world itself now faces a challenge to democratic governance that can no longer be ignored.

The expanding list of substantive challenges, from climate change to global pandemics, that the world must now address will sooner or later force a recognition that if we can't solve the problem of how to create effective global governance structures, there is no hope that we can solve the even more pressing problems that those structures will have to address. But this is truly a situation where failure is not an option. To put it more positively, the task of creating competent structures of global governance is as exciting a challenge as any democratic people could hope to encounter. And it is a challenge that can only be addressed democratically, with full and effective involvement from all the nations of the world. When I meet with the international students at the Mansfield Center, this is the challenge and this is the globally democratic approach to it that they seem most eager to engage.

In that setting it becomes unmistakably clear that this is not a task that lends itself to national arrogance from any quarter, or to any claim of exceptionalism. It is a situation, however, in which Americans should feel fully comfortable in playing our best democratic role at a global scale. The simple fact is that we have, as a nation, been blessed with a longer and sometimes deeper experience of democracy than most of the rest of the world. This is no time to be boasting about that experience, especially when so many of our own governing institutions are so clearly in need of healing or reform. But just as our deep, day-to-day, grassroots experience of democracy will be the most crucial element in the work of democratic renewal that now faces us here at home, so will it be our best contribution to the hard work of re-forming the outmoded institutions of global self-determination. America's greatest challenge is to learn to make that contribution more quietly and more humbly, not by proclaiming our democratic uniqueness, but by reclaiming and practicing it as the global citizens we are now called to be.

Notes

INTRODUCTION

1. *Buckley v. Valeo*, 424 U.S. 1 (1976); *First National Bank of Boston v. Bellotti*, 435 U.S. 765 (1978); *Citizens United v. Federal Election Commission*, 558 U.S. 310 (2010); *McCutcheon v. Federal Election Commission*, 572 U.S. 185 (2014).

2. Shanto Iyengar and Masha Krupenkin, quoted in Thomas B. Edsall, "What Motivates Voters More than Loyalty? Loathing," *New York Times*, March 1, 2018, https://www.nytimes.com/2018/03/01/opinion/negative -partisanship-democrats-republicans.html. See also Harry Enten, "Americans' Distaste for Both Trump and Clinton Is Record-Breaking," *FiveThirtyEight*, May 5, 2016, https://fivethirtyeight.com/features/americans-distaste-for -both-trump-and-clinton-is-record-breaking/.

CHAPTER 1

1. "Presidential Election, 2016," Ballotpedia, https://ballotpedia.org /Presidential_election,_2016.

2. Ibid.

3. Martin Kelly, "Presidents Elected without Winning the Popular Vote," *ThoughtCo.*, June 4, 2018, https://www.thoughtco.com/presidents-elected -without-winning-popular-vote-105449.

4. *Bush v. Gore*, 531 U.S. 98 (2000).

5. "Past Attempts at Reform," FairVote, https://www.fairvote.org/past _attempts_at_reform.

6. A Joint Resolution Proposing an Amendment to the Constitution of the United States to Abolish the Electoral College and to Provide for the Direct Election of the President and Vice President of the United States, S.J. Res. 41, 114th Cong. (November 15, 2016), https://www.congress.gov/bill /114th-congress/senate-joint-resolution/41.

7. Hamilton, *Federalist Papers*, No. 68, 412.

8. Ibid., 411–12.

9. Ibid., 412.

10. James Surowiecki, *The Wisdom of Crowds* (New York: Anchor Books, 2005), xxiii.

11. In exit polls following the 2016 presidential election, just 38 percent of voters had a favorable opinion of Donald Trump and thought he was "qualified" to serve as president. Chris Cillizza, "The 13 Most Amazing Findings in the 2016 Exit Poll," *Washington Post*, November 10, 2016, https://www .washingtonpost.com/news/the-fix/wp/2016/11/10/the-13-most-amazing -things-in-the-2016-exit-poll/?utm_term=.33badc66d672.

12. Hamilton, *Federalist Papers*, No. 68, 414.

13. U.S. Constitution, art. II, sec. 1, cl. 2.

14. Baron de Montesquieu, *The Spirit of the Laws* (New York: D. Appleton and Company, 1900), bk. 8, chap. 14, especially p. 146.

15. U.S. Const. art. II, sec. 1, cl. 3.

16. U.S. Const. amend. IX.

17. U.S. Const. amend. X.

18. U.S. Const. art. II, sec. 1, cl. 2–3.

19. Ibid., cl. 3.

20. National Archives and Records Administration, U.S. Electoral College, "Historical Election Results," National Archives and Records Administration, https://www.archives.gov/federal-register/electoral-college/scores.html.

21. National Archives, "Historical Election Results."

22. Ibid.

23. U.S. Const. amend. XII.

24. U.S. Const. amend. XXIII.

25. National Archives, "Historical Election Results."

26. Ibid.

27. Kurtis Lee, "In 1969, Democrats and Republicans United to Get Rid of the Electoral College. Here's What Happened," *Los Angeles Times*, December 19, 2016, http://www.latimes.com/nation/la-na-electoral-college-history -20161219-story.html.

28. "Past Attempts at Reform," FairVote.

29. Ibid.

30. Ibid.

31. "Agreement among the States to Elect the President by National Popular Vote," National Popular Vote, https://www.nationalpopularvote.com/.

32. Associated Press Staff, "Schwarzenegger Vetoes Voting Bill," *Orange County Register*, October 1, 2006, https://www.ocregister.com/2006/10/01/schwarzenegger-vetoes-voting-bill/.

33. "California," National Popular Vote, https://www.nationalpopularvote.com/state/ca.

34. "Status of National Popular Vote Bill in Each State," National Popular Vote, https://www.nationalpopularvote.com/state-status.

35. U.S. Const. art. I, sec. 10, cl. 3.

36. Andrea Levien, "Tracking Presidential Campaign Field Operations," FairVote, November 13, 2012, https://www.fairvote.org/tracking-presidential-campaign-field-operations.

37. Andrea Levien, "FairVote Maps the 2012 Presidential Campaign," FairVote, April 30, 2013, https://www.fairvote.org/fairvote-maps-the-2012-presidential-campaign.

38. Levien, "Tracking Field Operations."

39. "Following the Money: Campaign Donations and Spending in the 2012 Presidential Race," FairVote, February 3, 2013, https://www.fairvote.org/2012chart.

40. Andrea Levien, "FairVote's Presidential Campaign Tracker: Past, Present, and Future," FairVote, September 18, 2012, https://www.fairvote.org/fairvote-s-presidential-campaign-tracker-past-present-and-future-2.

41. Ibid.

42. Bob Dole, "Speech on the Senate Floor" (speech, Washington, D.C., January 15, 1979), FairVote, http://archive3.fairvote.org/reforms/national-popular-vote/the-electoral-college/solutions-and-the-case-for-reform/speeches-advocating-direct-election-for-president/#dole.

43. Ibid.

44. Ibid.

CHAPTER 2

1. National Archives, "Historical Election Results."

2. National Archives, "Historical Election Results."

3. Madison, *Federalist Papers*, No. 10, 78.

4. Sidney Blumenthal, *A Self-Made Man: The Political Life of Abraham Lincoln 1809–1849* (New York: Simon & Schuster, 2016), 209.

5. This phenomenon is at least as old as the republic itself. As the Supreme Court noted in *Rucho v. Common Cause*, 588 U.S. _ (2019), "Partisan gerrymandering is nothing new. Nor is frustration with it. The practice was known in the Colonies prior to Independence, and the Framers were familiar

with it at the time of the drafting and ratification of the Constitution." Indeed, the very word "gerrymandering" derives from the successful effort in 1812 of then-governor of Massachusetts, Elbridge Gerry, to redraw state legislative districts to benefit his Democratic-Republican Party.

6. Montana Constitution, art. V, sect. 14.

7. Ibid.

8. See Mike Dennison, "Legislative Redistricting Panel Gets Look at New Maps," *Missoulian*, February 17, 2012, https://missoulian.com/news /state-and-regional/legislative-redistricting-panel-gets-look-at-new-maps/article _2287056c-59f3-11e1-b69c-001871e3ce6c.html. For more on the communities plan, see Pat Smith and Joe Lamson, "Speak Up on Redistricting Maps," *Missoulian*, March 19, 2012, https://missoulian.com/news/opinion/columnists /speak-up-on-redistricting-maps/article_4f34d98e-71ce-11e1-afe8-001871e3 ce6c.html.

9. Montana Districting and Apportionment Commission, Meeting Minutes, March 13, 2012, Missoula, Montana, https://leg.mt.gov/content /Committees/Interim/2011-2012/Districting/Minutes/March%202012/DAC MISSOULA_3_13_12.pdf.

10. *Arizona State Legislature v. Arizona Independent Redistricting Commission*, 576 U.S. _ (2015); *Rucho v. Common Cause*, 588 U.S. _ (2019).

11. Citizens United, 112th Cong., 2nd sess., 158 Cong. Rec. S 108–10 (January 26, 2012).

12. Jim Messina, "We Will Not Play by Two Sets of Rules," *Huffington Post*, February 6, 2012, https://www.huffingtonpost.com/jim-messina/we-will -not-play_b_1258911.htm.

13. "Obama Forgoes Public Funds in First for Manor Candidate," *New York Times*, June 20, 2008, https://www.nytimes.com/2008/06/20/us/politics /20obamacnd.html.

14. Nominations, 113th Cong., 1st sess., 159 S 8294–97 Cong. Rec. (November 20, 2013).

15. Associated Press, "Supreme Court Timeline: From Scalia's Death to Garland to Gorsuch," *USA Today*, January 31, 2017, https://www.usatoday .com/story/news/politics/2017/01/31/timeline-of-events-after-the-death-of -justice-antonin-scalia/97299392/.

16. Ibid.

17. Executive Calendar—continued, 115th Cong., 1st sess., 163 S 2383–2417 Cong. Rec. (April 4, 2017). (Although this conversation takes place on April 6, 2017, it appears in the record as a continuation of a conversation started on April 4, 2017.)

18. Executive Session, 115th Cong., 1st sess., 163 S 2436–43 Cong. Rec. (April 7, 2017).

19. "Political Polarization in the American Public," Pew Research Center, June 12, 2014, http://www.people-press.org/2014/06/12/political-polari zation-in-the-american-public/.

CHAPTER 3

1. Marc Lacey and David M. Herszenhorn, "Representative Gabrielle Giffords and 18 Shot near Tucson," *New York Times*, January 8, 2011, https://www.nytimes.com/2011/01/09/us/politics/09giffords.html.

2. CNN Library, "Arizona Safeway Shootings Fast Facts," CNN, December 25, 2017, https://www.cnn.com/2013/06/10/us/arizona-safeway-shootings-fast-facts/index.html.

3. Barack Obama, "Remarks by the President at a Memorial Service for the Victims of the Shooting in Tucson, Arizona" (speech, Tucson, AZ, January 12, 2011), The White House, https://obamawhitehouse.archives.gov/the-press-office/2011/01/12/remarks-president-barack-obama-memorial-service-victims-shooting-tucson.

4. Frank James, "Bipartisan State of Union Seating Urged by Sen. Mark Udall," National Public Radio, January 13, 2011, https://www.npr.org/sections/itsallpolitics/2011/01/13/132888876/sen-udall-urges-bipartisan-seating-for-state-of-union.

5. Barack Obama, "Remarks in Tucson."

6. Ibid.

7. Theda Skocpol, *Diminished Democracy: From Membership to Management in American Civic Life*, (Norman: University of Oklahoma Press, 2003), 292.

8. Alexis de Tocqueville, *Democracy in America*, vol. II, pt. 2, chap. 8 (Chicago: University of Chicago Press, 2000), 501.

9. Ibid.

10. Ibid.

11. Ibid., 502.

12. Ibid., 501.

13. Benjamin Barber, *If Mayors Ruled the World* (New Haven, CT: Yale University Press, 2013).

14. "Quick Facts, Missoula City, Montana," U.S. Census Bureau, https://www.census.gov/quickfacts/fact/table/missoulacitymontana/PST045217 (as of November 2018).

15. Tax increment financing (TIF) is an economic development tool that municipalities and sometimes other jurisdictions can use to stimulate private investment and development in targeted areas by capturing the increased tax revenue generated by the private development itself and using the tax revenues to pay for public improvements and infrastructure necessary to enable further development. The municipality establishes a TIF area, usually after making an official finding of "blight" in that area, and dedicates future increases in taxes from the area within a specified number of years to the support of further development within the TIF area.

16. The journey to which the subtitle refers was a several years' journalistic trek across the nation, visiting a great variety of American communities,

documenting their challenges and their consistently resourceful response to them. James Fallows and Deborah Fallows, *Our Towns: A 100,000-Mile Journey in the Heart of America*, (New York: Pantheon Books, 2018).

17. Fallows, *Our Towns*.

18. John Dewey, *The Public and Its Problems* (New York: H. Holt, 1927), 149.

19. Ibid.

20. Ibid.

21. Ibid., 77.

22. Ibid.

23. Ibid.

24. Ibid., 149.

25. Light the Bridge Committee, "Missoula: Meeting to Explore 'Light the Bridge,'" *Missoulian*, November 4, 2012, https://missoulian.com /news/opinion/mailbag/missoula-meeting-to-explore-light-the-bridge/article _dde50d94–2e6a–11e2–8a86–0019bb2963f4.html.

CHAPTER 4

1. "Walter D. Kemmis," Ballotpedia, https://ballotpedia.org/Walter_D. _Kemmis.

2. There is a voluminous body of scholarship on the Progressives, of course, but readers seeking a quick overview will find an accessible and informative source in Walter Nugent's *Progressivism: A Very Short Introduction* (New York: Oxford University Press, 2010).

3. Jane Addams, *Democracy and Social Ethics* (New York: Macmillan, 1902).

4. Maureen A. Flanagan, *America Reformed: Progressives and Progressivisms 1890s—1920s* (New York: Oxford University Press, 2007), 81.

5. Ibid., vii.

6. Ibid.

7. Ibid., 35–39.

8. On temperance, Ibid., 190–1; on education, Ibid., 46.

9. U.S. Const. amend. XVI.

10. U.S. Const. amend. XVIII.

11. U.S. Const. amend. XVII.; U.S. Const. amend. XIX.

12. Flanagan, *America Reformed*, 77.

13. Edmund Morris, *The Rise of Theodore Roosevelt* (New York: Random House, 1979), 398–99.

14. "Theodore Roosevelt," Ballotpedia, https://ballotpedia.org/Theodore _Roosevelt.

15. Ellis Waldron and Paul B. Wilson, eds., *Atlas of Montana Elections 1889–1976* (Missoula: University of Montana Publications in History, 1978), 11.

16. Timothy Egan, "Backward, into the Future," *New York Times*, June 7, 2010, https://archive.nytimes.com/query.nytimes.com/gst/fullpage -9E01E7DF1130F934A35755C0A9669D8B63.html.

17. Ibid.

18. Center for Legislative Archives, "17th Amendment to the U.S. Constitution: Direct Election of U.S. Senators," National Archives, August 15, 2016, https://www.archives.gov/legislative/features/17th-amendment.

19. Egan, "Backward."

20. Ibid.

21. U.S. Const. art. V.

22. Center for Legislative Archives, "17th Amendment."

23. Flanagan, *America Reformed*, vii.

24. Waldron and Wilson, *Atlas of Montana Elections*, 45.

25. Ibid., 48.

26. Ibid., 45.

27. "Thomas J. Walsh: A Featured Biography," U.S. Senate, https://www .senate.gov/artandhistory/history/common/generic/Featured_Bio_Walsh .htm.

28. "1912 Presidential General Election Results," Dave Leip's Atlas of U.S. Elections, https://uselectionatlas.org/RESULTS/index.html.

29. Flanagan, *America Reformed*, 285.

30. "1924 Presidential General Election Results," Dave Leip's Atlas.

31. Ibid.

32. Ibid.

33. Mary Schons, "Woman Suffrage," *National Geographic*, January 21, 2011, https://www.nationalgeographic.org/news/woman-suffrage/.

34. Wyoming Const., art. VI, sect. 1.

35. Schons, "Woman Suffrage."

36. Ibid.

37. Martin Kelly, "Teddy Roosevelt's Progressive Party 1912–1916," *ThoughtCo.*, May 12, 2018, https://www.thoughtco.com/bull-moose-party -104836.

38. "The Montana Suffrage Story," Women's History Matters, Montana Historical Society, http://montanawomenshistory.org/suffrage/.

39. "List of United States Representatives from Montana," Ballotpedia, https://ballotpedia.org/List_of_United_States_Representatives_from _Montana?gclid=Cj0KCQiAgMPgBRDDARIsAOh3uyJvcjMY66VvrHni2gni -fCN5_02AX2S66zdT2eQdd01354In5KJpxQaAtpuEALw_wcB#1900s.

40. Carrie Hillyard, "The History of Suffrage and Equal Rights Provisions in State Constitutions," *Brigham Young University Journal of Public Law* 10, no. 1 (1996): 118–19.

41. Josh Altic and Geoff Pallay, "Ballot Measures: American Direct Democracy at Work," *New York Times*, August 31, 2016, https://www.nytimes .com/2016/08/31/opinion/campaign-stops/ballot-measures-american-direct

-democracy-at-work.html?mtrref=www.google.com&gwh=AFE2534411E0DB
1E9EC1A0316E16268C&gwt=pay&assetType=opinion.

42. Ibid.

43. Ray Ring, "Western Voters Love Ballot Initiatives—and Sometimes Make a Mess," *High Country News*, October 31, 2011, https://www.hcn.org/issues/43.18/western-voters-love-ballot-initiatives-and-sometimes-make-a-mess.

44. Waldron and Wilson, *Atlas of Montana Elections*, 35.

45. Ibid., 45–52.

46. Ibid.

47. *Citizens United*, 558 U.S. 310.

CHAPTER 5

1. *American Tradition Partnership, Inc. v. Bullock*, 567 U.S. 516 (2012).

2. *Western Tradition Partnership v. Attorney General*, 328 P.3d (Mont. 2011).

3. Ibid., 8.

4. Ibid., 10–11.

5. Ibid., 17.

6. Ibid., 18–22.

7. Ibid., 22–23.

8. *American Tradition Partnership v. Bullock*, 567 U.S. 516.

9. Ibid.

10. Ibid.

11. Brief of the State of New York et al. as amicus curiae, *American Tradition Partnership v. Bullock*. The states that filed this amicus brief were New York, Arkansas, California, Connecticut, Delaware, Hawaii, Idaho, Illinois, Iowa, Kentucky, Maryland, Massachusetts, Minnesota, Mississippi, Nevada, New Mexico, North Carolina, Rhode Island, Utah, Vermont, Washington, West Virginia, and the District of Columbia.

12. *Dred Scott v. Sandford*, 60 U.S. 393 (1856).

13. U.S. Const. amend. XIV, sec. 1.

14. For an example, see *Santa Clara County v. Southern Pacific Railroad Company*, 118 U.S. 394 (1886).

15. In Montana: Ellis Waldron and Paul B. Wilson, eds., *Atlas of Montana Elections 1889–1976* (Missoula: University of Montana Publications in History, 1978), 45–52.

16. Lewis F. Powell to Eugene B. Syndor Jr., memorandum, August 23, 1971, Attack on American Free Enterprise System, https://scholarlycommons.law.wlu.edu/cgi/viewcontent.cgi?article=1000&context=powellmemo.

17. "Justices 1789 to Present," Supreme Court of the United States, https://www.supremecourt.gov/about/members_text.aspx.

18. Richard Nixon to Henry A. Kissinger, letter, August 9, 1974, National Archives Catalog, https://catalog.archives.gov/id/302035.

19. An Act to Impose Overall Limitations on Campaign Expenditures and Political Contributions; . . . to Provide for Public Financing of Presidential Nominating Conventions and Presidential Primary Elections, S. 3044, 93rd Cong. (February 21, 1974), https://www.congress.gov/bill /93rd-congress/senate-bill/3044?q=%7B%22search%22%3A%5B%22%5C%22 federal+election+campaign+act%5C%22+public+funding%22%5D%7D&s=7 &r=18.

20. *Buckley v. Valeo*, 424 U.S. 1.

21. *Bellotti*, 435 U.S. 765.

22. *Austin v. Michigan Chamber of Commerce*, 494 U.S. 652 (1990).

23. Bipartisan Campaign Reform Act of 2002, H.R. 2356, 107th Cong. (June 28, 2001), https://www.congress.gov/bill/107th-congress/house-bill /2356?q=%7B%22search%22%3A%5B%22bipartisan+campaign+reform+act %22%5D%7D&s=1&r=1.

24. Ibid.

25. *McConnell v. Federal Election Commission*, 540 U.S. 93 (2003).

26. *Citizens United*, 558 U.S. 310.

27. *Speechnow.org v. Federal Election Commission*, No. 08–5223 (D.C. Cir. 2010).

28. *Western Tradition Partnership v. Attorney General*, 328 P.3d.

29. *McCutcheon v. Federal Election Commission*, 572 U.S. 185.

30. A Joint Resolution Proposing an Amendment to the Constitution of the United States Relating to Contributions and Expenditures Intended to Affect Elections, S.J. Res. 19, 113th Cong. (June 18, 2013), https://www.congress .gov/bill/113th-congress/senate-joint-resolution/19?q=%7B%22search%22%3A %5B%22SJR+19%22%5D%7D&s=4&r=1.

31. "Citizens United v. Federal Election Commission," Justia, https:// supreme.justia.com/cases/federal/us/558/310/.

32. Ibid.

33. Bipartisan Campaign Reform Act of 2002, sect. 203.

34. Ibid., sect. 101.

35. 530 F. Supp. 2d 274 (D.C. 2008) *(per curiam)*.

36. *Citizens United*, 558 U.S. 310.

37. "Citizens United v. Federal Election Commission," Oyez, www.oyez .org/cases/2008/08–205.

38. *McConnell v. Federal Election Commission*, 540 U.S. 93.

39. *Austin v. Michigan Chamber of Commerce*, 494 U.S. 652.

40. *Citizens United*, 558 U.S. 310.

41. Ibid., sect. 2.

42. Ibid.

43. *Speechnow.org v. Federal Election Commission*, No. 08–5223.

44. The Center for Responsive Politics reported that as of December 11, 2018, super PACs have raised $1,543,104,912 and spent $817,896,201 in 2018. Center for Responsive Politics, "Super PACs," OpenSecrets.org, https://www.opensecrets.org/pacs/superpacs.php.

45. Center for Responsive Politics, "Outside Spending," OpenSecrets.org, https://www.opensecrets.org/outsidespending/index.php?filter=&type=Y.

46. Center for Responsive Politics, "Dark Money Basics," OpenSecrets.org, https://www.opensecrets.org/dark-money/basics.

47. *Dred Scott*, 60 U.S. 614–5.

48. *Bush v. Gore*, 531 U.S. 158.

49. *Rucho v. Common Cause*, 588 U.S. _; 139 S. Ct. 2484 (2019).

50. *Citizens United*, 558 U.S. 310.

51. "Justices 1789 to Present," Supreme Court of the United States.

52. *National Federation of Independent Business v. Sebelius*, 567 U.S. 519 (2012).

53. Tom McCarthy, "Is John Roberts Poised to Become the Supreme Court's Key Swing Vote?" *Guardian*, July 15, 2018, https://www.theguardian.com/law/2018/jul/15/john-roberts-supreme-court-swing-vote-anthony-kennedy.

54. *Rucho v. Common Cause*, 588 U.S. _; 139 S. Ct. 2484.

55. *Franchise Tax Board of California v. Hyatt*, 587 US. _ 139, S. Ct. 1485 (2019).

56. *Franchise Tax Board of California*, , S. Ct. 1497.

57. U.S. Congress, S.J. Res. 19, 113th Cong. (2013).

58. Ibid.

59. U.S. Const. art. V.

60. U.S. Congress, S.J. Res. 19.

CHAPTER 6

1. Mass. Const., Preamble.

2. *Trustees of Dartmouth College v. Woodward*, 17 U.S. 636 (1819).

3. *Santa Clara County v. Southern Pacific Railroad Co.*, 118 U.S. 394.

4. Ibid., 410.

5. Ibid., 411.

6. Ibid., 396.

7. *Minneapolis & St. Louis Railway Co. v. Beckwith*, 129 U.S. 26 (1889).

8. Ibid., 28.

9. *Pembina Consolidated Silver Mining Co. v. Pennsylvania*, 125 U.S. 181 (1888).

10. U.S. Const., art. IV, sect. 2.

11. *Pembina*, 125 U.S. 187.

12. Ibid., 187–8.

13. An Act to Prohibit Corporations from Making Money Contributions in Connection with Political Elections, Pub. L. No. 59–36, 34 Stat. 864b (1907), 864–65.

14. *Pembina*, 125 U.S. 187–8.

15. *Lochner v. New York*, 198 U.S. 45 (1905).

16. Ibid.

17. Ibid., 53.

18. Ibid.

19. Ibid.

20. Ibid., 56–57.

21. Ibid., 68.

22. Ibid.

23. Ibid., 75.

24. Ibid.

25. Ibid.

26. Ibid.

27. Ibid.

28. *West Coast Hotel Co. v. Parrish*, 300 U.S. 379 (1937).

29. Powell, Attack on American Free Enterprise System.

30. Ibid., 30.

31. Ibid., 26.

32. Ibid.

33. Ibid.

34. Ibid.

35. Ibid., 27.

36. *Bellotti*, 435 U.S. 765.

37. Ibid., 771.

38. Ibid., 776.

39. Ibid., 784.

40. *Citizens United*, 558 U.S. 310.

41. *Bellotti*, 435 U.S. 803.

42. Ibid., 809.

43. Ibid.

44. Ibid., 822.

45. Ibid., 823

46. *Dartmouth*, 17 U.S. 636; *Bellotti*, 435 U.S. 825.

47. *Bellotti*, 435 U.S. 828

48. Jeffrey D. Clements, *Corporations Are Not People: Why They Have More Rights Than You Do and What You Can Do About It* (San Francisco: Berrett-Koehler Publishers, 2012).

49. Powell, Attack on American Free Enterprise System, 26–27.

50. Brief of appellant for *Citizens United*, 558 U.S. 310, https://www
.americanbar.org/content/dam/aba/publishing/preview/publiced_preview_briefs
_pdfs_07_08_08_205_AppellantAmCuACLUSupp.pdf.

51. Mary Ann Glendon, *Rights Talk: The Impoverishment of Political Discourse* (New York: The Free Press, 1991).

52. Arthur Conan Doyle, "Silver Blaze," in *The Penguin Complete Sherlock Holmes* (New York: Penguin Books, 1981), 335.

CHAPTER 7

1. Federal Election Campaign Act Amendments, S. 3044, 93rd Cong. (February 1, 1974), https://www.congress.gov/bill/93rd-congress/senate-bill/3044/actions?q=%7B%22search%22%3A%5B%221974+federal+election+campaign+act%22%5D%7D&r=145&s=6.

2. Gerald Ford, "Remarks on Signing the Federal Election Campaign Act Amendments, October 15, 1974," *Public Papers of the Presidents of the United States: Gerald Ford, 1974* (Washington, D.C.: Government Printing Office, 1974).

3. *Buckley v. Valeo*, 171 U.S. App. D.C. 172, 519 F.2d 821 (1975).

4. Powell, Attack on American Free Enterprise System.

5. *Buckley v. Valeo*, 171 U.S. App. D.C. 172, 519 F.2d 821.

6. *Buckley v. Valeo*, 424 U.S. 19.

7. Ibid.

8. Federal Election Campaign Act Amendments, S. 3044, 93rd Cong.

9. Mary Ann Glendon, *Rights Talk* (New York: Simon & Schuster, 1991), 4.

10. Ibid., 5.

11. For a seminal work on the theory and history of representative democracy, see J. G. A. Pocock, *The Machiavellian Moment: Florentine Political Thought and the Atlantic Republican Tradition* (Princeton, NJ: Princeton University Press, 1975).

12. Abraham Lincoln, Annual Message to Congress, December 1, 1862.

13. Thucydides, "Pericles' Funeral Oration," *The Peloponnesian War*, trans. Rex Warner, (New York: Penguin Books, 1972), 147.

14. John Locke, "Why Men Reason So Poorly," in *Of the Conduct of the Understanding*, sect. 3, in *Locke Selections*, ed. Sterling P. Lamprecht (New York: Charles Scribner's Sons, 1928), 23.

15. John Stuart Mill, "On Liberty," in *The Philosophy of John Stuart Mill: Ethical, Political, and Religious* (New York: Random House, 1961), 209–10.

16. An Act Declaring the Rights and Liberties of the Subject and Settling the Succession of the Crown, the Bill of Rights, Parliament of

England (December 16, 1689), http://avalon.law.yale.edu/17th_century
/england.asp.

17. Ibid.

18. U.S. Const. art. 1, sect. 6.

19. "John Adams and the Massachusetts Constitution," https://www
.mass.gov/guides/john-adams-the-massachusetts-constitution.

20. Mass. Const., art. XXI.

21. Ibid., art. IV.

22. Ibid., art. IX; art. XVI; art. XVII; art. XIX.

23. Pa. Const., art. XVI.

24. Va. Const., art. I.

25. This story and quote were originally found in the notes of Dr. James
McHenry, a Maryland delegate to the Constitutional Convention. McHenry's notes can be found in *The American Historical Review*, vol. 2, published
in 1906, as well as in *The Records of the Federal Convention* vol. 3, edited
by Max Farrand and published in 1911 and 1934. Benjamin Franklin, "Respectfully Quoted: A Dictionary of Quotations," Barleby.com, https://www
.bartleby.com/73/1593.html. This story is often recounted and rarely cited.
Although this quote seems to be generally accepted as true, its foundations
remain a bit hazy.

26. Virgil, *The Aeneid*, trans. Robert Fitzgerald (New York: Alfred A.
Knopf, 1992), bk. 1, 4.

27. Tocqueville, *Democracy in America*, 662.

28. Ibid., 663.

29. *Buckley v. Valeo*, 424 U.S. 52.

30. This book cannot begin to do justice to the scholarly literature on the
varieties of human speech as they bear on the practice of self-government.
A classic work on the subject, which has substantially influenced my understanding, is Jurgen Habermas's *Theory of Communicative Action* (Boston: Beacon Press, 1984).

31. Glendon, *Rights Talk*, 12.

32. Alexander Meiklejohn, *Free Speech and Its Relation to Self-Government*
(New York: Harper Brothers Publishers, 1948), 22–23.

33. In a *New York Times*/CBS News poll, 82% of American voters have
felt "disgusted" about the 2016 presidential election campaigns. A mere 13%
felt "excited." For more on voter distrust and distaste for the 2016 presidential election, see Jonathan Martin, Dalia Sussman, and Megan Thee-Brenan,
"Voters Express Disgust Over U.S. Politics in New York Times/CBS Poll,"
New York Times, November 3, 2016, https://www.nytimes.com/2016/11/04
/us/politics/hillary-clinton-donald-trump-poll.html. Favorability ratings for
both Hillary Clinton and Donald Trump were historically low; see Harry
Enten, "Americans' Distaste for Both Trump and Clinton is Record-Breaking,"

FiveThirtyEight, May 5, 2016, https://fivethirtyeight.com/features/americans-distaste-for-both-trump-and-clinton-is-record-breaking/.

34. Paul Waldman, "How Our Campaign Finance System Compares to Other Countries," *American Prospect*, April 4, 2014, https://prospect.org/article/how-our-campaign-finance-system-compares-other-countries.

CHAPTER 8

1. *Buckley v. Valeo*, 424 U.S. 19.

2. *Citizens United*, 558 U.S. 310.

3. See "National Issues Forum," Participedia, https://participedia.net/en/methods/national-issues-forum.

4. See Everyday Democracy, https://www.everyday-democracy.org/.

5. See "Deliberative Polling®," Participedia, https://participedia.net/en/methods/deliberative-polling.

6. See Journal of Public Deliberation, https://www.publicdeliberation.net/jpd/.

7. "About," Deliberative Democracy, http://deliberative-democracy.net/about/ (accessed December 29, 2018).

8. National Conference on Dialogue and Deliberation, *2012 National Conference on Dialogue & Deliberation*, Seattle, WA, October, 2012, http://www.ncdd.org/files/NCDD2012_Guidebook.pdf.

9. See "Citizens' Initiative Revew," Healthy Democracy, https://healthydemocracy.org/cir/.

10. Greg Munno and Tina Nabatchi, "Public Deliberation and Co-Production in the Political and Electoral Arena: A Citizens' Jury Approach," *Journal of Public Deliberation* 10, no. 2 (2014), art. 1.

11. Ross W. Gorte, Carol Hardy Vincent, Laura A. Hanson, and Marc R. Rosenblum, *Federal Land Ownership: Overview and Data*, U.S. Library of Congress, Congressional Research Service, R42346, February 8, 2012.

12. James Wilson to Gifford Pinchot, letter, February 1, 1905, https://foresthistory.org/research-explore/us-forest-service-history/policy-and-law/agency-organization/wilson-letter/. According to this source, "It is generally believed that Pinchot wrote the letter for Wilson's signature."

13. Multiple-Use Sustained-Yield Act of 1960, H.R. 10572, 86th Cong. (April 25, 1960), https://www.govinfo.gov/content/pkg/STATUTE-74/pdf/STATUTE-74-Pg215.pdf.

14. Carol Hardy Vincent, Laura A. Hanson, and Carla N. Argueta, *Federal Land Ownership: Overview and Data*, U.S. Library of Congress, Congressional Research Service R42346, 2017.

15. I will simply note here, without exploring any further, that what we are here calling the "public lands West" is almost exactly coterminous with

the region that we encountered repeatedly in chapter 4 because of the lead-ing role it played in the Progressive movement.

16. For an in-depth presentation of this statutory framework, see Sarah Bates, *The Legal Framework for Cooperative Conservation* (Public Policy Research Institute, University of Montana, 2006).

17. Andrus Center for Public Policy, "Policy after Politics: How Should the Next Administration Approach Public Land Management in the Western States?" *Journal of Land, Resources, and Environmental Law* 21 (2001).

18. *Conflicting Laws and Regulations—Gridlock on the National Forests: Oversight Hearing before the Subcommittee on Forests and Forest Health of the House Committee on Resources*, 107th Cong. (2001).

19. "The Lubrecht Conversations," *Chronicle of Community* (Autumn 1998): 9.

20. U.S. Forest Service (USFS), *The Process Predicament: How Statutory, Regulatory and Administrative Factors Affect National Forest Management* (USFS, 2002), http://www.fs.fed.us/projects/documents/Process-Predicament .pdf.

21. John Kania and Mark Kramer, "Collective Impact," *Stanford Social Innovation Review* 9, no. 1 (2011), https://ssir.org/articles/entry/collective _impact.

22. Grantmakers for Effective Organizations (GEO), *Working Better Together: Building Nonprofit Collaborative Capacity*, (GEO, 2013), 4, https://www.michiganfoundations.org/sites/default/files/resources/Working-Better -Together-GEO-2013.pdf.

23. Ibid., 13.

24. "Foundation Stats," Foundation Center, http://data.foundationcenter .org/#/foundations/all/nationwide/top:giving/list/2014 (data as of December 29, 2018).

25. See Philanthropy for Active Civic Engagement, http://www .pacefunders.org/.

26. "Mission," Philanthropy for Active Civic Engagement, http://www .pacefunders.org/mission/.

27. Ibid.

28. Ibid.

29. Ibid.

30. Ibid.

31. "About D5," D5 Coalition, http://www.d5coalition.org/about/.

32. "Why D5," D5 Coalition, http://www.d5coalition.org/about/why-d5/.

33. See Philanthropy Northwest, https://philanthropynw.org/.

34. "Grease and Glue," Philanthropy Northwest, 2013, 3, https://philanthropynw.org/sites/default/files/resources/Grease%20and%20Glue%2C %20Philanthropy%27s%20Unique%200pportunity%20to%20Strengthen%20 Communities-2013.pdf.

35. Ibid.

36. Ibid.

37. "PolicyWorks," United Philanthropy Forum, https://www.united philforum.org/policyworks.

38. Larry Kramer, "Tackling Political Polarization through Philanthropy," *Stanford Social Innovation Review* (2013), https://ssir.org/articles/entry /tackling_political_polarization_through_philanthropy.

39. Ibid.

40. Ibid.

41. Daniel Kemmis, *Philanthropy and the Renewal of Democracy: Is It Time to Step Up Our Game?* (Philanthropy Northwest, 2016), https://philan thropynw.org/resources/philanthropy-and-renewal-democracy-it-time-step-our -game. Some sections of this chapter are adapted from that monograph.

42. Kramer, "Tackling Political Polarization through Philanthropy."

43. Ibid.

44. Ibid.

45. "Foundation Funding for U.S. Democracy: Data Tool," http:// democracy.foundationcenter.org/.

46. See Moms Demand Action, https://momsdemandaction.org/.

47. Alan Blinder, Jess Bidgood, and Vivian Wang, "In Gun Control Marches, Students Led but Adults Provided Key Resources," *New York Times,* March 25, 2018, https://www.nytimes.com/2018/03/25/us/gun-march -organizers.html.

48. Ibid.

49. See Bloomberg Philanthropies, https://www.bloomberg.org/.

50. See "Mayors against Illegal Guns," Everytown for Gun Safety, https:// everytown.org/mayors/.

51. See Everytown for Gun Safety, https://everytown.org/.

CHAPTER 9

1. "History of the National Civic League," National Civic League, November 11, 2014, https://www.nationalcivicleague.org/history-of-the -national-civic-league/.

2. "History," League of Women Voters, https://www.lwv.org/about-us /history.

3. "About Common Cause," Common Cause, https://www.common cause.org/about-us/.

4. Robert D. McFadden, "John W. Gardner, 89, Founder of Common Cause and Adviser to Presidents, Dies," *New York Times*, February 18, 2002, https://www.nytimes.com/2002/02/18/us/john-w-gardner-89-founder-of -common-cause-and-adviser-to-presidents-dies.html.

5. Ibid.

6. "Let's Reclaim the American Dream," Reclaim the American Dream, http://reclaimtheamericandream.org/.

7. "History of the Campaign Finance Board," New York City Campaign Finance Board, https://www.nyccfb.info/about/history/.

8. Ibid.

9. "About the Program," Seattle.gov, https://www.seattle.gov/democracy voucher/about-the-program.

10. Bob Young, "M. Lorena González and Teresa Mosqueda Win Seattle City Council Seats," *Seattle Times*, November 7, 2017, https://www.seattletimes.com/seattle-news/politics/seattle-city-council-election-2017/.

11. Bob Young, "Seattle's Democracy Vouchers Haven't Kept Big Money Out of Primary Election," *Seattle Times*, July 30, 2017, https://www.seattletimes.com/seattle-news/politics/seattles-democracy-vouchers-havent-kept-big-money-out-of-primary-election/.

12. Ibid.

13. Ibid.

14. Mike Baker, "Amazon Tests 'Soul of Seattle' with Deluge of Election Cash" *New York Times*, October 30, 2019, https://www.nytimes.com/2019/10/30/us/seattle-council-amazon-democracy-vouchers.html?nl=today sheadlines&emc=edit_th_191031?campaign_id=2&instance_id=13420&segment_id=18380&user_id=f54a61a5bd32b2a530018135efb5c8f9&regi_id=694115731031.

15. Daniel Beekman, "Washington's Supreme Court Agrees to Review Case against Seattle's 'Democracy Vouchers,'" *Seattle Times*, December 21, 2018, https://www.seattletimes.com/seattle-news/politics/washingtons-supreme-court-agrees-to-review-case-against-seattles-democracy-vouchers/.

16. Ibid.

17. John Paul Stevens, *Six Amendments: How and Why We Should Change the Constitution* (New York: Little, Brown and Company, 2014), 78.

18. Ibid., 79.

19. For the petition, see "End Corporate Rule. Legalize Democracy," Move to Amend, https://movetoamend.org/ (accessed December 27, 2018). For more on Move to Amend, see Mark Karlin, "Call for Congress to Overturn 'Citizens United' through Amendment Picks Up Steam," Move to Amend, June 9, 2017, https://movetoamend.org/call-congress-overturn-citizens-united-through-amendment-picks-steam.

20. "American Promise," American Promise, http://www.americanpromise.net/ (accessed December 27, 2018).

21. "AP Council," American Promise, http://www.americanpromise.net/ap_advisory_council (accessed December 27, 2018).

22. "What Is Citizens United," End Citizens United, https://endcitizens united.org/.

23. Ibid.

24. Center for Responsive Politics, "2016 PAC Summary Data," OpenSecrets.org, https://www.opensecrets.org/pacs/lookup2.php?strID= C00573261&cycle=2016.

25. "History," The Concord Coalition, https://www.concordcoalition.org /history.

26. Ibid.

27. "History," No Labels, https://www.nolabels.org/history/.

28. "Who We Are," Bipartisan Policy Center, https://bipartisanpolicy.org /about/who-we-are/.

29. "Voter Turnout," FairVote, https://www.fairvote.org/voter_turnout #voter_turnout_101.

30. In 2014, 68 percent of the voting population in Oregon voted against Measure 90. "Oregon Open Primary Initiative, Measure 90 (2014)," Ballot-pedia,https://ballotpedia.org/Oregon_Open_Primary_Initiative,_Measure_90 _(2014).

31. Oregon Citizens' Initiative Review, "Citizens' Initiative Review of Ballot Measure 90," http://media.oregonlive.com/mapes/other/M90%20 citizens%27%20statement.pdf.

32. Ibid.

33. "Oregon Open Primary Initiative, Measure 90 (2014)," Ballotpedia.

34. Ibid.

35. Ibid.

36. "Ranked Choice Voting / Instant Runoff," FairVote, https://www .fairvote.org/rcv.

37. "Spotlight: Maine," FairVote, https://www.fairvote.org/rcv.

38. "Maine Supreme Judicial Court Advisory Opinion on Ranked-Choice Voting," Ballotpedia, https://ballotpedia.org/Maine_Supreme_Judicial_Court _advisory_opinion_on_ranked-choice_voting.

39. "Maine's 2nd Congressional District Election, 2018," Ballotpedia, https://ballotpedia.org/Maine%27s_2nd_Congressional_District_election, _2018.

40. "How Proportional Representation Elections Work," FairVote, https:// www.fairvote.org/how_proportional_representation_elections_work.

41. "California Proposition 11, Creation of the California Citizens' Redis-tricting Commission (2008)," Ballotpedia, https://ballotpedia.org/California _Proposition_11,_Creation_of_the_California_Citizens_Redistricting_Com mission_(2008).

42. Ibid.

43. Ibid.

44. "The Obama/No-on-11 Ticket," *Los Angeles Times*, September 12, 2008, https://latimes3.typepad.com/opinionla/page/336/.

45. "California Proposition 11," Ballotpedia. For election results by state for the 2008 presidential election, see "Election Results 2008," *New York Times*, December 9, 2008, https://www.nytimes.com/elections/2008/results/president/votes.html.

46. "California Proposition 20, Congressional Redistricting (2010)," Ballotpedia, https://ballotpedia.org/California_Proposition_20,_Congressional_Redistricting_(2010).

47. Ibid. For more on the failed Proposition 27, see "California Proposition 27, Elimination of Citizen Redistricting Commission (2010)," Ballotpedia, https://ballotpedia.org/California_Proposition_27,_Elimination_of_Citizen_Redistricting_Commission_(2010).

48. "Did the California Citizens Redistricting Commission Really Create More Competitive Districts?" FairVote, https://www.fairvote.org/did-the-california-citizens-redistricting-commission-really-create-more-competitive-districts.

49. "Ohio Bipartisan Redistricting Commission Amendment, Issue 1 (2015)," Ballotpedia, https://ballotpedia.org/Ohio_Bipartisan_Redistricting_Commission_Amendment,_Issue_1_(2015).

50. Peter Miller and Annie Lo, "Support for Ohio's Issue 1 Ballot Measure in the 2018 Primary Election," *Brennan Center for Justice*, November 7, 2018, https://www.brennancenter.org/blog/support-ohio-issue-1-ballot-measure-2018-primary-election.

51. "Arizona Creation of a Redistricting Commission, Proposition 106 (2000)," Ballotpedia, https://ballotpedia.org/Arizona_Creation_of_a_Redistricting_Commission,_Proposition_106_(2000).

52. Ibid.

53. *Arizona State Legislature v. Arizona Independent Redistricting Commission*, 576 U.S. __; 135 S. Ct. 2652 (2015).

54. U.S. Const., art. I, sect. 4.

55. *Arizona State Legislature v. Arizona Independent Redistricting Commission*, 576 U.S. __; 135 S. Ct. 2677.

56. Ibid., 135 S. Ct. 2678.

57. *Cooper v. Harris*, 581 U.S. __; 136 S. Ct. 2512 (2017).

58. Ibid.

59. *Rucho v. Common Cause*, 588 U.S. __.

60. *Dred Scott*, 60 U.S. 614–5.

61. *Rucho v. Common Cause*, 588 U.S. __, 6.

62. *Rucho v. Common Cause*, 588 U.S. __, 12.

63. *Rucho v. Common Cause*, Kagan dissent, 1–2.

64. "Broad Support for Renewed Background Checks Bill, Skepticism about Its Chances," Pew Research Center, May 23, 2013, http://www.people-press.org/2013/05/23/broad-support-for-renewed-background-checks-bill

-skepticism-about-its-chances/. Also, see, Paul Steinhauser, "Public Opinion Gets Trumped in Gun Control Defeat," *CNN Politics* (blog), April 17, 2013, http://politicalticker.blogs.cnn.com/2013/04/17/public-opinion-gets-trumped-in-gun-control-defeat/.

EPILOGUE

1. See https://www.umt.edu/mansfield/.

2. I am indebted to Jane Mansbridge for the reminder that there is actually a long and strong tradition of American scholarship pursuing exactly this open, inquiring approach into what made America so fortunately receptive to democratic theory and practice. Louis Hartz's *The Liberal Tradition in America* (New York: Harcourt, Brace and World, 1955) became a classic of this literature, followed by Seymour Martin Lipset's *The First New Nation* (New York: Basic Books, 1963) and then Lipset's *American Exceptionalism: A Double-Edged Sword* (New York: W. W. Norton, 1996.)

3. Madeleine Albright, interview with Matt Lauer, *The Today Show*, February 19, 1998, U.S. Department of State Archive, https://1997–2001 .state.gov/www/statements/1998/980219a.html.

4. The White House, "U.S. National Security Strategy: Overview of America's International Strategy," September 2002, https://2009–2017.state .gov/documents/organization/63562.pdf.

5. Ibid., 1.

6. Ibid., 15.

7. George W. Bush, "President Bush Discusses Freedom in Iraq and Middle East" (speech, Washington, DC, November 6, 2003), White House Archive, https://georgewbush-whitehouse.archives.gov/news/releases/2003 /11/20031106–2.html.

8. Barack Obama, "Remarks by the President to the White House Press Corps," August 20, 2012, White House Archive, https://obamawhitehouse .archives.gov/the-press-office/2012/08/20/remarks-president-white-house -press-corps.

9. Mark Landler, "Obama Threatens Force Against Syria," *New York Times*, August 20, 2012, https://www.nytimes.com/2012/08/21/world /middleeast/obama-threatens-force-against-syria.html.

10. "Syria Crisis: Cameron Loses Commons Vote on Syria Action," BBC, August 30, 2013. https://www.bbc.com/news/uk-politics-23892783.

11. Steven Erlanger and Stephen Castle, "Britain's Rejection of Syrian Response Reflects Fear of Rushing to Act," *New York Times*, August 29, 2013, https://www.nytimes.com/2013/08/30/world/middleeast/syria.html.

12. Barack Obama, "Remarks by the President in Address to the Nation on Syria" (speech, Washington, DC, September 10, 2013), White House

Archive, https://obamawhitehouse.archives.gov/the-press-office/2013/09/10/remarks-president-address-nation-syria.

13. Ibid.

14. Vladimir V. Putin, "A Plea for Caution from Russia," *New York Times*, September 11, 2013, https://www.nytimes.com/2013/09/12/opinion/putin-plea-for-caution-from-russia-on-syria.html.

15. Ibid.

16. Barack Obama, "Remarks by President Obama in Address to the United Nations General Assembly" (speech, New York, N.Y., September 24, 2013), White House Archive, https://obamawhitehouse.archives.gov/the-press-office/2013/09/24/remarks-president-obama-address-united-nations-general-assembly.

17. Putin, "A Plea for Caution from Russia."

18. Obama, "Remarks by President Obama in Address to the United Nations General Assembly."

19. Putin, "A Plea for Caution from Russia."

20. Obama, "Remarks by President Obama in Address to the United Nations General Assembly."

Index

CPSIA information can be obtained
at www.ICGtesting.com
Printed in the USA
LVHW041016200820
663648LV00004B/433

9 780806 166292